TO SAVE A LIFE

To Save a Life

Stories of Holocaust Rescue

ELLEN LAND-WEBER

UNIVERSITY OF ILLINOIS PRESS ～ URBANA AND CHICAGO

Publication of this book was supported by the Sheldon Drobny Family Endowment for the University of Illinois Press and by grants from Richard Hamburger, Simon Moss, and the California State Library Foundation.

Library of Congress Cataloging-in-Publication Data

Land-Weber, Ellen.
To save a life : stories of Holocaust rescue / Ellen Land-Weber.
p.   cm.
ISBN 0-252-02515-6 (cloth)
1. Righteous Gentiles in the Holocaust—Interviews.
2. Holocaust survivors—Interviews. 3. Holocaust, Jewish (1939–
1945)—Personal narratives. 4. World War, 1939–1945—Jews—
Rescue. I. Title.
D804.65.L36   2000
940.53'18'0922—dc21   99-050499

C   5   4   3   2   1

CONTENTS

My inspiration for undertaking this work was the study of altruism by Samuel and Pearl Oliner, professors at Humboldt State University. For their Altruistic Personality Project the Oliners organized interviews with hundreds of Holocaust rescuers, all of whose stories have been authenticated by Yad Vashem, the world's premier Holocaust museum, memorial, and archive.

Since shortly after the end of World War II, Yad Vashem has collected and authenticated thousands of testimonials from Jewish Holocaust survivors who asked that the non-Jewish people who risked their lives to save them be remembered. Yad Vashem honors these rescuers with a medal designating each as a "Righteous Gentile." The institution also plants a tree marked with a commemorative plaque for each rescuer in a special grove at the Holocaust Memorial in Jerusalem.

As an interviewer for the Oliners, I was struck by the special personal qualities of so many of the rescuers. The Altruistic Personality Project is a broad sociological study of human behavior. I envisioned writing a companion volume to the Oliners' study that would reveal a few of the rescuers' stories in rich detail. To do so I returned to seven of the fifty rescuers I had interviewed for the Oliners, to record their stories at greater length, and I spoke with a Jewish rescuer who passed up her chance to save herself in order to save a great many others. I chose this group not only for the variety of their stories, but also because I could interview some of the Jewish people they had rescued. Beginning in 1985, I traveled to Canada, Israel, the Netherlands, Czechoslovakia, Denmark, France, Poland, and several locations in the United States to photograph and conduct new interviews with the rescuers and the people they rescued.

For the people in this book, telling their stories stirred profound memories and emotions. Although the events they recalled occurred more than forty years earlier, the traumas, anxieties, fears, and joyous moments of their wartime experiences remained intense and vivid, so much so that two of the subjects preferred to remain anonymous. Therefore, "Erika van Hesteren" and "Rachel Litowitz" are pseudonyms.

Since I began this project several of the people whose stories are featured have passed away, including Bert Bochove, Herman Feder, Dr. Olga Lilien, Joseph Heinrich, and Jerry Chlup. I dedicate this book to their memory.

ACKNOWLEDGMENTS

I am deeply grateful to my Humboldt State University colleagues Pearl and Samuel Oliner, whose pioneering work in the study of rescuers was the impetus for this book. Julie Landweber, Stephen Miller, Alison Bond, Gale Cohen, and Tom Pettipiece have given valuable editorial assistance. Marilyn Murphy of the Eureka Public Library has been an inestimable resource for research questions. Many others who have provided vital support, advice, and assistance include Julia Scully; Marise Rinkel; Karen Simonetti; Klaus Meyer-Dettum; Ab, Mia, and Wim Ikkersheim; Richard Hamburger; Andy Grundberg; Sigrid Casey; Mead Kibbey; and Mordecai Paldiel. In addition to the people whose stories appear in this book, I give heartfelt thanks to the forty-three other rescuers who allowed me into their homes to record their stories and make photographs.

To Save a Life: Stories of Holocaust Rescue is a collection of personal memoirs and photographs that reveals how certain individuals acting upon their own moral convictions—while endangering their own and their families' lives—saved the lives of Jewish people from Nazi-occupied Europe.

In the following pages you will find true stories narrated by seven rescuers, accompanied by the narratives of ten people whom they rescued. Three stories take place in Holland; the others are set in Czechoslovakia and Poland. I made the contemporary photographic portraits of the rescuers and the people whom they helped and I photographed many of the sites that figure in their stories. The vintage photographs and other documents relating to the individual rescue accounts came from the subjects' personal albums and from historical archives. I have included descriptions of the conditions that Jewish people endured under Nazi occupation in Holland, Czechoslovakia, and Poland. An appendix provides background information about many of the larger political events, important places, and some of the individuals mentioned in the stories.

The fact of six million Jewish deaths, plus millions more of non-Jews, is well known. However, very little has been told about the approximately two million Jews who survived the Nazi era in Europe, many entirely because of aid given freely by men and women who, asking for nothing in return, sometimes died for their efforts. It is estimated that these rescuers comprised only one-tenth of one percent of the population of Nazi-occupied countries, although the actual number can never be known.

Rescuers came from every walk of life. They were teachers, students, shopkeepers, factory workers, housewives, and farmers. They ranged in age from their late teens to their eighties. By protecting Jews they were forced into a life of deception in their daily relations with friends, neighbors, and family. For years they lived in constant fear of betrayal or accidental exposure, knowing full well that the most severe punishment would be the consequence of helping Jewish people, if they were caught.

The self-effacing men and women who performed these incredible deeds of heroism were quite unexceptional in most other ways; they were ordinary people who responded to extraordinary circumstances in a morally exemplary fashion. In a world forever changed by the devastating horror of the Holocaust, their personal stories reveal the potential of the human spirit.

PART 1 ～ Holland

Few Jews survived in Holland, but those few

were saved as a result of the most strenuous efforts,

for Holland was the one territory of the occupied

West in which the Jews did not have an even

chance to live.—RAUL HILBERG

Everything worked against the Jewish population in Nazi-occupied Holland. The terrain is flat and there were no natural hiding places. With the open sea to the north and west, the German Reich to the east, and occupied Belgium to the south, escape beyond the borders was difficult and dangerous. Even before the occupation, most Dutch Jews lived in close proximity to one another in a few large urban centers, over half in Amsterdam alone.

Far worse for the Jews than the geographic disadvantage, the German-imposed government was civil rather than military and was therefore concerned primarily with control of the civilian population rather than with military matters. The governing body was headed by Arthur Seyss-Inquart, an Austrian veteran of the Anschluss known for his severity and efficiency in promulgating Hitler's idea of "racial purity." He closely followed the pattern of economic and social anti-Jewish measures carried out in Germany, which were designed to gradually destroy Jewish culture and eventually eliminate all trace of the Jews themselves.

There were three key factors to the success of such anti-Jewish measures in Holland. First, the initial wave of public protest by the Dutch population was immediately and ruthlessly suppressed through extremely severe reprisals. From that point on, protest became a more private matter, conducted largely by small underground groups engaged in sabotage against the Germans or in aiding Nazi victims, particularly Jews, to hide or escape. As public protest disappeared, the Germans were encouraged to proceed with their systematic plan to empty Holland of the Jews.

*Jewish Council
workers registering
Jews for "jobs" in
camps, Amsterdam,
c. 1943*

The second factor was the German device of setting up a Jewish Council, the Joodsche Raad, composed of prominent middle-class Jewish leaders, for the purpose of conveying German commands efficiently to the Jewish population. As in other occupied countries, the leaders reasoned that by keeping open the channels of communication with their German oppressors and by maintaining law and order in the newly formed chaotic ghetto population, they would help the bereft Jews more than harm them. In retrospect it is easy to see how wrong they were, as the council quickly became the unwitting tool of the German destruction machinery, actually delivering the Jews directly to the German deportation trains.

The third factor was the gradual nature of the implementation of the anti-Jewish measures, which lulled Jew and non-Jew alike into believing that despite the difficulties and inconveniences, things were not that bad and the Germans' demands could be accommodated. The common feeling was that the Germans would certainly lose the war and it was just a matter of waiting it out as best one could. With this in mind, a great many Dutch Jews willingly reported to the trains, which they believed would take them to work camps where they would labor for the Reich.

Schouwberg Jewish Theater, where Nazis detained Jews in Amsterdam, 1996

Of the 140,000 people who registered with the Germans as being Jewish, 107,000 were deported. Only 5,500 of them ever came back. Approximately 24,000 went into hiding, of whom about 8,000 were caught.

The following chronology of events shows how the German occupation government gradually imposed its will upon the Jewish population of Holland.

May 14, 1940   Holland surrenders to Germany. Dr. Arthur Seyss-Inquart appointed Reichskommissar, the highest governing authority.

October 1940	Every government official must sign an affidavit that neither he, his wife or fiancée, parents, or grandparents are Jewish. Jews are not to be promoted or appointed to government jobs. All businesses owned or operated partly or fully by Jews, or in which Jews have a financial interest, must register with German authorities.
November 1940	Jews in the Dutch Civil Service are dismissed.
December 1940	Persons of German "blood" are not allowed to work in Jewish households.
January 1941	All Jews residing in Holland must register with German authorities. Failure to do so is punishable by five years in prison or confiscation of property, or both. The Jewish Council, Joodsche Raad, is established, consisting of twenty members, including rabbis, lawyers, and middle-class businessmen.
February 1941	The Amsterdam ghetto is established following a series of incidents arising from an attack on the old Jewish quarter by groups of Dutch Nazi sympathizers. Several counterattacks by Jewish and Dutch youths set off severe reprisals by the Germans. A resultant general strike lasting several days is ruthlessly suppressed. This is the last large-scale public civilian protest in Holland to Nazi policies.
March 1941	Germans begin to "Aryanize" Jewish property. The Jewish Council is given authority over all Jewish organizations. Jews can no longer travel without a special permit from the Jewish Council, participate in the stock exchange, hold cultural posts, or enter public parks.

April 1941	German identification cards issued to the Dutch population.
July 1941	Jews who registered have their identity cards stamped with a large "J."
August 1941	Jewish children are barred from public and vocational schools.
	All Jewish assets, including bank deposits, cash, and securities, are blocked in order to be confiscated. A maximum of 250 guilders per month is made available to a Jewish owner of such assets, for his own use.
January 1942	Forced labor camps for Jews are established.
May 1942	Jews must wear a yellow star with the word *Jood* ("Jew") printed on it.
	Jews must observe a curfew between 8:00 P.M. and 6:00 A.M.
	Jews are allowed to shop only between 3:00 P.M. and 5:00 P.M.
	Public transportation is forbidden for Jews.
	Telephones are forbidden to Jews.
	Jews are forbidden to enter the homes of non-Jews.
	German government is authorized to confiscate all Jewish property except for wedding rings and gold teeth.
July 1942	Deportations of Jews out of Holland begin.
	Two transit camps are established in Holland, Westerbork and Vught, from which Jews are shipped to other camps, primarily Auschwitz.
September 1943	In the last major roundup, five thousand Jews, including the Jewish Council leaders, are sent to Westerbork.

1 ⌣ Like Violets in the Woods

Tina Strobos was not quite twenty years old when the Nazi army invaded Holland, in May 1940. She was living with her mother and a maid in their large, comfortable Amsterdam home and had just begun her medical school studies. Several years earlier she had decided to become a psychiatrist, the profession she practices in the United States today. During the last years of the war, when the daily business of buying food had become increasingly difficult, Tina's maternal grandmother, Maria Abrahams, came to live with Tina and her mother, Marie Schotte.

Although their home was a frequent target of raids by the Schutzstaffel—the Nazi elite guard known as the SS—Tina and her mother provided shelter for many Jews in hiding, in some cases for as long as a year. As an active member of the Dutch underground, Tina helped many Jews to survive by finding them places of refuge with other Dutch families, providing food ration coupons and false identity papers, and helping separated family members stay in contact with one another. When four of her Jewish friends in hiding were betrayed and arrested, it was Tina's cool wit and presence of mind that convinced a highly placed SS officer to release three of them, saving their lives.

Bram (Abraham) Pais was a close friend of Tina's before the war. Young, Jewish, he was described as brilliant by all in his circle. Bram was a physics student at the University of Utrecht when the Nazis came to power. Managing to finish his Ph.D. just days before Jews were barred altogether from the universities, he earned the distinction of being the last Jew to receive a doctorate in wartime Holland. His dissertation attracted the attention of Nils Bohr, who sent a message inviting him to work with Bohr in Denmark. With Tina's help he went underground for the duration of the war, unable to leave Holland to accept Nils Bohr's invitation until 1946. Tina helped Bram and his family to survive the war by finding them a succession of hiding places, arranging to supply Bram with books during his many months of enforced seclusion, and serving as a courier for messages between Bram and his family.

Before the war, Erika van Hesteren's parents were friends of Tina's mother, Marie. Erika's father was an important Jewish businessman with many contacts. But when the Nazi regime threatened arrest and deportation, Erika's parents were reduced to hiding in an Amsterdam attic, with food brought to them every day—like Anne Frank's family. It was Erika's father who sent Tina to prevail upon one of his friends—who happened to be Hermann Goering's friend—to release Bram Pais from jail.

Through her boyfriend, Erika had been associated with an underground resistance group that engaged in terrorist activities. Eighteen members of this group were caught and summarily executed by the Nazis. Erika was imprisoned. Escaping from prison, Erika was taken in by Tina and her mother, where she lived with other Jews in hiding for nearly a year.

Among the dangers of protecting Jews from the Gestapo was the difficult job of finding proper medical attention when necessary. Erika suffered from a back condition that worsened while she was staying with Tina and her mother. Tina made arrangements for her to have an illegal hospital operation.

Erika van Hesteren remained in her native city after the war. She gave this interview on July 15, 1986, at her historic canal-side home in Amsterdam, where she lives today.

In 1947 Bram Pais arrived in the United States where he became a colleague of Einstein at the Institute for Advanced Study in Princeton. In 1982 he published a critically acclaimed biography of Einstein; in 1986, a definitive history of the study of modern physics; and more recently a biography of Nils Bohr. He is presently a physics professor at Rockefeller University in New York. He and Tina remain close friends. Bram gave this account at his second home in Taagense, Denmark, on July 20, 1986.

After the war Tina Strobos emigrated to the United States, where she married, raised a family, and established a successful practice in psychiatry. She told her story in her home in Larchmont, New York, on June 23, 1985.

Tina Strobos

Our involvement with helping people began right away, the first day after the invasion. A friend of my parents, Henry Polack, was a famous labor leader and newspaper columnist. As a prominent socialist he was afraid he would be arrested. He felt he had to go into hiding. So my mother and I were immediately called into action.

We thought it would be safer for Polack at my grandmother's house. She had an extra room, and being over eighty, who would be suspicious?

Tina Strobos with portrait by a Jewish artist in hiding whom Tina was helping, 1984

We intended to make up a story that she was renting the room to a stranger. She said it would be hard for her to say she didn't know who Polack was, not only because he was so well known, but she even subscribed to the socialist paper where his picture regularly appeared next to his column. We told her to say she never read his column, but then she showed us her closet shelves, all nicely lined with that particular newspaper! We decided to take it out. But when we set to work, we discovered she had glued it on exceptionally well. My mother was so angry at her for not buying regular shelf paper! It was the day after the Nazi invasion and there we were, working like mad in my grandmother's apartment, peeling off those old newspapers.

My grandmother had sheltered people in her house during the First World War, refugees from Belgium. I thought that was interesting—a woman so old willing to take risks. She was a fighter. She was my model, my mother's mother. When she was a young married woman and had eight young children of her own to care for, she still had room to take in refugees.

Maybe it was selfish, but we thought my grandmother's house was a safer place than ours. Polack stayed there for a couple of weeks, but then, like other people in his situation, he came out of hiding, because in the beginning they weren't arresting anyone. That came later.

Soon after that the underground took form, and among the first to hide in our house was one of the leaders—Johan Brouwer. My mother admired him very much, so she wasn't against helping by giving him shelter for a couple of months. She certainly knew what work he was engaged in, although he never told her exact details, and that was just as well.

Brouwer got me interested in joining his group of about ten people, the BS, or Binnenlandse Strydkrachten. We read *Mein Kampf* and Marx together. One of the first jobs he gave me was to write out a thousand copies of a poem by a man who was in jail at the time for having written against Hitler. He was a very second-rate poet and I couldn't see that it would help our cause for me to risk my life by making a thousand copies of that awful poem. I refused.

Maria Abrahams, Tina's maternal grandmother, 1941

Brouwer was furious. He said, "You're in an army now. You either obey the rules or you're thrown out!" I said, "Well, I can't obey orders," and I was ousted from the group. But then they would call on me for a job or to hide some weapons for them. We had guns stolen from the Wehrmacht [German army] in our house. They were in big boxes, half the size of a sofa, with the names of the guns written all over them. I also did some courier work for Brouwer: one time I brought a radio sender to an address. I was only with this group for a couple of months. They frightened me to death.

I never told my mother about them. If I was scared, I figured she would be even more so. They went into action making bombs, and all of them were killed, including a friend of mine. They were very impetuous, very impulsive, very heroic and brave. I was none of those. I've always been a cautious person. If I did something, I always did it very carefully. I survived and they didn't.

Then I joined the Landelyke Organizatie, which means "Country Organization." They were involved with peaceful activities, such as placing people in hiding and making passports. The organization would call on me and my friends to deliver Jews or Jewish children to safe addresses in the country. I remember spending a lot of time each week on my bike, bringing false passports to people in hiding and providing them with printed food stamps. Then, too, when Jews came to my house, I would call the LO to find a more permanent place for them.

Our house became kind of a transit station; we didn't keep people too long because we were raided so often. And then, my mother was always terribly scared. Whenever the Gestapo visited she would tremble, really tremble. I've never seen anybody tremble as much. I would hiss at her out of the side of my mouth, "Don't show them you're afraid. You have nothing to be afraid of. You've done nothing wrong. They have nothing on us. They can't prove a thing." I sort of hypnotized her by talking like that. And then she would become somewhat reassured, and I'd hold her, you know, take her arm. That you could do, because they knew that everybody was scared of them.

Our house was not very safe because we were involved in too many activities—the medical school, the radio listening, hiding people, making passports. We always had contraband in our house, under the rug—a pretty stupid way of hiding things. My grandmother had a radio sender in her house, so we could send messages from the underground to the BBC. We would listen to the BBC broadcast and then go to her house to send our messages back in code.

The Germans decreed the death penalty for anyone having a radio, but we kept ours and hid it. When Churchill or the queen of Holland would speak on BBC, we had as many as thirty or forty people come to our house after dark to listen, mostly Jews in hiding who lived within walking distance. That's how many people we knew were in hiding. In Holland it's dark in the winter around three or four o'clock in the afternoon. The broadcasts were usually around 6:00 P.M. so they had time to go back home before curfew at 8:00 P.M.

I had many Jewish friends. Then there were the friends of friends, and their families, and so forth. They would often ask me how to get a non-Jewish ID card. First, I had them give me a photograph. I put their fingerprint on the back of the photo, using a little machine I had which was made for this purpose. Then I would steal a passport of the appropriate age group, soak off the seal, put their picture in it, and seal it again. They looked good.

I usually stole passports from people I knew. For example, when I went to my aunt's funeral in the spring of '41, I noticed that a lot of people were leaving their pocketbooks beside their coats and jackets in the hallway. I stole a couple of passports by going through the pocketbooks. No one saw me. It was very inconvenient to have had your passport stolen: you had to go through a lot of misery to get a new one, but it was small potatoes compared to not having one at all, or worse, having one that had a "J" on it. There was no way to get that "J" off. It was large.

The university students had to sign a loyalty oath to Hitler in the spring of '41, or was it '42? The exact chronology for all this is not good because I didn't keep a diary. About 95 percent of the students refused, so the universities closed. After that, we held underground medical classes in our home. That was forbidden with the death penalty too, but I thought it was worthwhile to continue our studies. We had to be organized, to contact all these people, telling them to meet at a certain place and time. And we didn't always know who could be trusted, but even so, we had at least eighteen people coming once a week, all through the war. When the hospital had a corpse to dissect, they would call us and say we could send six students over to learn pathology. Gradually they rotated through all the enrolled students. I attended quite a few of those sessions. It was quite a marvelous organization.

The hospital also arranged for medical students to serve as interns. When I was asked by the chief of internal medicine to fill an internship, I accepted even though I had not yet taken the qualifying exams. I had to do it over again after the war, but still I learned a lot. I tried to study every day.

The Jews should never have registered themselves with the Germans. They were afraid not to. They were afraid that the Germans would find them through synagogue records, which should have been immediately destroyed. There were, of course, signs posted all over the city saying that if you didn't register, terrible things would happen, and if you did, they wouldn't bother you. In retrospect, who would believe that?

All my Jewish friends registered. There was this very good friend of my mother's, a journalist. He was not an observant Jew, and he didn't happen to look Jewish. He wore the Jewish star but he would also go in the streetcar, which was one of the things forbidden to Jews. He just put his coat on over his star and thought that he was safe. Well, he was caught on the streetcar. They were constantly trying to catch people. If you didn't look Jewish, and you didn't register, and you didn't wear a star, nothing happened to you. But do you know, I don't know anybody who did that? Not one.

Before the Nazi occupation there were no anti-Semitic regulations in Amsterdam that I know of; Jews lived all over the city. But there was an old Jewish quarter, which happened to be one of the nicest neighborhoods

Identity card stamped with incriminating "J," for "Jew," issued to a Dutch Jew during Nazi occupation

in Amsterdam, not at all poverty-stricken. It was a lower-middle-class merchants' neighborhood, full of seventeenth-century houses situated on beautiful little canals. They had a wonderful market there each Sunday, and everybody I knew always went to it. Somewhat like New York's Lower East Side, there were stalls where you could buy clothes, and wonderful food—pickles, Jewish delicatessens. It was a great place to buy fresh bagels and bread on Sunday. In fact, it was the only place, since the bakers' union required that all the other city bakeries close on Sunday. But the Jewish bakers observed their sabbath on Saturday, so they were allowed to be open. We all went there for a good time, and for the bread.

In '41 the Germans closed off the Jewish quarter and forced into it all the Jews living in other parts of the city. They put up barbed wire all around, but they left the main thoroughfares open, so there was still lively communication and trade. We could go in and out, and the Jewish people could go in and out, but that didn't hinder the Gestapo raiding procedures at all, because everyone had to be home by the 8:00 P.M. curfew.

They used the Jewish theater, not far from where Rembrandt lived, to hold people they rounded up before deporting them to the camps. Once you were in there it was very hard to get out—but it happened. In the beginning, you could still get out with the right kind of passport, or if you knew how to sew German uniforms, or if you were important in the diamond trade, or had some other important job. If you belonged to the Jewish Council, you were excused. But in the end, they went too.

I visited many of the people that I hid. Sometimes I was their only contact with the outside world, especially those who were hidden in attics on isolated farms. They generally didn't have much in common with the farmers, and the farmers thought they were pretty odd people, too. Sometimes my mother and I went together, which was a relief, because the visits could be so painful. They couldn't receive mail. A month could go by with no news from anyone. Anything, like mail from a son or daughter, or news, I smuggled to them, which, in a way, was dangerous. The farmers didn't especially appreciate my visits, and I didn't appreciate having to travel all over the country to make these visits, either. It was hard. Off-hand, I would say there were seven people I regularly visited like that.

You felt you had to help the children. Everybody felt that, and then too it was easier to find places for children. For instance, the parents of a little three-year-old girl called me. They had a hiding place, but they couldn't bring their child with them. So I said, "Tell me when you're hiding and I'll come pick her up. She can stay in my house until I find a better place for her." I couldn't tell them about our house, that it wasn't really safe.

I would immediately call one of my contacts and say, "On the eighteenth I will have a visitor, age three. Can you find a place for her? Let me know." Then we would get a call back. "About that three-year-old—we have a place. On the twentieth I'll send you instructions on where to bring her." I went to the ghetto and brought her out on my bike. My mother once brought a child home like that, on the back of her bike, without telling me about it.

The trains were still running at that time, so I brought her by train to a farmer. As time passed, this little girl became very attached to her step-mother. The father was caught, but later on when the mother came back, the child no longer recognized her. It was a very wrenching experience for all of those concerned. Sometimes these farmers didn't want to give up the Jewish children, even though, as in this case, they were blond and the child had dark hair, dark skin, and black eyes. Tamar Melkman was her name; I remember her quite well.

Once, we had a large family with five children staying with us. They were very religious Orthodox Jews, refugees from a small Polish village, who had brought their own bread and food in a big bag. They stayed in their room, leaving only to visit the bathroom. They didn't talk to us. All they wanted from us was water, which we handed to them through the door; they would open it just a crack. They had never met people like us and didn't quite trust us. I guess they were afraid of heathens, or pagans. We had a few families like that, that had fled Poland or Germany in '39 and stayed with us just a short while. The religious groups had their own network and they would come and go without us knowing who they were, where they were from, or where they were going.

LOU

In July 1942, the Germans began periodic raids on the Amsterdam ghetto, seizing tens of thousands of Jews in house-to-house roundups, shipping them first to Westerbork transit camp in Holland, and from there to other destinations, most often Auschwitz. As the Jews were emptied out of the ghetto, new ones from other parts of Holland were forced to move in.

Family friends asked Tina to go to the ghetto to bring out a fourteen-year-old boy named Lou, to find a safe place for him. But finding a family to take him in proved difficult because of his age. He was too old to elicit the protective sympathy commonly extended to younger children, too young to be on his own, too big to go to school, and too conspicuous to be out on the street.

I talked to ten families before I got a place for him; it was one of the few addresses I found on my own. They were not at all eager to take him, either. I had to talk to them three times, in the company of a mutual friend, before they agreed. They explained to me, "We have a Nazi living in our apartment building, so the boy will have to stay home at all times. He must always wear slippers, and cannot make any noise at all when we're away. He must remember to not flush the toilet when we're gone." And they were concerned about how to buy food for him with only their own ration cards. So I replied, "We'll provide you with money, food stamps, and a very fine passport. He'll pass as your boarder. He doesn't look Jewish."

They asked me to show them his picture. Luckily, he didn't look too Jewish. But this boy happened to be rather shy, not somebody you would easily take to your heart. He was standoffish. I guess fourteen-year-olds are strange people anyway, but Lou couldn't afford to be like that.

All his rebellious instincts had to be suppressed. He had to be a good boy and a perfect boarder. They weren't such warm people, either. They took him in from their sense of duty, and maybe because the extra coupons helped a little bit with their expenses, although they wouldn't get rich from it. Partly they did it because they were pressured by us. We told them it was their job as good citizens to save a life, which kind of appealed to them. We told them that he was quiet and wouldn't cause them too much trouble, they'd be fairly safe, and it wouldn't cost them any extra money.

I had to find money for him, plus all the documents, as well as talk to this couple three times, which altogether took a good week's work—one placement. Meantime, he's staying in our house.

So I got this not-so-fine place for him with people who didn't really care all that much. They weren't the warmest people, and they never opened their hearts to this lonely kid. I know he had a hard time there because I would visit at least once a month bringing food cards and things like that. The bikes were so awful, it took an hour to get there—all the way to the other end of Amsterdam. Pneumatic tires were not available by then, and pedaling the heavy, solid tires over cobblestone streets was hard work. On one occasion, when I arrived, these people took me aside and said, "All right. He's a very good boy. He doesn't give us any trouble. He's obedient, but he eats so much!"

Well, after all, he was a growing adolescent. I would try to get some extra food coupons for them. Then they told me that his feet smelled terribly. I said, "Why don't you tell him? Let him bathe and powder his feet once or twice a day."

"Well, we're embarrassed to talk to him about it."

"But you must tell him, otherwise you'll start hating him." They wanted me to tell him what was bothering them. That's the kind of job I had! Isn't it pathetic?

They were decent people, in a way, or else they wouldn't be keeping him, and they didn't want to embarrass him or hurt his feelings. But they weren't doing him or themselves a favor, because they started disliking him and disliking being with him.

I explained to Lou that he had to wash his feet and wear clean socks every day and that solved the problem. They suffered for nothing all that time. But it was true; after she told me, I noticed an odor when you came into their small apartment. It's an example of how these relationships weren't always very comfortable.

Lou's mother was a person who never attempted to find a hiding place. She couldn't accept the idea of hiding. She also couldn't accept the horrible truth that it might be the end of her life if she went to work in a "factory," the myth that the Nazis held up to the Jews. She was one of those who didn't return.

Amsterdam ghetto, 1941

Lou stayed with them until after the war. By then he was eighteen. He found a job in a printer's office and a little room to rent somewhere. He made a living. He was handy and smart and he did a good job, but he was awfully quiet, still. I think his sojourn in this house with these uncommunicative people didn't do him much good. I felt I should have visited there every day. But it was an hour one way and an hour back and I had a lot of other things to do. And anyway, it was hard to have rapport with this child.

After the war he got meningitis and died. I felt a little bit cheated. Look at all the things we went through—he went through. Then he dies. I really think that life was just too hard for him. I can't help but think that.

THE DE LEEUW FAMILY

My mother went to the ghetto one day to see some good friends and was caught in a raid. When she came home she looked like a ghost, trembling from head to foot. She never forgot what happened that day, nor will I ever forget what she said. She was on her bike in the ghetto, starting to leave.

On a loudspeaker they were saying, anybody who doesn't belong here, doesn't live here, if we catch you, you will be transported to Germany too. We didn't know they were going to Poland. We didn't really know about the concentration camps.

As my mother was leaving the ghetto, trembling with fear and with misery, a couple of times people stopped her to ask, "Would you please take my baby on the back of your bike?" She told them, "Do you have papers for him, otherwise he will be stopped at the gate, and I will be too, for trying to get him out. If you know a way I can meet him outside, a place where you can get him through the barbed wire, then I can help." But lined up every ten feet were flares and lights, plus machine guns on the roofs, and on every street corner. There was really no way she could do that. It would certainly have endangered our own lives. There was no question about it, because we knew the risks we faced and we knew that if Jews were found in our home, we were going too. We didn't believe in the "factories," but we didn't know about gas chambers until after the war. I can swear to it. It wasn't in the underground press. The Jews didn't know. Many went willingly.

The next morning my mother went back to the ghetto to see her friends—De Leeuw was their name. Arriving at their home, she called out to them. It was deathly quiet. They were a family with seven children. Five were registered in that home, and those five children had been caught. But visiting them was a married daughter and son-in-law, Siegfried and Suze Pekel, only seventeen or eighteen years old, who were registered at another address in the ghetto. This young couple had hidden in a closet and were not found by the Gestapo. My mother brought them home.

They were so bereaved and upset, we felt we had to keep them a while. They stayed in our house, I guess, for a couple of months, but then we had a warning that we would be raided ourselves so I found a place for them very quickly, in one of the hothouses in Aalsmeer where they were growing tomato plants and flower bulbs. I brought them by train. They were hiding there from 1943 until 1945, sleeping on mattresses beneath the flower beds. It was a warm place to hide and they were together. They were lucky.

ARREST

Between 1942 and the end of 1944, Tina and her mother's home was "visited" eight times by the Gestapo, Tina was arrested three times, her mother, twice. Their maid was arrested once for black marketeering.

One day a man came and announced he was a carpenter, sent by the underground to make a hiding place for us. My mother looked at me, "Do you know this man?" I said, "No, of course not, but if we can't trust him, who can we trust?" So she agreed: "Okay, show him the attic." That's how I found out I was part of a network. They didn't give you an official certificate. This carpenter built sort of an attic within our attic, almost inaccessible. In one or two of the raids the Gestapo went up there and knocked around, but they never discovered it.

My mother and I were cautious. We didn't want to jeopardize ourselves or anyone else. Our house was well known, so in a way it was not such a great place to hide, but nobody was ever found in our house. Nobody was ever caught.

We did have a spy in the Gestapo headquarters, who would warn us with a phone call saying, "I've heard you're going to have visitors within the next few days." Then I would call on all my resources to let them know that we had to empty out our house and find places for the people who were staying with us. Then we would check all the hiding places to make sure there was nothing they could get us for. Once our house was clean we would just sit and wait for them.

Hans De Jong was an industrialist who hid in our house for a whole year, during '43 and '44. The Nazis were eager to get people like him because of their money.

One day we heard that his bookkeeper, who was in the habit of occa-

sionally coming by to bring him money, was under arrest. We didn't trust this man not to betray us, so we very quickly found De Jong another hiding place. We just assumed that the bookkeeper would have mentioned our address to the Gestapo.

I thought it might be a good idea for my mother to go out of town on a little vacation. So she went to visit her two very dear friends in Leiden while I stayed at home. We figured it might be valuable for Hans De Jong to know what his bookkeeper blabbed to the Gestapo, so I had the task, if they came, to ask about him, to find out what they knew. Sure enough, they came.

You always knew when it was the Gestapo coming to visit. They rang the bell hard and banged on the door. All at once, they opened the door wide and jumped in, two men in mufti, civilian clothes, with hidden guns. They wouldn't say their business until they had closed the door behind them. I acted very naive. I told them my mother rented rooms and I was taking care of her business while she was away on vacation.

Suddenly, there were six men in the house. Two of them, one on each side, took me by the wrists and threw me against the wall.

"You're under arrest!"

"I don't speak German, I can't understand you."

So they yelled again, "We need a translator!"

I speak perfect German, but I had been trained that if arrested, to ask for an interpreter. To hear the question in German, then the translation, gives you more time to think of a good answer. It worked pretty well. So I said to them, "Hans De Jong? Sure I know him. He rented rooms from us. Did he do anything wrong?"

The Gestapo said, "He's a Jew," as if I should know that that was a terrible thing.

"But he has blue eyes and blond hair. How could he be a Jew?"

Then he went on, "Some Jews are like violets in the woods. They hide by having blue eyes and blond hair," as if they were doing this on purpose.

"Really? I can't believe it."

"I will show you pictures."

And he did. He showed me pictures of eye corners. That's right. There were about sixteen pictures of the corners of eyes. "That's what we're looking for in the streets," he said. They did, too. They arrested Jews and half-Jews in the street, even though they didn't look Jewish. A half-Jew they could recognize. To me these people didn't look Jewish at all.

I was sitting during this interrogation, nervously crossing and uncrossing my legs. It was summer and I was wearing shorts. At one point he said, "You don't have to show off your legs to me. That doesn't impress me at all." Well, that remark reminded me that he was just a man. I had nice legs, fortunately, and he was noticing. Realizing that, it relaxed me no end—I can't tell you how much. Suddenly I was no longer this beaten-down person under arrest, threatened with punishment. Because they *were* very threatening. Now I became a young girl, not too bad looking, who apparently was seductive to them. I felt so much more at ease that I even became fresh; I noticed this was a good tactic. I took the attitude that I had no idea what they were talking about, I hadn't done anything wrong, and what was all the fuss about, anyway? They saw I wasn't scared anymore, and somehow it turned into a more human intercourse with someone who was being nasty, giving me the right to be nasty back.

I was too tactful to get them angry. But I recovered a lot of confidence and I stopped trembling. Finally he said, "You and your mother had better come to Gestapo headquarters in The Hague. We're going to pursue this further. We want to find this man and we think you know how."

Later, when we went to The Hague, we dressed to the nines, and we were both speaking fluent German, to flatter them. These were different people now, highly placed Gestapo officers, who were polite and doctrinaire. They weren't at all suspicious that I had learned German so well in just a few weeks. They weren't that smart, really. They were only interested in finding out where this Hans De Jong was. We were supposed to let them know immediately if we saw him or got a message from him. While we were there, we heard our interrogator say to an underling, "Go to the Haverstraat." We knew that was De Jong's other hiding address, where he had been before, and where indeed he might have been now, except that luckily we didn't send him there this time. So as soon as we returned to Amsterdam I got a message to the Haverstraat to warn them. The people there didn't take anyone in for a long while after that. And we didn't either. This was in 1943. De Jong got caught in '44. He was in jail and was shot in 1945.

Bram Pais and I were engaged until 1943. My mother wasn't too thrilled with him when we broke up. She thought it was odd for us to be friends after that, but we've always stayed friends. I found hiding places for a lot of his relatives: his father and mother, a cousin, his sister-in-law, and I would have hidden his sister and her husband if they had let us, but the husband couldn't bear the idea of going into hiding. He was sure he would go crazy. He said, "I'm young. I'm strong. They'll select me to work in a factory." We talked and talked with Bram's sister but she was absolutely adamant about staying with her husband. We pleaded with her to let us find her a hiding place, but she refused. They died in the concentration camp.

Bram's parents were among those whom I regularly visited while they were in hiding. They were on a farm, living in an attic with steeply sloping walls; you could stand up straight only in the middle of the room. All they did was complain about the food, about the farmers, about how unfriendly they were, how uncommunicative, how they never came to sit and talk with them, how lonely and isolated they felt. This was all very understandable, but it was not pleasant. There was nothing I could do except come more often.

When Bram decided to go into hiding I helped him to find a place— actually four different places, because he was almost caught three times; three times the house he was hiding in was raided. One time the Gestapo were in there for six hours, searching everything. Another time he hid himself in a footlocker, and they never found him. Bram Pais was very lucky and very courageous. He could shake off these experiences and forget about them. He's an optimist person.

We had a close-knit group of friends, which included Tirtsah Van Amerongen and her sister Jeanne, neither of whom looked at all Jewish. They had the best false papers you could get, with a whole history memorized about where they came from and who their families were, and even copies placed in the city hall register. It all checked. They had that in place by '44.

Jeanne was married to Lion Nordheim, who was a wonderful person and a very dear friend. I would say he was the spiritual leader of our group. He was also one of the leaders of the Dutch Zionist movement, and a man of fantastic intellect, very able as a speaker and writer.

He wrote a paper for the underground press about what to do with the great number of Jewish children who were in hiding, whose parents would not be coming back after the war. The children being so much safer than the parents, he foresaw that this would be a serious problem later on. Lion and Bram were close friends.

In the summer of 1944, yearning to be free and on their own instead of being unwelcome guests in people's homes and attics, Bram, Tirtsah, Jeanne, and Lion rented an apartment together. They weren't unwelcome in our house, but they were guests nevertheless. It was a burden for both sides. So they were delighted to rent an apartment, just the four of them, all young—still in their twenties and early thirties, and good friends. They were happy to be by themselves.

But Bram Pais had an ex-girlfriend who betrayed this place. In February 1945, they were all caught.

As soon as I heard they were arrested I tried to find out what had happened, where they were, what I could do to help. I went straight to their apartment and rang the doorbell; unknowingly I had entered the lion's den. The Gestapo grabbed me immediately, yanking me inside.

"You're under arrest!"

Again I asked for a translator. I made up a story that I was selling potatoes, going door to door.

"So! You're in the black market!"

"Well, we have to eat." They knew we didn't have anything anymore.

They showed me pictures and passports of my four friends, but of course I didn't know any of them. By good luck during this ordeal, I found out the name of their boss, because they were mentioning his name all the time—Herr Obersturmfuhrer So-and-So. I buttoned that name in my ear. Unfortunately, I was carrying a picture of my boyfriend in my pocketbook.

"You're Jewish!" they said. "You're a Jew! This is your boyfriend and he's hiding. Where is he?" He was a doctor, listed in the telephone book, and they could call him, which they did. He wasn't Jewish. If he had been, I wouldn't have carried his picture. The questioning went on for nearly five hours, and then at last they let me go.

Amsterdam home of Tina Strobos and her mother, 1986

The next day I brought Tirtsah a package with food and clean clothes and a pair of very special, very beautiful pajamas that my aunt in the United States had sent me years before. Later Tirtsah said she was so happy to get those things, because she knew then that somebody was working on her case. It was the beginning of her liberation.

Because she and Jeanne had such good papers I was able to help them get out of jail in about a week. The first thing you had to do was find out who was the Gestapo official dealing with the case, the Sachbearbeiter. The Germans were always quasilegalistic. I went to this Sachbearbeiter, whose name I already knew from my interrogation, and insisted to him that they were not Jewish. How dare they, in heaven's name, keep these friends of mine who had done nothing wrong? It helped that the jail was quite full by that time, and also that they knew they were losing the war. This man wanted to do me a favor. I noticed that. He wanted to do some good for people he thought were influential, or do a favor for a pretty young girl. Maybe he wanted to go out with me or something. He let them go.

But Bram and Lion were still in jail. They were caught in February '45, but it was not until early March that I could get Bram Pais out, too. It happened like this.

First of all we had this letter from Nils Bohr inviting Bram to study with him in Denmark. Then, too, I knew a man who was in hiding who had been a big *macher* all his life, an important rich Jewish businessman. This man thought I should go to see this friend of his who was a high official in the German army—maybe he was a colonel—a close friend of Hermann Goering, the head of the German Luftwaffe. He thought if I showed him the Nils Bohr letter, since he knew they were losing the war, he might want to do a good deed and let Bram out. This Jewish man wanted to do something for me because his daughter, Erika van Hesteren, was staying in our house. He also knew Bram; he knew that he was considered a young genius. Somehow people feel the loss of a genius more keenly than of an ordinary person. I guess we all feel like that, like that's a greater loss. Of course, it's not true.

I thought, well, maybe I'll have to sleep with this friend of Goering or something, but if I have to, I'll do it. I had this girlish fantasy that you had to be submitting to all kinds of favors. I made an appointment to see him.

This man looked like a caricature of a German—bald, with a big fat neck and a red face. He was extremely repulsive to look at. On his desk was a large portrait of Hermann Goering inscribed "to my best friend, So-and-So." Well, it was true. At least it's true, he's Goering's friend, I told myself. When I spoke to him I said, "They caught Bram Pais, but I understand that he was caught without identity papers," something I had learned from the Sachbearbeiter. That was in Bram's favor, that he had not tried to pass as a non-Jew. They could understand hiding, but they could not forgive trying to pass as a non-Jew. He didn't have papers because he was in the process of getting these very fine new ones, like Jeanne and Tirtsah had, where you had a duplicate in the city hall. So that's why he had temporarily given up his documents. The Gestapo thought it was terrific that when they asked, "Where are your identity papers?" Bram said, "I don't have any."

"You're a Jew!"

"Yes, I am."

They thought that was very good, too. Bram is very bouncy and very

Tina Strobos, Bram Pais, and Marie Schotte, 1941

intelligent. He knew how to respond to them, unlike Lion, who was in a total panic all the time, sure he was going to be killed. And so he was. Maybe you help it along by being so afraid. Lion wanted to commit suicide when the war started. I said to him, "Well, at least try to escape." His reply: "I'll never make it." Even though he was so intelligent he didn't have the courage that Bram had.

Tirtsah van Amerongen and Tina Strobos, 1938

So I gave Hermann Goering's friend the Nils Bohr letter and told him that his prisoner was a young genius in physics. "Hmm," he said, "what jail is he in?" And I told him, "Weterings schans." He asked the secretary to look up the telephone number, dialed the phone, and said, "I want to speak to Oberst So-and-So," the head of the jail. "Heinz, I want you to look up a young man, a Jew named Abraham Pais, and let him out." Then he hung up the phone.

An hour later Bram Pais was free. I told this story to Bram at the time, but years later he didn't remember why they had let him out. Isn't that strange? He forgot the whole story. He suppressed the whole thing from his mind, I'm sure, because he felt guilty that his best friend was killed because of his girlfriend's carelessness. They shot Lion.

Coming out of jail, he headed straight to our house. He told us, "I was probably the only Jew in years who walked down the middle of the street in broad daylight." This was typical for Bram Pais. The Germans were losing the war, and he was in the best of spirits. That was like him.

Bram knows that his ex-girlfriend betrayed the four of them. He knows it, but he doesn't want to talk about that. I have never, except now, spoken about it. My friend Tirtsah and her sister won't speak to him because of this, which you can understand.

His ex-girlfriend was the only person they could suspect because there weren't that many people who visited them. This girl broke up with him and was very angry, maybe threatened somehow. I've never found out exactly because Bram won't speak about it. He has now forgotten this. We sometimes speak about the past and he has a lot of interesting stories to tell, but this is not one of them.

ERIKA

Erika van Hesteren was part of an underground group I was afraid of—the Soldiers of Orange. She had been caught in a house where they were making bombs. Her boyfriend, her brother-in-law, her boyfriend's brother, everybody was shot to death, except her. Why? Because her Sachbearbeiter, who was still a young man, and a protégé of Himmler, fell in love with her. He dyed her hair blond and set her up in an apartment for himself. He was hoping to enlist her services as a counterspy and she went along with him. She was seventeen and scared to death. All her best friends were shot. She was hardly in a position to say no, so she was no hero in that sense, but as far as I know she didn't betray anybody. She contacted the underground and told them the true story. They began feeding her information to bring back to her Gestapo friend, so that she could keep up the game. It was in their interest too.

But she became terribly ill. She started having severe backaches and just couldn't take it any longer. It's odd; when she was arrested in the summer of '44, she had been wearing sandals and a summer dress. She escaped in December, and for some crazy reason she was wearing the same dress and sandals. She had a kind of superstitious idea that she should not take anything her Gestapo friend had given her. Then she was brought to us and we gave her winter clothes.

She arrived in our house a sick little girl, bedridden. She was, of course, a dangerous person who was sought by the Gestapo. After a year, I was able to get her into a hospital under a false name with good papers, where she was able to have an operation on her spinal disc—a laminectomy and fusion. The Catholic hospital was very good to us, because anyone could see she was a Jewish-looking girl. They were doing these things for sick people who were in hiding. They delivered babies, too. I visited her regularly during the two months she was recovering in the hospital, until the end of the war. Fortunately, she was the only one in our house who became sick.

THE LAST YEAR: THE HUNGER WINTER

We lived under such terrible strain during the war, but then practically everything we did was punishable by death: listening to the radio—which we did faithfully—even buying potatoes. If they wanted to, the Gestapo could kill you for that. They usually didn't because people were really hungry. The Germans took everything that last winter, after D-day.

They simply emptied out the north of Holland. Below the Rhine it was liberated. They attempted to cross the Rhine at Arnhem in the fall of '44, but it failed, and after that we were totally isolated. Fortunately, no more transports could get to Germany, so the Jews in hiding were relatively safe after that, but the Germans did take all our food, all our cars, all our factories. They dismantled everything. It was as if a plague of locusts had descended upon us.

That last winter there were no more cats in Amsterdam. People ate them. Before the war our maid's family were big importers and exporters, using the Rhine boats for transport. Now, when everything in Holland was being sent to Germany on these boats, her family was surviving by stealing things from them to sell on the black market. That's how we managed to get fairly well fed. Fairly well. Mostly we ate potatoes. But occasionally we had smoked eel, or a box of biscuits, or perhaps cookies or a bottle of Dutch gin.

We had heat in only one room that winter. Just a little fire in a can about the size of a two-pound coffee tin, that was our stove. Everybody would congregate in this one room; it was tolerable. On top of the little stove, we always kept a kettle boiling with water and sugar beets.

We could still get sugar beets, although there was very little sugar in them, mostly they were fiber. We ground them up in a meat grinder and then boiled them to get the sugary water. Every house in Amsterdam smelled of sugar beets. I still can't stand the smell.

I tried to study every day, and then too I was spending time at the hospital as an intern. It was wonderful to be there, a lot better than running around to all the people in hiding. You have to be a little bit selfish and look after yourself, too, otherwise you just die inside, you burn out. There's just so much you can do for other people.

My room where I studied was cold, so to stay warm I would put on a fur coat and gloves and go under the blankets with a hot water bottle. We used empty Dutch gin bottles, made from earthenware; they made good hot water bottles.

One day I came into the living room to refill my bottle from the boiling kettle. As I was emptying the old water into the sink, I noticed something smelled different. I stood there absolutely frozen with horror. It was gin! Just then, Lion Nordheim walked into the room, saw what had happened, and started to laugh. He laughed and laughed, and pretty soon everybody came to look, and they all burst out laughing. As it turned out, Lion and my mother had paid sixty dollars for that gin, and had planned to get drunk to cheer themselves up. A fortune! We laughed a lot in those dark days. It's very strange.

I've been asked in recent years why my mother and I did these things. Historically, how did I grow up to be a rescuer? I never asked myself that question because it was a natural assumption for both of us that we would do this. We never questioned the premise, as if this was a tradition in the family. Well, it was. For us it was the right thing to do. We never argued with my grandmother about it. We just assumed she would do this. I never asked my mother if she thought it was all right to bring these people in the house. She once said to me, "You know, this could get us killed." I said, "Yeah, I realize that." That was the only sort of hard discussion we had on whether it was dangerous or not, or whether you should do it or not.

Breaking up a building for firewood during the Hunger Winter, Amsterdam, 1944–45

You should do it. That it was dangerous, we really didn't want to focus on that.

Religion was not a factor. We're atheists. My mother was a very militant atheist. My grandmother was even more militant. My parents were in the socialist movement. Most of my generation went to the university, but my parents didn't. My parents knew and spoke four languages fluently, but all from night school studies and traveling.

My mother and I, we didn't talk about these things until much later. When my children were small I couldn't tolerate even thinking about it. I had to give my energy to becoming a doctor in a new country, finding a home, finding schools for the children. I couldn't deviate from those goals and I couldn't afford to dwell on those wrenching experiences. They were survival techniques. But now it's not so bad anymore. I can distance myself from it. In the beginning, when I was first interviewed about this, I couldn't sleep all night. I had recurring nightmares like I used to have, about being arrested, about Nazis persecuting and following me.

I remember May 1945, when we were waiting for the Canadian army to come and liberate us in Holland. We knew the war was won but the Canadian army had not reached us yet. The rumor was they would come from the east, from Germany. Day and night, people were lined up, waiting at the eastern entrance of Amsterdam to pass the word. I had gone to take my exam in pharmacology, underground, at my professor's house, which was all the way in the easternmost part of town, only two blocks away from the road they were supposed to be coming on. My professor said right as I entered, "You know this could be the day. They're expected to come any time." Sure enough, right in the middle of the exam his wife shouted out, "They're coming! They're coming!" and we all ran out of the house.

Everybody ran to the road. We heard the tanks rolling in. Thousands of people were standing there, at the entrance of the city. We stood there and cried and waved, and a lot of people had flags and handkerchiefs. Some people climbed on the tanks. You've seen the pictures. You have no idea how the pent-up fears and emotions suddenly fall off you. That

Tony van Renterghem, now a US citizen and declared a "Righteous among Nations" by Israel, guides the first Canadian unit into Amsterdam on the day of liberation, May 1945

moment. It was maybe the most wonderful moment you ever have in your life, except giving birth to a child.

My daughter and I went to Amsterdam for a visit in April 1986. As we were passing by my old house, I began telling her about this house where I was born, where my grandparents had lived, where we had hidden people. I asked her if she'd like to see it.

We saw a woman going inside, so I knocked on the window next to the door. I said, "I used to live in this house during the war. I would like to show it to my daughter," and the woman invited us in.

I told her, "I was here once before with my husband, looking for the hiding place for the Jews, but we couldn't find it. Do you know where it is?"

"Of course I know. We found it when we made the bedroom in the attic. By the way, there is a portrait sculpture of your head—a bust—here. Did you know about it? I recognized your face when you knocked just now. It's a beautiful Jugendstil sculpture."

"I knew it was there but it was too heavy for me and my husband to carry home."

Immediately, my daughter said, "I'll carry it."

"I'm sorry to say that the nose is broken. I've always wanted to fix it. I'm a sculptor and know how, but I've never gotten around to it." A wonderful woman. Personally, I never liked the thing; it was too idealized. So my daughter carried it all the way home, and now it is in my living room.

I had forgotten everything. I had forgotten all about the attic. I'm sure it was because I didn't want to remember all those things. So you just close the whole attic of your memory. Now I can remember it again.

Bram Pais

There was a family in Amsterdam, three sisters and one brother, who were all very active in one way or another in the Zionist youth organization. Their name was Van Amerongen. That's where I met Tina, in their home,

Bram Pais, Taagense, Denmark, 1986

around 1939 or '40. Tineke is not Jewish, but she was a close friend of the youngest of the sisters, Trusha [Tirtsah], and was also interested in the Zionist movement. I was a physics student; she was beginning to study medicine. We saw a fair amount of each other. She was what you might call my girlfriend.

I knew Tina's mother, Marie, and I knew her grandmother. The grandmother was a fairly well-to-do widow. Her mother was divorced long before I met her. That whole family was simply spectacular!

Tineke was a very beautiful young woman. She's still a beautiful woman. She was dark haired, with dark eyes. Her mind is quick, but she talks rather slowly. My father, who was Orthodox, was furious that I had a girlfriend who was not Jewish. "Not in my house," he said. Then one day, by chance, Tina and I were walking along the beach and my parents were there. I said to her, "Come on. I will introduce you." They were courteous people, my mother and father. They didn't make any fuss. It ended up that nobody, including myself, loved Tineke more than my father. He just worshiped her. He thought she was so wonderful.

TINA'S FAMILY

Tineke and her mother, Marie, lived in a pleasant house. Tineke was the only child. It was a rambling house with quite a large number of rooms. I would say they were pretty well off. I don't quite know how they came about it, perhaps through a family inheritance. I wouldn't say there was wealth; they were well off, but they were socialists.

I don't know all the details about the family, but they did a great deal during the war. They gave their own home to so many people coming into hiding. They did not keep people there for a very long time, because they felt they were too exposed, but their home became a transit place from which people went on to other places.

Tineke was fantastic. Her mother was an absolutely marvelous woman, and so was her grandmother. Her grandmother was one of those early expatriates for whom atheism was a religion. She was an old woman when I knew her, a very fat little lady, but with tremendous vigor—a wonderful person. They were just a very fine family. I can say that they are among the finest people I've known in my whole life.

Tineke's mother, Marie, was a cheery person, but perhaps a little bit too self-deprecating. She was always doing things for other people. It was sort of natural in that family. She was pretty old, but you know, I was quite young, so every person more than ten years older than me looked archaic to the ultimate.

There was something tireless about Marie. She was tirelessly active on behalf of other people. She was a hospitable person. In times of difficulty she would be running around, doing errands, bringing messages, bringing things to people. There was a certain special quality in her home. It was like a haven. She didn't, as they say in America, make a production out of it. It was a natural thing for her. People would come and she would help them. She was always doing things: she would hide items of value in her cellar, or personal effects that people wanted to keep, which the Germans would have confiscated. I think she was also a little bit restless. She was a woman of deep conviction, but she didn't make speeches. She translated her convictions into actions, without making a fuss about it. Tineke was not a fussy woman either. She just did it. In these respects I think Tineke and her mother had quite a bit in common. Marie and Tineke both had that general sense of helping.

There were measures against the Jews almost from the day the Germans marched into Holland, in May 1940, but it was a gradual thing, which was very clever on their part. They didn't immediately start transporting the Jews to camps. They did it step by step by step. The very first rule, in September 1940, I think, was that Jews were no longer allowed to go to the cinema. We said to ourselves, "So what? So we can't see movies anymore." We could live with that. Then there was the next thing, then the next. My memory is that it was the beginning of '42 when we had to wear the star. It was not at the start of the war. Non-Jewish people would come up to

Sieg Gittler, Bram Pais, and Lion Nordheim at Bram's Ph.D. defense, 1941

you in the street and say something friendly, like, "It's terrible that you have to do this," something like that. We had a very small National Socialist [Nazi] organization in Holland, very small.

The fourteenth of June 1941 was set by the German authorities as the last day Jews were allowed to get a Ph.D. in Holland. I was working toward my degree in physics at the University of Utrecht. I told myself, I must get a Ph.D.

Bram Pais and his family at his Ph.D. ceremony, 1941

before this date because as soon as the war is over I want to be out of Holland, to study abroad. I think that I was quite certain I would get through the war. On the ninth of June 1941, I got my degree.

I'm a hard worker, but I hope I never work as hard again as during that time. I spent every night until four in the morning on my dissertation, until I came to the point when I could not write another word, not even the next letter. I went to bed. Eight o'clock the next morning I was up writing again. For weeks I slept four hours a night, trying to finish in time. Anyway, I got through with it. It was printed, as was necessary in those times. It was also the custom to defend your dissertation before the faculty in a formal ceremony, attired in white tie and tails. You had two assistants, called "paranymphs," who were also dressed in white tie and tails. I came in, flanked by my good friends, one of whom was Lion Nordheim. We stood up and the whole senate of the university came in and sat down, to witness the defense of the dissertation. Then I got my degree.

There was a reception, after which we went to Tineke's home to celebrate, where her mother had made a dinner. My parents were there. My sister was there. I think they are all in the picture. I was so tired. Following that, Tineke and I took a vacation together for about two weeks. I was completely exhausted. I've never been so tired. We just went for walks in the country, things like that. She could recite poetry very well. One poem she was fond of began: "They were not the Jews, Jesus, who put you to the cross." It was a medieval Dutch poem, very old. It's typical that that was a poem she would know by heart.

What was so special about these people who did so much for the Jews? What made them do it? It was partly a moral thing. They had incredibly

Sixteenth-century Portuguese synagogue, Amsterdam, 1996

deep convictions. That that poem was important to Tineke says something about her personality.

In December 1940, all Jews who held positions at universities—professors, assistants, lecturers—were dismissed. I was an assistant, a very low, low rank. We had our ID cards with the "J" prominently stamped on them. But people who had had positions at the university also got a special stamp which said, "The owner of this particular ID card is, until further notice, exempt from being sent for labor." I had the very highest ranking for a stamp of this kind, so I felt fairly safe. Then in early '43 there was an announcement that said, "Since we can no longer guarantee your freedom of movement"—because the Germans had begun to pick up Jews to be sent to camps—"we have arranged that all of you will be housed in a chateau near a little village called Barneveld. Be there at such and such a time." So we were to go to Barneveld.

For several years there were no deportations. When that began, I, for one, knew that if the Germans were taking the Jews out of the Netherlands, it was going to be really bad. I decided I would never go anywhere where the Germans wanted me. The university people who went to Barneveld were sent later on to Theresienstadt, which was a high-class concentration camp, and, in fact, most of them did come out of the war.

In the Netherlands we had a difficult situation because the highest German authority was civil, unlike France and Belgium where the highest authority was military. In those countries the main German concern was to keep the roads to the front open, but in Holland the idea from the start was to prepare for the annexation of Holland into the German Reich. A civil authority meant that the highest power in the country was the Gestapo, which was disastrous for the Jews.

HIDING

When they announced the deportation to Barneveld, I talked it over with Tineke and she said, "You will go in hiding." A friend of hers had a big house on one of the canals in Amsterdam where I could go. Then on a certain day, I vanished from the earth. I had been living in my parents' home. They simply told people who asked about me that I had gone to the camp, to Barneveld, but in fact, I had vanished. I was in hiding. Of course, Tineke knew where I was; it was not so far from where she lived.

I lived altogether in nine different places while in hiding, because whenever something happened, either someone betrayed the place or something happened to someone who knew where I was, I had to move. The rule of the game was never assume that anybody, however honorable, would be able to stand up under torture. If Mr. X, who knew where I was, was caught for some reason, I should move.

I was in that first place for nine months. Then the Gestapo came. I ran to the attic where I had a hiding place between the walls. There was a false piece of wall that you lifted out. Once inside you had to push the piece of wall back in position to make it look like a regular wall. I had done it so often, but this time I couldn't quite get it back in the right place; it was a little bit off, a little piece was open. At one point this German fellow came searching up there with a flashlight. I could see him, but he couldn't see me. It was unbelievable. I was sitting there, crunched up for three hours. The funny thing was, when I came out I had the feeling I had only been there ten minutes. I remember that so well. I had no idea of the time. But then I had to move.

I moved to the house of a psychiatrist in the summer of '44, the summer of the invasion. That whole summer I was inside a small home, never once on the street. But there was no time to go crazy, there was too much work to do. I had big piles of books: I was reading, I was calculating. After I woke up in the morning, I did forty-five minutes of calisthenics, and again before dinner, at around five o'clock, I exercised for another forty-five minutes, in front of an open window with the curtains drawn across it. I used two little dumbbells. Before going into hiding I had taken exercise and calisthenics classes to learn how to keep fit. I did that as a precaution, because I knew I would be in confinement.

The families I stayed with were pleasant and kind. I have nothing but good memories about them. At the first place I stayed, there were two children, a girl and a boy. Another family had two daughters, one of whom was epileptic. They were people of quite modest means; the father was an office worker and they lived in a very small house.

Now, Tineke always knew where I was. She arranged for food coupons. As long as somebody could take the ID card to some office or other, you could get ration stamps. Tineke would see to it that I had books to read or to study. She got these from the library or through friends. There was a man who lived near my last hiding place who sent me a long list of all the books he had in his library. I checked off the ones I wanted to read and he would arrange for them to be delivered to me, but not by him. I've never ever read so much as I did then. I read *War and Peace,* I read all of Dickens, everything. Also—it's a very strange thing—when you are out of circulation for a long time, the mind comes to the rescue in peculiar kinds of ways. You are capable of reading for entire days.

One of the things I learned, one of the strangest things, is how to think. There was nothing else to do. I couldn't see people, or go for a walk in the forest. All I had was my head and my books, and I thought a lot. I learned, because there was no interruption. I had access to myself, to my thinking. I wouldn't say that I particularly matured. The thinking was physics thinking. I was just short of twenty-two then.

I was in hiding for two years and two months, something like that. In all that time I went out very, very little, just once in a great while, after dark. Once I even took the train to Utrecht, forty miles from Amsterdam, with my yellow star, this star which I still have. Why did I go? I just wanted to visit some friends. I was a little bit crazy, a little bit insane.

At first the Jews were scattered all over Amsterdam. Then the Germans concentrated a very large number of them into a de facto ghetto in the old Jewish quarter of Amsterdam, because it was easier to round them up when they all lived crowded together in one area. My parents did not move into this ghetto, but my sister and her husband, Hermann, did. They had no choice.

One day they got picked up by the Gestapo but were let go again. I was already in hiding at the time. Talking it over with Tineke, she said, "We will find them a place." So I sent a message for my sister to come to my parents' house on a certain night, and I came out of hiding to meet her. I said, "Look, this can't go on. You and Hermann have got to go into hiding. Tineke has found a place and in a few days we will get you out of here." But she wouldn't go. Her husband was a businessman who traveled a lot, selling things. "I can't," she said. "Hermann can't do it. He will go crazy. We're young and strong. We will work for the Germans."

That was an indelible moment in my life. I couldn't tell her, "You are going to a camp and will die in the gas chamber." We didn't even know anything about gas chambers. We just didn't know about that. But my instinct was, you must not go where the Germans can put their hands on you. It was a substantial belief. So I was in this quandary. She was insisting, "I can't go in hiding because my husband won't do it and I must stay with him." I didn't know what to say. I should have said, "Sophia, I don't care what anybody says. Don't do it!" I remember that evening well. It was the last time I talked to her. They picked her up soon after, and she never came back.

FAMILY

I would say my childhood was a good and happy one, in a typical middle-class environment, not poor, not rich. Everything was fine. I never had any problems. I was awfully bright, a miserably bright kid in school. I was physically healthy. I swam. I had friends. I went to the beach. I had nothing in particular to be afraid of. The Dutch formed such a solid society, with everything in its proper place.

My father was first a schoolteacher. After the war he became the secretary of the Sephardic Jewish community in Amsterdam. I'm Sephardic, of which I am, like all Sephardis, immensely proud, even though I am not particularly practicing as a Jew.

My father was a man who felt a very deep solidarity with the Jewish faith. One day he said to my mother, "If they pick me up, I will go, because I want to share the fate of the Jews," to which my mother answered, "All right, go. Share the fate of the Jews. But I'll stay here!" My mother was a very determined lady, so of course he didn't go. They went into hiding and made it safely through the war.

They were living on a farm somewhere outside Amsterdam, a safe place Tineke helped them find, but I didn't know where, and they didn't know where I was either. One of the absolute rules I learned in the war was, don't know anything you don't need to know, because if you ever get caught they will get it out of you. But Tineke knew where we both were, and she was our courier, bringing my letters—I think, on her bicycle—to my parents. Of course, we couldn't use the mail because we didn't know the addresses. It was a very special thing she did for us.

Through this correspondence system I taught my father English while we were in hiding. We each had a copy of the same little book. He would do the exercises and send them over to me, perhaps once a week or so, and I would correct them and send them back to him.

My parents were of fairly modest means but we had one tremendous asset: my father was a stamp collector, and stamps, during the war, were an extremely important investment, as valuable as diamonds, because you could make them safe from fire and bombing. So now and then we would sell something from my father's collection to keep us going.

I knew all the time I was going to get through the war. It was completely irrational, a silly idea, but I was not going to lie down and get myself killed. I was going to get out of it.

ARREST AND IMPRISONMENT

My last hiding place was an apartment in Amsterdam where I was living independently with my friend Lion Nordheim, his wife, Jeanne, and her sister Tirtsah, Tineke's good friend. The girls were blond with blue eyes, the whole family was very Aryan-looking. So they could go out, go shopping, all those things. But Lion and I were staying strictly at home.

In some way or other, we were betrayed. Somebody knew. One day the Germans caught us and we went to prison. That was late; I think it was March '45. How they found us I do not know. I have always been too scared to find out. Somebody may have followed the girls, or may have thought they were Jews after all, because superficially they didn't look Jewish, but if you knew a little bit, then there was no question about it. But what actually happened, I do not know.

I was lucky because the same week that I went to prison the Americans crossed the Rhine and cut off the northern part of Holland, so there was no longer any possibility of being shipped out to a concentration camp. The rail lines were cut. So I was in prison in Amsterdam during the very last days of the war. We were sent to the men's prison and the girls were sent to a women's prison in a different place.

But first we were taken to the Gestapo headquarters for interrogation. Alone in a room with this man, he said, "Well, we don't have that much against you. If you just tell us all the things you know, we will treat you well." He was pacing up and down. I didn't know how they caught us. I have never known. And I did not know what they knew of our involvement with the Zionist youth organization. I didn't quite know what to expect. They were convinced that we had some connection with the resistance movement. They always asked, automatically, are you Jewish? "Yes," I said. So this man interrogating me is walking up and down the room. Then he walks by me and suddenly strikes me in the face! Now that is an experience I can never forget. Imagine that you are sitting, having a civil conversation, and suddenly the other person just hits you, but then keeps on talking as if nothing happened! It's not such a terrible physical hurt. It's the shock. They had these techniques to throw you completely off balance. They interrogated me again. For thirty-six hours they gave me no food. Normally I'm a very healthy eater and cannot live for more than three hours without food. But for those thirty-six hours I was never hungry.

Never in my whole life was I more afraid than on the day I went into that prison. The fear was like a physical pain. I couldn't tell you where it hurt, but I remember everything hurting. My body hurt with the pain of fear. They hadn't tortured me or anything, but it was such an incredibly intense fear I had.

Jeanne and Tirtsah were let go. I was also let go, but Lion was shot, just ten days before the war was over. There were several reasons. First of all, I'm Jewish-looking, but Lion had almost the caricature of a Jewish look: the nose, the mouth. If you were a real anti-Semite you would pick on him. Secondly, he was an extremely frightened person. When you are very scared in the face of an animal, the animal smells it, he knows it instinctively. I was scared out of my wits but somehow I kept myself looking unafraid. I cannot prove it, but I'm sure it made some difference. There is something in this style of fear, a certain faith you have to have. So I had this. Tina had it too. We would not lie down, we wouldn't take it. It was completely irrational. I could have been shot many times. I could have been caught any number of times. I think to have that sort of faith helps keep your mind sane.

But lastly, and most importantly, on the day that we were caught, Lion and I had been talking about writing a memorandum on the fate of the Jewish war children living in hiding or among Dutch families. The question was about their legal position if their parents didn't come back after the war. Should they be brought back to the Jewish community, stay where they were, or be given a choice? All these kinds of things needed to be discussed. On the same day that we were caught, a Dutch gentleman living in London, who was working on this problem, had come to consult with us about it, as we were the representatives of the Zionist youth organization. He was a well-known figure who later became a cabinet member in the Dutch government.

Lion, who had been taking notes of the discussion, put these papers in his jacket pocket when we took a break for lunch. When the Germans caught us they discovered his notes. If those papers had been in my pocket

I would never have lived to be seventy. I have led a strange life, a set of complete coincidences.

Tineke told me how she went to the Gestapo to try to get me out, but how that happened I do not quite know. I was in prison for over a month, and then one day they let me go.

It was only a few days before the war was over. I was standing outside the prison door. I knew the war was nearly over. What was I going to do? I decided to go to Tineke's house. I will not forget it, ever. I rang the bell. They didn't know I was out of prison. When they saw it was me—free— they just pampered me like a baby. They brought me inside the house. They cuddled me. They put me in a chair and made me eat.

For several months I was incapable of feeling anything, completely inaccessible to my feelings—I did not laugh, I did not cry. The second thing was this amazing trauma, where I forgot the names of everyone I knew. That was very strange. I knew who everyone was: this was a friend from high school, this was my cousin, but I had to relearn every name. It was quite striking, that very strong reaction that I had. They have a name for it, I think: posttraumatic stress syndrome.

I don't sit here conquering great resistance to talk. It is not my way. I don't suffer the reliving of these memories with tremendous pain. It's very odd, but it's finished for me. That, of course, is never quite true. It isn't finished. I am like all of my generation; we are marked people. But I don't suffer; I can talk to you about it. Most of my family was killed. All my father's and mother's sisters and brothers and their children, my sister and my old grandfather, they're all gone. Four out of five Jews in Holland never came back after the war—80 percent.

THE WAR ENDS

Holland's liberation came just a few days after I was released from prison. I was in Tineke's home. We had seen so many planes flying over. So many times in the daytime, we had heard the sirens, and at night, too, with air alarms and antiaircraft guns going like mad. And now those American planes were there, dropping food. Imagine, a whole city being on the rooftops of houses, and all of us crying. We were so incredibly hungry. The great moment of liberation was the planes coming and dropping food. Then came the Canadian troops. All the women went mad. From every walk of life—the finest families and the not-so-fine families—it seemed like all the women got laid by the Canadians. The Dutch men, we were worn out! It was unbelievable. I remember that. I have no statistics, but it was truly a phenomenon.

I sit here listening to myself, being sort of a split personality, talking casually about all these people who got killed, as easily as saying the Danes lost against Spain in the World Cup. It's very odd. I have certain pictures in my mind about the situation that are so incredible, when I listen to myself I can't believe I'm telling the truth. How can I tell the truth about those times while I am sitting in this beautiful room with lovely people. It makes no sense. But I swear to you that I'm telling the truth, every word. It was such an incredibly strange time.

The thing which is very hard to understand is that, whatever the level of danger or terror may have been, there were good days and bad days. Even when I was in prison, there were days I had a great time, and there were days that were terrifying. It is never all bad; at any level of human existence you find there are peaks and valleys.

It's a very funny thing to say, but I think for Tineke, her experience is more undigested than mine is for me. It has always struck me how for her it's almost as if the experience was more deep than it was for me. It's a very deep thing in her life. She struggles with it. I sometimes think that I am a little bit strange, that I can talk about it as if I'm talking about the weather.

I feel very strongly about Tineke's involvement. That family was simply glorious. The memory I have about them is sort of an overall memory, not a series of anecdotes. There is so much I have lost. I wish I had kept a diary. In fact, I did keep a diary during the war, and it was a very good diary, but then a little bit after the war was over, in a melancholy moment, I threw it away. I wanted to be done with it.

We have a feeling, Tineke and I, we have ties that will never break. We have this shortcut for telling each other things that people with a common experience have. You don't have to explain. You move right in. Every time we get together, once in a year or two, I find that I am so happy to see her. We spend a couple of hours talking, having tea or a drink, and then we move on in our respective lives again. We will never lose each other.

There were many people in Amsterdam who helped one way or another, but I would say there were very few who had the single-minded dedication of Tineke and her mother. I wouldn't say that they were unique. I simply do not know, but I don't think there would be very many like them.

Erika van Hesteren

Until seven years ago, I never talked about any of these things. I just couldn't. Then something happened, a very trivial event, really. The police stopped me on the highway and asked to see my papers. That young policeman affected me dreadfully; it was so similar to the way I was arrested during the war. Suddenly, it all broke open again. Later on, when I was more calm, I realized that it was essential to examine these memories I had kept hidden for so long. I think it's especially important to write these things down now, or else it will soon all be lost.

I am Jewish. Miraculously, my family all came out of the war. Before the Nazi invasion, our family lived in the southern part of Amsterdam. On a certain morning in 1941, the Germans moved all the Jews from the other parts of the city and drove them into the ghetto in the center of town. But even before that happened, a German officer had decided he wanted our house. My father, always direct, said right off to him, "All right. You can have the house. But see to it that we get another." My father said that, even though there was nothing we could have done about it, because they were going to take our house anyway. But this officer actually did find us a house, a very fine house with two spacious floors, situated just across the street from the ghetto. Soon after we began living there, we could see the ghetto filling up with all the Jews who were forced to move in. Then before long, the Nazis began taking them out again, deporting entire families to "work for the Fatherland," and new Jews were moved into the vacated houses.

We had to wear the yellow star. The only discussion about it at the time was what color thread should be used to sew it on: the color of your garment, or the yellow of the star. Everyone hated wearing it, to be marked like that, but it had to be done. There was the constant fear that your neighbor might report you to the authorities if you took it off. We thought, oh, well, if this is the only thing, it's not so bad. But then came the rule that Jews were not allowed out after eight o'clock in the evening. Gradually, from one day to the next, there were more and more restrictions.

There came a time when I could no longer attend my secondary school. Jewish pupils and Jewish teachers were dismissed. So a Jewish school was organized, and we enrolled. I didn't hate going there at all. Actually, it was very nice to be in a Jewish school. But in no time at all, we could see that each day more children were missing. They took the Jews from their homes, from the streets. Every day we were asking one another, "How did you manage today?" We lived like they must live in Israel today.

I had a non-Jewish boyfriend named Gideon, who had already been working for an underground organization. Gideon and I were very young— I was about sixteen—and we were very much in love. He and his brother had tried to cross the channel to England and were caught, but then the Gestapo let them go again. So nothing happened that time, but afterwards Gideon was always afraid the Germans were looking for him. We thought what a wonderful idea for him to hide with our Jewish family, because who would think to look for him there? Still, he knew he couldn't stay with us for very long since we were obviously in danger ourselves.

"Jewish street,"
Amsterdam, c. 1943

Being a young boy, with nothing much to do, he was bored to death staying on our top floor. To keep himself busy, he made us a wonderful hiding place, in a triangular space under our eaves. He fixed up a small wooden door that opened from the bottom, and then hung different things in front of it. You would never suspect an entrance there. Inside, he put cushions and medicine, and all kinds of supplies. A couple of days after he finished, when he felt a little bit safe from the Germans, he left us.

One day there was a tremendous raid, in my memory the very biggest raid of all. Starting quite early in the morning, the Germans threw a cordon around the ghetto, then drove in their big trucks, yelling, "All Jews must come out! Bring only hand luggage!" Something like that. They were going from house to house. When we realized what was happening, all of us—my parents and the five children—hid in the place Gideon had made; there was room for seven, easily. We locked ourselves inside.

The raid went on and on, all day long. At one point we thought perhaps they had finished and moved on. We came out to take a look through the window but then quickly went straight back to the hiding place, because there were still plenty of their cars and trucks all around. It was really dreadful; I don't want to think about it too much. Around six o'clock we saw that their cars and trucks were finally gone and thought that it was probably finished now.

My mother and my elder sister went down, while we stayed back and watched. They crossed the street. It seemed to be all right; there were no police anymore. Then I took my younger brother and sister and went down. We crossed the street to join them. But my father and eldest brother were still in the hiding place. They looked the most Jewish of the whole family, and they didn't dare to move.

I met Gideon right there in the street. When I told him what had happened, he sent his brother and his friend to bring out my father and brother. All the doors of the house were open. They walked straight up to the top floor room we told them about and started searching for the hidden door.

"I'm sure it must be here," one was saying to the other. My father and brother didn't know who it was in the room, so they were keeping very quiet. The two boys looked and looked but couldn't find the hiding place, even though it had been explained to them just where it was. After a while they gave up and left. My father and brother waited another whole hour before they dared to come out.

After that traumatic event, we all went into hiding. We had it arranged already beforehand. We each had separate places, and we all came out alive.

I joined Gideon and his underground group. He talked with his leader and asked if I could come and work with them. At first he said no, but in the end he agreed.

We lived in a tiny little house which was being used by the group for making false identification cards. It's quite close to where I live now. I even went inside again just a few years ago. The kitchen was on the ground floor, and there was a little sleeping and living room on the first floor. At the top was the room where we made false identity cards, in a rather primitive fashion, I must say. There was also an attic, where we kept the organization's papers and supplies. We lived in that little house for maybe nine months, perhaps a year, until we were caught and sent to jail.

But these are all complicated stories. In short, there were altogether eighteen young men in this group. Well, some had been in the Spanish civil war already, so in my eyes maybe they were not so young. Soon after we were caught, the Germans shot to death all eighteen of them, including Gideon and his brother. They killed them.

IN HIDING WITH TINA AND HER MOTHER

I was in jail for about six months before I was able to make an escape. I went first to my parents for a short time, to their hiding place in an attic. From there I came to Tina's house, because my parents and her mother knew each other.

Tina's mother, Marie, was the most extraordinary woman you could ever meet. She took everyone who needed a place into her house. She didn't have any prejudices; she just helped everyone. Marie lived there with Tina, who was a medical student at the time, about twenty-four years old and an absolutely gorgeous woman. She looked almost like an American Indian, with a wild, beautiful face. I knew Tina before the war, but not very well, because she was older than me; she was already grown up while I was still a teenage girl.

Arriving at their house, I found myself among a wonderful group of people; each one was fascinating to talk with. Marie and Tina had taken all of them in. And every person in that house just loved Marie. She was a lovable person, so easy to get along with. She never got upset. Whatever you talked about, it was all right. You could talk with her about anything at all; any subject, no matter how strange, she wouldn't be astonished. She would take it in her stride. But I don't think I talked with her about what happened to me in my captive days in prison. I don't think we talked about that.

They did something to me in prison that injured my back, and while I was staying at Tina and Marie's house it grew steadily worse and worse. Most of the time I was lying in bed. I could get up and take a few steps, but I was in so much pain, I really couldn't walk. So there was no question of going out.

Dutch resistance worker making false German occupation identity cards, c. 1943

Staying in the same room with me was a most extraordinary man, possibly the ugliest-looking man I've ever met. He looked almost unhealthy. But the moment you talked with him, you forgot all about his appearance, because he was truly a philosopher, so gentle and so wise, and very charming as well. A wonderful person. He was thirty-seven or thirty-eight years old, an old man in my eyes. He looked so peculiar and so Jewish, he could never leave that house. This philosopher, Lion Nordheim, was actually the easiest person of all to talk to in that household.

Lion's wife, Jeanne, was there, and she was great fun. She had the best sense of humor of anyone I knew, unlike Tina, who was more serious. Tina didn't always see the funny side to something right away, but Jeanne did.

Also staying there was a peculiar woman and her two admirers, a father and son. I didn't exactly understand the arrangement, but I noticed that when one came in one door, the other would leave right away by another door. I'm sure Marie knew what was going on, but she never said a word. A man named Hans De Jong was also staying there.

We observed certain unwritten rules. For instance, you stuck to your own room as much as possible, because with so many people in one house, we could get on each other's nerves. After dinnertime, we all went together to Marie, to sit on her bed and talk. It was a very lively house; there was always something going on, and a lot of laughter, even though there was nothing much to eat. Well, we always had food, but nothing very healthy.

While I was there, I never really appreciated how exceedingly difficult it was to get food for all of us. It was the Hunger Winter, 1944, and there was almost nothing left to eat in Holland. It was Tina who regularly went out to the farmers on her bike, without rubber tires, taking for barter valuables she got from her grandmother and that I got from my parents. She was so very slender, yet she rode out in the bitter cold for hours and hours on her bike, coming back with all her bags loaded with food. I don't know what other things she was involved with at that time, but she definitely looked after us for food.

Tina is very talented, very bright, and has always been interested in people and involved in helping people. She's sweet and she's understanding—a wonderful person—but she is a difficult person to get along with.

She was studying medicine, illegally, because she had refused to sign the Nazi loyalty oath. She told a doctor with whom she was studying about my worsening condition, a herniated spinal disc. On his advice, Tina arranged for me to be taken to a Catholic hospital and operated on illegally under a false name. This was a tremendous risk for everyone, but the nuns couldn't have been more sweet or kind. I am sure that they knew I didn't belong there. And then, too, this was a new operation in Holland. The surgeon who performed it learned the procedure only from reading articles in journals. Luckily, everything went well.

I stayed in that hospital more than six weeks, right up to the day of liberation, so by then my days of hiding at Tineke's house were over. I never went back. I will always remember the people in their house as being friendly, fascinating, and lively, and not scared, except perhaps De Jong, because he was the most intelligent and the most wise; he knew the dangers. I never had time to think about danger or dwell upon what could

happen to us. Like the others, I just lived by the day, by the minute. One thing which I think is very important to remember now: there was no doubt in our minds that we were going to win the war. It never occurred to any of us that the Germans could win, or that we could lose. I don't know anyone who doubted it.

I was very surprised when, a few years ago in the United States, I heard myself referred to as a "survivor." It's so strange. I would never use the word. "Are you a survivor?" I was asked. "We are all survivors," was my reply, but in fact, we didn't survive, we just went on living.

2 ⌒ You Have It in You

When Hitler declared war on Poland in 1939, Bert Bochove was working in Finland as a mill manager. He was advised to return home to Holland. At first he joined his two older brothers in running the family retail business in their native town, Woubrugge. Bert was twenty-nine years old and engaged to be married to Annie, a pharmacist living in Amsterdam. Wanting to be his own boss, he borrowed money to buy a drugstore in Huizen, a fishing town of ten thousand on the Zuider Zee, about eighteen miles from Amsterdam. The drugstore was on the ground floor of a fine corner building, with spacious living quarters above.

Henny Juliard and her husband, Pam, were living in The Hague at the outbreak of World War II in Holland. Henny lost her job as a department store office manager in June 1941 because, bowing to German pressure, the company she worked for was dismissing all Jewish employees. Pam continued to run his business until he was no longer able to work due to the escalating anti-Jewish German decrees. Like his wife and so many others, he was a victim of the Nazi plan to destroy the economic livelihood of the Dutch Jews.

During the war Henny was in regular contact with her friend Annie, whom she had first met in 1933. Both young women had been treated in a sanatorium in Switzerland for several months, recovering from tuberculosis.

Threatened with deportation in 1942, Henny and Pam were the first of twenty-six Jewish people who came to live under the protection of Bert and Annie Bochove. They remained for three years, initially in the Bochove home, then, after the birth of their first child, in a safe house Bert arranged for them.

Henny, her sister Ans, and their four brothers and sisters were children of their father's first marriage. After their mother died, their father remarried and had two more children, Yettie and John. The second marriage is remembered with great fondness by Henny and Yettie, who enjoyed growing up with all of their siblings in an atmosphere of loving affection.

In 1942, as the Nazi noose tightened around the Dutch Jewish community, Yettie fell in love and married Bob Wolf. Before the German occupation he had been a specialist in aeronautic electronics. When the Nazis forced professional Dutch Jews out of their positions, he took a job as an electrician in a Jewish old-age home in The Hague, where he and Yettie lived in one small room.

That same year Bob Wolf was rounded up in a surprise raid and deported, leaving Yettie pregnant and alone. When her baby was only three and a half months old, mother and son were separated because no family could be found that was willing to risk hiding them together. Young and inexperienced, Yettie used a succession of subterfuges to conceal her Jewish origins. Although she stayed under his roof for only one night, Yettie credits Bert Bochove with saving her life over a period of several years. At the same time that Bert's house was filled to overflowing with Jewish people in hiding, including Yettie's older sisters Henny and Ans, Bert was helping Yettie make the right contacts to assure her safety and survival.

In 1951, Yettie visited Israel as a participant in a short-term nursing program and decided to stay. Today she lives in a pleasant suburban setting, a short walk from the hospital where she has worked for more than thirty years. Yettie Malachi Mendels related her story on June 20, 1988, at her home in Beer-Jaacow, Israel.

Henny Juliard was interviewed at her seaside home in Scheveningen, The Hague, on July 16, 1986. Since then she has married her second husband. After living several years in Amsterdam, the couple now reside in Israel.

In July 1945, two months after Holland's liberation, Annie Bochove gave birth to their second child, Marie Louise. Very soon afterwards Annie collapsed with a recurrence of her prewar tuberculosis. She spent the next two years recuperating in a sanatorium in the Swiss Alps. Hoping to settle their family in the warm, dry climate of southern California, Annie and Bert Bochove applied early in 1946 to emigrate to the United States. Their papers didn't arrive until July 1949, on the same day that Annie died. Bert settled in southern California, where he established a small upholstery business and eventually married his second wife. He gave his interview at his home in Lomita, California, on June 23, 1986. He passed away in 1991 at the age of eighty-one.

Bert Bochove

The Germans came over the border into Holland in May 1940. One year later, on the very same day in May, Annie and I married, and traveled to

Bert Bochove, Los Angeles, 1984

Huizen to open the store. Pretty soon we had our first guests in the house, but they were not Jews. They came because of my friend Jaap van Rijn, who helped me with the soap.

By then we had ration cards that allowed people maybe half a pound of soap a month, but it was seldom in the store to buy. Later it was the same with food, too. In a town like Huizen, the women kept their kitchens *clean.* They waxed and polished the counters and made everything shiny and spotless, and then didn't use any of it, so it would all stay clean. They never ate in the kitchen, shoes stayed outside—slippers only allowed in the house. They washed the whole day long and used a lot of soap. I think their souls were not so clean, however, but that's another story. The point is, soap was almost impossible to get.

Jaap, my friend from Woubrugge, owned a paint factory. The Germans had already requisitioned all of his stock to be sent to Germany, but before they came for it, he had changed the measuring sticks, and managed to keep several thousand liters of linseed oil in barrels buried in the yard.

"Here's what I'll do," he told me. "I'll make soap for you to sell in the store."

He made highly concentrated pieces of hard soap, about twenty pounds each; I made small bars of soft soap from these, the stuff the housewives wanted most. I could make about a hundred and twenty pounds of soft soap from each of Jaap's pieces, and I got two or three. On Saturdays the customers brought me a plate with their name on it. On Mondays they picked it up filled with soap. For a big family I put on a little bit more. And I sold it for the normal price, which in those times was unbelievable.

Having that soap in my new store was a tremendous advertisement. Jaap taught me several other tricks, too, that made my store well known in nearby towns. People came from all over the place, sometimes as many as sixty in a day.

One time—it was late in the morning—I went to pick up more soap from Jaap. His wife was a strong woman and didn't show much agitation, but I could see that something was wrong. Early that morning they had

had a telephone call from the bookkeeper at the factory saying that the Germans were there looking for Jaap—he must stay at home.

Jaap had said to his wife, "I've got nothing on my conscience. I'll go."

Brought up in a small town, he had a lot of self-confidence; he was a proud man. Whenever he passed an NSB'er [member of the Dutch Nazi party] on the street, he would say things like, "Better be careful! It will be a short war!" He was not ready for those Nazi fellows. Even though he was ten years older than I was, in some ways he was absolutely like a child: he didn't understand things. It would have been easy for him to stay home a couple of hours that day, but, no, he went to the factory. They arrested him instantly, and he never came back.

Staying in Jaap's house were a young Dutch couple who had done quite a lot of underground things. They had good false papers, and they were coming and going all the time. After they arrested Jaap at the factory, the Germans came to their house, so of course the couple hid.

As I was leaving, Jaap's wife said, "What should I do about them?"

"I'll take them out of your way. There's enough misery here." So I took them with me to Huizen, and they stayed in our house for a couple of months.

They were very well educated people, but they played a lousy trick, which I didn't find out about right away. The man told me stories about how he had supposedly brought Jews over the border to Spain, but it was pure fantasy. He knew how to talk about it, but he didn't know how to do it.

He took money from Jewish people and then did nothing, while the Jews waited to hear from him. Slowly, I found these things out—that they were a bit like parasites—and then I put them out of the house.

THE JULIARDS

Just a short time later, early in the summer of 1942, Henny Juliard came. She and my wife, Annie, had become close friends before the war, when they were both in the same sanitarium recovering from tuberculosis. Henny was from a poor Jewish family living in The Hague.

Selling in the store was very easy, but it was the hardest thing to get new stock. I had to go to Amsterdam almost every week. One day, coming home from a buying trip, I found Henny Juliard in the house.

"Can I talk to you?" she said.

All at once, I sensed why she came. I never thought it over. I knew immediately that she would stay with us.

"I hope Annie has already told you that it's all right," I said.

I had never met her husband, Pam, but of course he had to stay too, although he didn't come until three months later because he was trying to save his little nephew. It did not work out. On both sides, their parents were already gone; there was plenty of misery around them.

Henny is very special—real quality. Coming from a poor family, she had only a little formal education, but she is a very intelligent woman and speaks absolutely perfect French, German, and English. Her husband, Pam, was a terrific fellow to have in the house. He had a way of making everyone laugh; even if he didn't feel good himself, he still joked around. He knew that his optimism helped everybody in the house.

Henny had a sister, Ans Mendels, a home-economics teacher living in a small town in the south. She was about forty years old—sort of an old maid—and a little bit sour, but she had a heart of gold. When Ans got in trouble with the Germans, she came straight to us. She knew it was time to leave, and we had room.

We had a big kitchen and living room, two bedrooms, and a very large hall. At first Henny, Pam, and Ans were living with us on the second floor, over the store. Later on, when we had more Jewish people, we used the attic on the third floor.

My wife was smarter and much more practical than I was. Right away when Henny came, she told me to build a hiding place, in case the situation got worse. She and Henny were really pressing me, but I was busy and couldn't see the use of it. Maybe I was more optimistic than they were. I took things easy and let the consequences come later. But they were simply trying to help themselves. Finally it penetrated that they were right, and I built it. It's good that our family had that place, too, because later on it saved our lives.

THE HIDING PLACE

Bert's building shared a wall with the house next door. The brick fire wall dividing the two structures was actually behind the place where the two rooflines met, under what appeared from the outside to be the neighbor's roof. At the point where the two roofs met in his attic, Bert built a new wall, creating a large triangular room behind it, under the neighbor's roof. He camouflaged the new wall by exactly matching its wood and joinery to that of the rest of the attic. The hanging door he built swung open from the bottom. To conceal the seam, he added shelves along the top edge of the door and filled them with drugstore goods. The bottom edge was hidden by a beam placed all the way across the floor. Bert stapled old packing paper on the inside of the new wall so that to someone knocking on it, the sound was the same as the other attic walls.

There was plenty of room in the hiding place. It could easily hold ten or twelve people, or more. We put in a big, old mattress, and when the house was really full, the kids slept in there. And all the radios—ours and the neighbors' that we were supposed to destroy, or turn over to the Germans—I had them in there, too.

One day in '42, my brothers called asking me to help a business acquaintance of theirs who was in trouble. Abraham Rodrigues was a salesman for women's apparel. His family were Portuguese Jews, known as Sephardic. They had been living in Holland for maybe 250 years but still proudly maintained their Portuguese heritage. Abraham and my father had met by chance on a streetcar, around 1915, and a business relationship developed between them that continued on with my brothers after our father died. I had never met him.

"Can you take Rodrigues and his wife and two kids?" they asked me. "Well, I'll see what I can do."

I went to the Rodrigues house in Amsterdam to talk it over and found out that they were ready to go. It was high time, too; they really were in danger. There were parents and others in that family that were already caught. Back in Huizen, I arranged with a skipper who had a delivery business to go the next day and load up all their possessions onto his boat. Meanwhile the Rodrigues family came to my house by train. Two days later the Gestapo came to pick them up, but their house was empty.

Across the street from us was a little grocery store with a big, long attic above; you couldn't see it from the outside. We told those people that we all had to help the Jews. And since they had extra room, and we were happy to pay for it, could they please store the Rodrigues family stuff. They said yes, fine, only the piano they couldn't have; it was too big to get up the stairs. Well, I had a commercial building with a wide staircase and a big hallway. It took four strong fellows to get it up, but we were glad to have it. Annie liked to play the piano, and the guests, too.

After the Juliards and the Rodrigues family, it was all unknown people coming into my house. There was a network in the underground that brought people to us; I didn't understand how it worked and was never interested either. After all, with so many strangers coming into my house, the less I knew the better. Sometimes it wasn't until years later that I knew their real names; with some, I never learned them.

The next to come was Peter—his real name was Lou—Ikkersheim, with his wife and three kids. They were from The Hague. He was a large, happy man, with a strong Hague accent, uneducated, but he had a good set of brains—that type. Peter was a Jew, but with his blue eyes and bald head, you couldn't really tell. He was a very fine fellow. His wife was very quiet.

The postmaster in Huizen, who was a friend of ours—well, let us say, an acquaintance—knew what was going on; when there was trouble we could count on him. He lived in a huge place on top of the post office,

Annie Bochove wearing her pharmacist's coat, in front of the Bochoves' store, Huizen, 1941

which was ideal. When we were overcrowded, two of the Ikkersheim kids often stayed there, although most of the time they were at our place.

With the Juliards, the Rodrigues, and Ikkersheim families all living in the house, it was becoming a little crowded, so I built two large bedrooms in the attic. Then I added a balcony on the second floor. On fine days the Jews who couldn't leave the house could take sunbaths, concealed by the bedding hung over the railing to air out. So we were all in the house together, plus a girl from Woubrugge—Diet Rosendaal—who also worked in the store. She knew everything and was dependable.

JOPIE

A short time later, we hired Jopie to be a clerk in the drugstore, to make it easier for my wife. The only weak spot was that Jopie came from the east, near the German border. She had an accent, but that didn't mean anything; it was typical of border regions. She didn't make a bad impression, but she was one of those people you feel you never get through to. Most people, when you meet them for the first time, they talk to you; you feel they are normal. Jopie wasn't like that; she was a bit of a mystery, although she did become friendly with Mrs. Rodrigues.

After Jopie had been with us for about a year she asked my wife if she could take a week's vacation. I went off to Amsterdam for a buying trip the same day she left. When I came back the house was very quiet. It was after closing time. Only my wife and Diet were there. "What happened?" I asked. Annie told me the story.

That morning Peter had helped Jopie carry her suitcase to the street-car. When he came back he said, "That suitcase was awfully heavy. I don't trust her. And, she left this box for me to drop off at the post office. I think we should take a look." So they opened the package, and it was all stolen stuff: toothbrushes, nice pieces of soap—prewar quality, and all from the store. She must have been stealing and hiding those things for months. But that was nothing compared to the letter they found.

"Dear Jopie, When you go away on vacation we'll get the Jews out of the house." It was written in German. She was engaged to a German soldier!

What could we do? Diet immediately brought Rodrigues and his wife to Utrecht, where Diet's aunt lived. There was no time to warn the aunt; she just brought them, and they were accepted. This aunt's apartment shared a staircase with the apartment next to it. They had just arrived and were halfway up the stairs when down from the other apartment came a National Socialist wearing his black boots and black shirt. Rodrigues, seeing the fellow coming, spit on the stair in front of the man. It was tremendously dumb, but Rodrigues was impulsive. The NSB'er said nothing, but a few days later they picked him up, and his wife, too. They went to the concentration camp and never came back. No trace.

We sent all of the Ikkersheims directly to the postmaster, except Peter, who stayed in the store because he had good papers and didn't look Jewish. Diet took the two Rodrigues kids to her family in Woubrugge, where they lived for the rest of the war. Our Dr. Van den Berg, who was taking care of all the Jews in the community, came right over to our house with an official sign: "Quarantine, Typhus." It was already hanging on our door by the time I got home from Amsterdam. The whole neighborhood knew the typhus sign didn't mean anything and still came to the store, but the Germans were afraid and stayed away.

The next day my wife took the train to pay a visit to Jopie's family. I couldn't go because, being near Germany, that area was closed to Dutch men. Jopie was not there, so Annie spoke to her mother, making it very clear to her that if anything happened to the Bochove family, or to the *Jews* in the house—and Annie didn't know if this woman might be half-German or not—her Jopie would be killed, and not to forget it. The mother nearly had a heart attack.

That's how Annie was: she saw what needed to be done. I think it was a good thing that she went, too. We never saw Jopie again. The quarantine sign hung on our door for about fourteen days. By that time everybody was back in the house. The Germans never came.

MEYER

The Rodrigues drama was already over when Meyer, the German banker, arrived. They brought him in the middle of the night, with his twelve-year-old son, Gerd. They had caught his wife, and he and Gerd had just barely escaped, so of course we had to take them. The boy was a nervous wreck—he had seen some things that day. He was in such terrible shape, I never did ask him about what had happened.

Meyer was a big, self-confident man, more like a German than a Jew. What I mean is that he had a few of those German qualities that we Dutch never liked. For example, they liked the wife to always walk a step behind them. They are the boss, momma is number two. You still find that a little bit in Germany: the working-class poppa who has his glass of beer in the bar before coming home, and momma waiting in the kitchen with everything ready for him. Maybe not in every household, but I think that was common, even among better-educated people, though in a more refined way. I found that out about Meyer.

In '33, when Hitler started pestering the Jews, Meyer was smart enough to take his money and possessions and move his family to Amsterdam, where he went into banking. But business was too good, and he forgot to go to America before it was too late. They went underground in a small town about an hour by bicycle from our place and had been living there, under very hard circumstances, until they came to us.

Having Meyer in the house was not easy. Pretty soon he was in trouble with everyone, but especially with Ans, the old maid. She irritated him. Ans was a very good person, but a bit cranky, and somewhat easy to upset. Meyer

Bert and Annie Bochove, 1941

was more or less a gentleman, but he was used to having things his way, so he and Ans had a lot of battles. They couldn't stand each other. I didn't see much of this because I was always in the store during the day, but Ans had complained to me about him. Then one day Meyer said to me, "This cannot go on much longer, Mr. Bochove. That woman has got to go."

"Wait a moment. You have money. It will take half a day to find a place for you." For money, you can always find people to help. "It will be much harder to find a place for Ans."

"Well, then I will have to go."

We found a place for Meyer and Gerd with a grocery-store keeper, a nice man, but without much character. He did what "momma" said, and she was a stinker. In Meyer, she saw money. They let him pay them very well, and kept them in a tiny room upstairs where they had to be completely quiet. If they made any noise at all, a warning knock immediately came from downstairs. Meyer also had to work in the cellar to help the man restock his store.

That cellar was filled with cheese and all kinds of extra food. The store-keeper was not to blame for that; people were hoarding, but Meyer and Gerd got none of it. Every three days they came back to us, after dark, when they could go out for a walk, and we stuffed their pockets with sandwiches. Otherwise they would have starved to death. The storekeeper and his wife were orthodox Christian people, but they fed them practically nothing. I was so mad recently because everybody wants to say now that this man behaved well, but I cannot see it. After the war I wanted to make a bit of publicity about him, but Meyer, who had stayed with them until the end of the war, said please don't do it. Maybe they were mean, but they had saved his and Gerd's lives.

The underground was pretty good at directing people to our house; there were always strangers coming in. One time they brought an old couple, very quiet, very Jewish, the type that cannot eat your food—strictly kosher. Their stay was short, only one night, but they left a big impression on me. I remember them because I got a strong feeling that these people gave themselves up. Many Jews don't believe that that happened.

I know a Jewish man who wrote a wartime story about his mother. His father was already dead, and she was living alone in a small place. When her son went to see her she told him she was going to give herself up. He talked her out of it, but when he came back later on, she was gone. Living in a small community with well-behaving people, everyone knows you; you always have someone with a sympathetic ear to turn to. When she had to go out of circulation, she couldn't handle it. She gave herself up and ended in a concentration camp.

KETS DE VRIES

The Bochoves hid the parents of a man named Kets de Vries, who was a Dutch Jew, raised in Germany, and married to a Christian German. His marriage and textile business gave him a certain degree of protection during the Nazi occupation. As long as it supplied German needs, he was allowed to keep his large mill in operation. He was often seen on the streets of Huizen, wearing a yellow star.

Kets de Vries was an important person. He knew how to do everything the right way, and he was very involved. After the war, I got the feeling that certain people knew all along what I was up to, but Kets de Vries was the only one that I recognized as such at the time.

His parents were up north in Friesland for a long time before they came to our house. They were in their seventies, old-fashioned people. Sometimes I joked with his father, a simple man.

"You are a tailor." I said, "How did you get that expensive name?"

"Oh, I just have it."

It doesn't mean anything in another language, but in Dutch it's a venerable old family name. He showed me his papers, false of course, but with a genuine picture.

"Look. I am not Jewish-looking. I can go out."

We always tried to keep him in the house. He was a certain type you could say absolutely was a Jew. At night, if the situation was normal, he could walk to his son's house, but sometimes he would wander out to the beach in the middle of the afternoon.

"Uncle Karel," I said, "I know you don't look Jewish, but you are not so young anymore. Why should you go out?" Then he gave [it] up.

Even though we were living in the same house, we didn't see too much of them. They led a quiet life. Sometimes Karel came more or less to the surface and told Jewish jokes and kept things going a little, but Sarah was never happy. Her type is not easy to live with, and Kets de Vries knew it. He wanted them to stay up north where they had a good place, but she was old and wanted to be close to her son and relatives, so they came to my already full house. It didn't help with the so-called harmony. She didn't bother me much, but it was hard on the other people, and they were depending on me to keep the peace.

She was one of the champion sufferers of the world. I think she felt good when she could complain, mainly about herself, about her suffering, things like that. That caused trouble for the other people; they really didn't need it. There was no one in the house who had not lost parents or children, and they did not want to bring it up all the time. They had enough dealing with their own struggles. I could see that there was less suffering when Sarah was not around, but she and Karel stayed until the end. It wasn't easy.

BETRAYED

Bochove installed an electric alarm under the store counter to alert the people upstairs in case of an unexpected Gestapo raid. Later, when there was no longer any electricity, the household devised an alternate plan. Someone would excuse himself to go to the small kitchen behind the store, where pharmaceutical bottles were washed. Passing by the hallway stairwell, he would signal a warning to the people upstairs.

One day, midmorning, we had a terrible situation: we were betrayed. The incident with Jopie was long past; this was another betrayal.

It was just a normal weekday, and very, very busy in the store. I was talking with a customer, facing the counter, when I happened to look over at Joost, one of my helpers. I could see by his expression that something was wrong. By the time I took this in, there was a hand on my shoulder.

"Bist du der hausmeister?" ["Are you the boss?"] It was an officer from the Grunepolizei [German police]. Whew! Then you shrink a little bit.

I didn't understand German, of course; you let them repeat what they said, and by that time Joost had left through the back door into the hallway of the house.

"What is that fellow doing?" the officer said.

"Oh, he is just going to clean the bottles."

He checked it out, and there was Joost in the back kitchen, cleaning bottles. But on [Joost's] way through the hallway he saw Mrs. Ikkersheim on the landing. He gestured to her, and she took off to warn the rest. There was no electricity anymore, so this was the system, and it worked! Joost was a dependable fellow.

A few minutes later they ordered me upstairs; the room was much more empty than it had been five minutes earlier. Sitting there was my wife, my mother-in-law, who had come to live with us about a year before, and my son Erik, in his highchair. Then there was Ans. She had blue eyes and tinted hair and had very good papers; she called herself the maid. Her being there didn't worry me too much. But then I looked farther, and there was old Sarah, looking like she was straight out of the Bible! That was wrong. She had had plenty of time to hide and could easily have done it—she was quick as a bird. Karel and the Ikkersheims were out of sight in the hiding place. It was just Sarah.

One of the Germans walked right up to her and said, "You are a Jew!" She snapped back, "That's an insult!" She got so mad, she jumped up. "I won't take that!"

The leader of the gang said, "Okay. Okay. Leave her alone."

But they didn't go away. I glanced down at the floor and got a chill. Left there quite carelessly was a bag filled with food ration cards—enough for about thirty people. Why hadn't it been put away? You cannot let things like that lie around. Like making up the beds that we had all over the building, the whole place had to be cleared and looking normal every morning. Mainly, we did pretty well, but this time that bag was there!

Ans was very cool. She said to the fellow, "I was just leaving to shop for the family. Can I go now?"

"Go on," he said.

Calmly, she picked up the bag with all the cards inside and walked out of the house with it on her arm. Ans had guts. Later on I learned that she went first to find Peter to tell him not to come home. So he stayed away, but Ans returned. For two more hours the Germans were busy looking all over the house.

They ordered me up to the attic. I had to sit there with a fat fellow who was running the business, while two others were knocking on all of the walls, listening for a different sound.

I had a strong feeling someone told them we had a hiding place. The cellar was very small, so it was natural that they would look in the attic, especially since it was a very big attic, over the whole house. All this time inside the hiding place were old Karel de Vries, Peter Ikkersheim's wife, and their three children, right behind the wall where they were knocking. Just those five. Luckily, the Juliards were away at that time.

I had a dead-sure feeling that they would never find the door. But I had a knot in my stomach, thinking about the little kids in there, and my wife and kid downstairs; so there was worrying. Still, I had a strange feeling that it would come out all right. I was not afraid.

In the attic were three big willow baskets filled with potatoes—an unknown luxury—and I had to explain it to those Germans.

One of them said to me, "Look, there is hunger everywhere in this country. What are these potatoes doing here?"

"Well," I explained to the fellow, "to begin with, I am a farm boy. I have relatives who give me food from their farm. There are several people here in town who will be very angry if they don't get these potatoes, because when my family sends me food, then I help them, too." He believed it.

Meanwhile all this time—I could hardly believe it—the fat one was sitting right on top of three or four thousand Dutch flags. They were neatly folded into a package—a bundle about one yard square and one yard high. If they had discovered that, it would have been the end of everybody. Oh, yes. It was about that same time that a church had to pay a $30,000 fine for playing the national anthem. If a radio announcer made double entendre remarks that even slightly touched the Germans, they put him in jail. Flags? Then they had you as a political agitator and you had to go; and the chance that you would come back was very small.

Luckily, they didn't touch the package of flags, and everything went fine; after two hours they gave up. I had to hand over my identity papers, and maybe that helped too; they could see that I had been living in Finland before the war. At that time the Germans still thought the Finns were their friends. Later the Finns were fanatic against them.

Finally they left, and then Annie and I opened the hiding-place door.

Diagram of Bochove store and home showing hiding place Bert built

Firewall

Hiding Place

Neighbor's House

Bochove house and store showing balcony Bert built for Jews in hiding, Huizen, 1987

"Everything is safe now," we said to them, "but please stay in for a while more." A half hour later we let them out.

Bochove house and store before Bert added balcony for Jews in hiding, Huizen, 1941

Peter's wife was never normal again after that experience. When she came out she was more quiet than ever. It was already close to the Hunger Winter, and then that May they were free. By the end of May, Peter was back in The Hague. His store was still there, a lot of his stuff had been saved, and it all turned out pretty good for him. Half a year later I was in The Hague, and we had dinner together. Peter's wife was eating very little, she was staring, and didn't talk at all. I could see by the way the kids and Peter handled her that her mind was gone. I think it started that day. Maybe she had had too much: the hours she was in the hiding place wondering if her husband was caught in the village, afraid that the kids would make a noise. It was enough to help her down, and she never came out of it. About a year later she died.

After the war we never could trace who betrayed us. The people in Huizen pointed to a fellow, but nobody could say for sure if it was him, so we let it go.

THE GARBAGE TRUCK IN THE HUNGER WINTER

During the last winter of the war, known as the Hunger Winter, people in small towns like Huizen weren't quite as desperate as those in the cities, where many were dying of hunger and cold; they could keep small gardens, and fish in the Zuider Zee. Maintaining a hidden population of Jews, however, put a severe strain even on their relatively greater resources.

Huizen had two garbage trucks: each one could handle five thousand kilos—about five tons. During the war there wasn't much trash, so only one was in use. When you have only one newspaper—just a few pages now— you used it in the bathroom, or the stove. One truck was enough. In any case, there was no gasoline either.

We had an idea for that other garbage truck; we built an extra carburetor, so it could burn wood. As the wood burned down to charcoal, a gas formed that ran the engine. It worked so well, it didn't even take much fuel; you could put enough wood on top of a truck like that to last for five days.

In charge of that garbage truck was the director of the gas factory and Johan Kappelhof, who was number two in Huizen's distribution office— he was in charge of all the scarce things. He did absolutely whatever he could to help people out. Whenever there was a newcomer—a Jew, or someone else who had to go underground—he got them a ration card; he supplied us with food cards for all the extra people in our house. He had such good contacts that if someone needed shoes or something like that, you could go to him and he would work on it. I had the feeling that helping out the Jews was much more important for him than his distribution-office work.

Since we had invented the wood-burning carburetor, I asked him for the use of the truck to bring my pharmaceutical stuff from Amsterdam.

"No. You can find other ways," he said.

"But, we need it to get potatoes from the farms up north, too."

"Okay. That's different."

Kappelhof arranged for his assistant, a retired Dutch army officer, to provide us with all kinds of false papers, showing that we were driving for the Wehrmacht and were allowed to stay out after curfew.

Kets de Vries was mixed up in this business, too. He arranged for Gerrit Veerman, a farm boy working in his textile factory, who was well acquainted with the wood-burning system, to be the driver. Gerrit was my age, around thirty-five, with a round, red, healthy face, though his hair was already white. In the village his nickname was Silver Gull. So we were all set to go out to the farmers, looking for five thousand kilos of potatoes. Seems like a lot of potatoes, but when you consider all the Jews hiding in Huizen, some of them in situations where people could not give them enough to eat, it wasn't so much.

We took off for the first run. Along the road we saw a lot of people wrapped up in all kinds of shabby old clothes, trying to keep warm, some pushing baby carriages with a child or a little bit of food or clothing. They were walking from farm to farm looking for food. But they had to spend such a long time on the road, they seldom came home with anything; they ate it on the way. The farmer we went to had a big place. He was a very good man. Because it was for the Jews who couldn't go for themselves, he filled up our truck.

There were other things that came our way with that famous garbage truck. One time I went back to Woubrugge, my birthplace. Along with me were the post-office director and the Dutch chief of police. Gerrit drove, of course. Our destination was a farmer, an old, old friend of mine, who always took care that he had something for us. That trip we got nine hundred kilos of wheat from him, and he wouldn't take a dime for it—not a dime.

The last trip—I'll never forget it—was the most unusual one ever. It was between Christmas and New Year's in the Hunger Winter. We arrived at a farm we had been to twice before, but this time we couldn't go in: the farmer had strung up barbed wire all around. We honked. When they saw it was us, they opened up and let us in.

"This time, I don't know if I can help you. I don't have much anymore. It's so hard," the farmer said.

Still, he wanted to help. Having nothing else, he decided to give us the small seed potatoes he had been saving to plant in the spring. They were stored for the winter in deep holes, covered with straw and earth. His farmhands had to dig them up for us, but we got our five tons.

"Don't worry. I'll get more from the other farmers' surplus. I can make it," he said.

I paid him 140 guilders—far, far less than you would pay in the store today. He could have sold those potatoes for hundreds of thousands of guilders, which some stinkers did, but he was a very fine man, a normal person.

When winter threshing was finished, his barn floor had been covered, as usual, with dirt, gravel, and chaff, but there was always a little bit wasted, and there was some grain mixed in there too. Because it was wartime and shortages, he had gathered it all up in bags, saving it for the hogs. When he showed it to us, we said, "Please, give it to us. We have hundreds of people around with plenty of time on their hands to sort it out." So we got eight or nine bags to take home, each one at least seventy-five pounds.

We drove off with our load of potatoes and extra bags. With us this time was the director of an Amsterdam shipping company, who was living in Huizen. He had to sit on the potatoes; I was sitting in front with Gerrit. For miles we were driving alongside a famous canal, used in the old days for ships bound for Indonesia. The air was bitter cold. We had been on the road maybe an hour and a half when Gerrit said, "We'll get to a bridge pretty soon. On the other side live some relatives of mine. We can get a hot cup of coffee." I thought I would like that; besides, coffee was hard to come by. When he mentioned their name, I realized I had known a man from this family in Finland—Jaap Langendijk, a famous ice skater. So I wanted to meet them, too.

Pretty soon Gerrit turned the truck onto the bridge. That very same moment, I saw the sign, "Weight Limit Three Tons." Oh, God. We had five tons of potatoes and a ton of other stuff.

That bridge was on pontoons, the whole business hanging from heavy poles with chains. We rolled on down. Halfway across, all of a sudden there was a lot of noise, and water flooded over the bridge floor. The moonlight shone through the clouds. We were hanging there.

"What now, Gerrit?"

I looked over and saw his undisturbed face.

"Well, we seem to be a little bit heavier than the thing was built for."

"All this work and all this food? How dumb!"

I was getting mad. He knew darned well that the bridge was not strong. But I couldn't stay mad; after all, it wasn't something he really wanted. So there we sat, with a lot of water under the truck.

In a very short time we heard the unmistakable sounds of marching feet and singing; it had to be Germans. Only Germans would be singing—it was required. They came closer and closer, until Gerrit—who could barely read or write, but in his own way was very philosophical—shouted out in a tremendously loud voice, "Hey, there!"

It was a group of maybe twenty men with their sergeant. They stopped. Gerrit boomed out, "Over here!" And over they came. They had to; when they heard such a loud mouth, they would automatically do whatever they were ordered. Gerrit yelled to them again, "We drive for the Wehrmacht! We have to take these potatoes to Amsterdam! It will be pretty bad for you fellows if we don't get there!" They understood that. There was no question of being suspicious. They figured a fellow with such a big mouth must be somebody important.

"What do we do?" they asked.

"I'll start the motor, and you men get behind and push."

So all the fellows got behind the truck to push, and we stayed inside and kept our feet dry. The way Gerrit handled those soldiers, he was not afraid of the devil.

I always had the feeling that without Kets de Vries, Kappelhof, and Dr. Van den Berg, a lot of things would have gone wrong. Kets de Vries was a supersmart man; he always did just as he pleased. One time he told everyone, "I have to go to Westerbork [the German transit camp in Holland from which Jews were deported to Auschwitz] to show the National Socialists running around here that they cannot take me; they need to understand that." I told him he was crazy.

For a couple of days he was gone; I didn't know where he was. Then he came back, and everything was normal again. Later, I thought it over and realized he fooled us all. No other Jews were coming back from Wester-bork. He never went anywhere, of course—just stayed in his house—and that way he got the Dutch National Socialists off his back.

Kappelhof, the distribution man, brought a lot of people to our house, including Meyer and his son. Ans said that at one time we had twenty-six people. Of course, that included my mother-in-law, my wife, and baby Erik, and maybe my sister and youngest brother, Kees, who came to us when the war got worse, but most of them were Jewish people. With so many women around, Annie never had to clean or look after the house; they were glad to help. When you have bad years behind you, and so much to worry about, the more you have to do, the better.

Dr. Van den Berg came to our house very often. He took care of all the Jews in the community and never wrote out a bill, a very special man. No one in our house actually got sick, but they often had complaints, and if he was in the neighborhood he would come by and give them something. I think sometimes they were happy to have an ailment just so the doctor would come.

Henny had a baby while she was in our house. That happened, too. It was less than a year after Erik, our first child, was born. We brought her to the hospital where Annie gave birth to Erik. To be safe, the doctor didn't record the baby's birth until after the war was over, so Marion is actually older than her birth certificate says.

We were friends with the Sickens family, who lived in a little house close by that belonged to a doctor. Sickens was a journalist for a Dutch news-paper. They paid no rent—they were that poor—and the doctor didn't go after it; he was happy enough to have a tenant, because otherwise his place would have been broken up for firewood. Every house that wasn't in use was torn down that winter for stove wood. The house was in a lit-tle forest, an ideal place to put a mother and young baby. So Pam, Henny, and the baby moved in there, and Sickens's wife took the very best care of them until the war was over.

Pam had been writing some stories he wanted to publish. He went to a man in town who printed underground things and talked him into doing it. Borrowing the man's typewriter, Pam typed it all out, and it was printed: a little book, in Dutch, and there was not a good word for the Germans in the whole thing. I kept a few hundred in stock that I sold under the counter for one and a half guilders. Pam kept about three hundred copies at Sickens's place.

Annie Bochove with her son Erik, 1943

One morning, looking out, we saw two Germans roaming down the street, and then a moment later Pam passed by pulling a little four-wheeled cart behind him. On the cart were all the books and the typewriter. I thought, "Oh, Pam Juliard looks scared!" There was a raid on the outskirts of town that day, and before he knew what was happening they were in his house. They picked him up along with his whole stock of books. They rounded up several other people as well and brought them all to a cafe in the center of town, very close to us.

Now Pam's face was a little bit pronounced; he had blue eyes, but there was something typically Jewish about him. By then I was not an outsider anymore; over the years I learned to recognize certain things, like—especially when Jews are together—their accent has a little bit of Yiddish in it. The Amsterdam Jews, especially, were very lively; they had all these interesting points of view. It could be about art, music—anything. I always recognized them as people with a certain blood in them. Pam, as blond and blue-eyed as he was, had that character. Still, the Germans were never smart in these things.

At that little cafe they questioned him. According to his papers, he was a seminary student, studying to become a minister. The people they were picking up were going to be sent for forced labor in Germany, but Pam, as a seminary student, was supposed to be exempt. They weren't sure what to do, so they made him and some others they had picked up walk about twelve miles to the queen's Summer Palace at Soestdyk, now a German headquarters. The thing was, they forgot the books. The German fellow in Huizen had looked at one. He couldn't read Dutch, but he recognized the word "God." Pam told him it was about the Bible, and he believed him; but really it was a curse against the Germans. At the Summer Palace, they questioned him again, checked out his story, and let him go.

We were eating dinner that evening when Pam passed by our house again, on his way home to Henny. He was mad: after all that walking, he hardly had shoes left anymore.

I think he had quite a lot of guts, Henny too, and Ans—all of them. I have the deepest respect for them. It could have been the end of Pam's life. There are very few people like the Juliards. In the house, they could always settle disputes the right way, talk hate away, things like that. They are very wise.

Yes, it could have been the end of my life many times too, but I was slowly growing into it. It was like walking in a mine field; you're halfway into it and all at once you recognize that you are in a mine field. What can you do? Keep walking.

After that episode I still sold the books in the store. It was a little dangerous, but I knew my customers, of course. When the war was over I still had a few copies. I have one or two around here somewhere; they're fairly small.

Huizen was a small, close-knit community; families lived in harmony there for generations. We never explained anything to our neighbors and they never asked. They knew about us. I found that out whenever there was a small emergency and we needed a little help; I never had to tell them about it. I don't know for sure, but Kets de Vries once told me that a hundred and fifty Jews were hiding in Huizen.

There must have been at least twenty families involved, maybe more; I knew of about ten or twelve. I think perhaps more people were helping in Huizen because, being so close to Amsterdam, where most of the Jews came from, there was a kind of relationship with many of them. Then, too, there was the quality of the people—the most stubborn in their hate against the Nazis—and their orthodox beliefs that the Jews were God's chosen people. They took the Bible literally; I think that had an influence. Personally, I don't believe that a snake has spoken, or things like that, and I don't worry about it, either.

My feeling when doing it, and Annie's too, was that it had nothing to do with religion. If I was not a Christian, I would still do it. You have it in you. The first woman to come to us was a good friend of Annie's, and likable, the last person you could say no to—it was impossible. Then you see that your house is more or less the right place for giving help; you have the feeling that you can do a good thing.

Annie never objected, but it was all very hard for her the last months of the war. If your body is not strong, and your system is a bit nervous, if you get very weak and close to being sick, and every time the doctor comes he is worried about you, then you begin to wonder: how long can it go on? You cannot put the people out in the street. So sometimes you cry to get a little bit of relief. That was hard on me. There were days, moments, when it was very hard, but then it would pass, and we went on.

We always had enough to eat but when the war was over I was still quite a bit underweight, about thirty pounds less than my normal weight, and the same for Annie, too. It was from the strain, from all the struggles you go through. The strain was with us day and night, especially after the Germans came to the store that time; we lived with the thought that any day it could happen again. Yet, when I think back, I can see that I have always been an optimist. I can easily remember the good things and forget the rest.

Recently I was talking to a man who said people helped either for money or because they hated the Nazis. I had to say my piece: "Well, hate of the Nazis and money are two different things. You help people because you are human and you see that there is a need. There *are* people who do it just for the money, which is really terrible, but in the case of someone who badly needed money, well, that was different—I could understand it." I was lucky that I didn't need their money. I was not rich, but the store brought in enough to feed everyone, and I had a good feeling that we could make it with what we had.

If someone, like Meyer, came into my house, who could pay for his food, then fine. Ans and Henny didn't have much, but they were always telling Annie that they wanted to pay something. Annie said, "Take it easy. We don't want your money." At one point Ans sold her piano, and then she was so happy because she could give some money to Annie. Annie kept that money separately, and when it was the Hunger Winter we used it to buy a little extra food.

LIBERATION

The day that the war was over, I'll never forget it. The air was electric. The news reached everywhere, of course, that the Germans had lost. They signed the peace treaty on the fifth of May, which is still a celebration day in Holland. That morning the Jews in our house decided to go out in the street. It was still not completely safe, but even so, they all went to the little forest where the Sickens and the Juliards were living, to gather fir boughs to decorate the house. I brought down the three thousand Dutch flags from the attic. The first person in the store that morning was the schoolteacher.

"I need some decorations," she said. "Do you have enough paper for us to make about thirty flags?"

Little did she know what she would be getting: real flags! Then, while most of the helpers and the Jewish fellows were busy hanging the flags up all around, more people came in the store. All of a sudden the customers realized that we had had these Jews in the house all the time; it was surprising, but there were still plenty of people who didn't know.

Everyone was busy stringing up wire on the streetlights, hanging flags and candles. There were a lot of people around. By noontime, two German officers on a motorcycle with a sidecar came through the crowd; I don't think they had cars to drive anymore. They stopped in front of the house, and one of the fellows stepped out. Seeing all the people and the decorations, he got mad.

"Break it up!" he yelled.

We didn't do it, of course. They drove off, and we never saw them again. Then the police came by.

"Bochove, don't do it. It's too early."

"Well, can I stop these people?"

I could not stop them. Several people got nervous, but they didn't want to stop.

Before it was night, Huizen's musicians were in the road, marching endlessly through the town, playing the national anthem, with all the kids following behind them. It was tremendous.

A few days later, Pam Juliard brought a sergeant from the English secret service to the house. We asked him if he could find the hiding place. He looked through the whole attic for at least thirty minutes and couldn't find it. Years later, needing some building materials, I tore out the wall of the hiding place. Then I thought to myself, why did I do that? It was dumb.

In 1980 I was in Holland with my brother and sister-in-law, in Naarden, only twenty minutes away from Huizen. They said, "Let's all go there." Well, I did not have happy times there; I didn't want to go, but they insisted. We drove over, stopping close to the drugstore—only it's not a drugstore now; it's back to being a store that sells knitting wool, the same as before we took it over. My brother took a few photos, then he said he wanted to go inside. I said no. I don't know why, but it was too much for me. I was thinking about how my wife died after we had done all those things. Up until just a short time ago, it was just too much. But now I feel differently. Now that I've told so many stories, that it's being recorded—I think I've aired it out. Now I can see it the way it was.

Henny Juliard

In 1942, the Jewish people in Holland got invitations from the Germans asking us to please be so kind as to show up at the train station so they could take us away to the concentration camps. We told ourselves, "If they find us, so be it, but go on our own? Never."

Before our particular invitation arrived, my husband, Pam, and I moved away; we went to live in The Hague with my brother. But then he and his family got the famous letter and went into hiding, and we had to move again. Someone had given us the address of a very nice old lady—a Socialist—also living in The Hague. She took us in. But there were other people staying in her house as well, one of them a Dutch man who was working for the German army. We were in her house only two days when this man said to the old lady, "Those people are Jews. You'd better get rid of them or I will go to the Germans about it." I immediately phoned my friend Annie Bochove, and that same day she came to get me and took me to her home in Huizen.

Pam felt that since the Bochoves were newly married, he would find a different place for himself; he didn't want to cause any extra trouble for Annie and Bert; one of us was enough. With the help of a friend he found an address in Rotterdam, but his stay there ended in a tragic drama.

By 1942, everyone needed false papers, but not many people knew how to arrange for them; that came later, with the so-called Resistance. To supply identity cards, Pam's Rotterdam friend was in the practice of stealing them from other people's pocketbooks. One day a woman caught him in the act and yelled for the police. He was so afraid he would be tortured and betray his secrets, before the police could even arrest him, he shot himself. But the policeman—this was a Dutch policeman; I'm telling this story to show that some Dutch people had a very bad attitude—found a

Henny Juliard, 1938

receipt in his pocket that led him to a mattress shop, and there the police learned where he had lived. Searching his home, they discovered lists with names and addresses of people in hiding, including those of Pam, Pam's sister, and my brother, who was married to Pam's sister.

Because it was crowded, Pam had already moved into Rotterdam's Chinatown, so he was not at that house when they came for him, but they picked up his sister and my brother and their four-year-old boy, and took them away. When he found out, Pam came to us in Huizen, in despair. We learned years later that they were sent from Holland to Sobibor, where they were murdered on March 26, 1943.

From August 1942 until May 1945, we lived under the care of the Bochoves, both in hope and despair. We were thankful for the shelter but depressed knowing that our presence was putting our best friends in deadly danger. And then, too, we were always thinking about our family, wondering what had happened to them. Of course, we didn't know any of the things we know now, but we recognized that we were all in danger. We were very lucky to have had the Bochoves, that in spite of everything, they somehow managed to help us live a rather normal life.

We weren't always in their home. From time to time the police warned us that the house was under suspicion, and then we went to another address for a while.

Annie Bochove, 1940

The Bochoves were exceptional. Bert was an even-tempered man, always kind, liked by everyone. Annie was introverted but easy to talk with; she was kind and soft-spoken. She never said very much, but she always did what she thought was right. They didn't congratulate themselves for being good; it was just natural for them. Bert, as nice as he was, seemed to always have everything under control; he arranged everything. You knew he was the boss; he ran the shop and Annie ran the house.

I did a lot of the housework and cooking. I wanted to do as much as I could to help out, of course, and in a large household there's always plenty of work. Pam gave a hand to Bert in the drugstore. In the evenings everyone sat around the warm stove while Flippy, their little white dog, jumped from lap to lap. There was a good feeling among all of us together; we weren't always crying.

My first child, Marion, was born in those black days. Born seven months after Annie gave birth to Erik, we called her the black baby. It was Bochove's friend, Dr. Van den Berg, who made the secret arrangements for me to have the baby in a hospital, under false papers. No one ever asked me for money or for food cards; even after the war, neither the doctor nor the hospital would accept payment. Pam came to visit me every evening. When he was late, I became afraid. Most of the doctors hated the Germans and were reliable, but still, it was dangerous for me to be there.

In December '44, during the Hunger Winter, food was scarce; you had to go to distant farms to find it. The men couldn't go—it was much too dangerous: they were picking up all the boys and men for forced labor in Germany. One time Annie and I went out on our bicycles to a farmer the Bochoves knew. It was snowing, and the tires on the bicycles were bad; we had to stop every few kilometers to fix them. Usually we traded whatever we had for food—even my husband's shirts—but this particular farmer was not like most of them; he wouldn't take anything. We tied the bags he gave us to a cart pulled by Annie's bicycle and pushed the bicycles home. We were gone for three days, but we got a lot of food: potatoes, grain, all kinds of things.

Annie always did what she thought was right, but she made a bad mistake that year, going on another trip like that one. In September or October, she had seen her doctor for a lung examination. She explained to him what her home life was like—having all the people there. She could talk to him about these things because the doctors were very good about being against the Nazis. This was after Arnhem, and everyone thought the war would end soon. The doctor said to her, "If the war is over in a few weeks, what you are doing is all right. But if it lasts much longer, you must send the people away. It's too much for you. You can't take it." But she

Two women searching for food in the Dutch countryside during the Hunger Winter, 1944–45

Henny and Pam Juliard on their wedding day, August 18, 1938

didn't follow his advice. The winter was long and there was very little to eat. She made a second journey to a distant farm, this time with another woman friend. By then she was pregnant with her second child, but she didn't tell anybody; she wanted to make the trip.

She didn't listen to anyone's advice, and she never complained about anything. Not long after the war ended she became ill again with her lungs and was sent to Switzerland. She came back in 1947 and died.

Near the end of the war, Pam and I were living in a little house in the woods that Bochove found for us; with our newborn baby, it was a better place to be. While we were living there, Pam published a little book, underground, to help earn some money. In it were two anti-Nazi stories. It was a dangerous thing to do, but it was all right with me. I even helped him with the typing.

By then we had practically no food in the house. There were some Dutch SS in our village—Dutch, not German—who were in the habit of searching houses, looking for food to confiscate. I can't say that we lived in fear of them as much as anger, and we were very angry about this. One day they came to our little house, looking for food, and what did they find? My husband, me, our little child, and the books.

"What is this? You'll have to come with us!"

They made Pam pile the books on a cart. Then they made him pull the cart, and they took him away.

I was certain I would never see him again. I was so sure he wouldn't come back, I began to pack a suitcase to go to Annie Bochove's. Then a few of the SS came back to the house.

"You are leaving? Oh, what a nice little girl you have," said one.

Then he started to rip up the place. I got really angry.

"What are you doing? I shouted. "I just cleaned up and you're making a mess again. Get out of here!"

And he went away. He was so surprised that I stood up to him. Usually in such circumstances you don't have the courage.

They took Pam to a different town for interrogation. It was only two weeks before the end of the war. We could hear the cannons of the Canadian army, they were that near.

The German questioning Pam said, "This is Jewish libel!"

"No, that is not libel."

Pam made up a story that someone from the Resistance had asked him to hide the books for him. The German said, "Wait until the Russians are here. Then you will see what life will be like. Go home! Go home!"

Pam walked all the way back to Huizen. He was just very lucky. The next day they shot a boy there because they had found a gun on him. Pam's great danger, of course, was that they might have discovered he was Jewish.

By then we had no money left at all. The first years of the war, before we went to Bochove's, we lived from our savings and by selling every possession of any value. By the end of the war, all Pam had left to wear were his pajamas. We had traded my gold wedding ring, his watch, even his underwear. But we were lucky. I know of other people in hiding who were told to leave when their money was gone. One person told me that when he wanted to go to the bathroom he had to pay for a piece of toilet paper.

Yes, some Jewish people we knew had very bad experiences in hiding, but because of our friends the Bochoves, it was not so terrible for us. That we had to hide, that we were treated like criminals, that we couldn't feel like a *mensch, that* was awful.

My husband and I are from large families. Almost everyone was murdered—parents, brothers, sisters, uncles, aunts, and their children. May they rest in peace. The Bochoves saved our lives.

Yettie Mendels

From the moment I came to Huizen in January '44 until the end of the war, everything that happened to me went through Bert Bochove. He al-

Yettie Mendels, Beer Jaacow, Israel, 1987

ways knew; he always helped; he did all the arranging. I'm sure he forgot all about it because I was such a small part of all the work that he did, but I remember quite well; the things he did were very, very important for me.

I was in Bochove's house for only one night because his house was already completely filled with Jewish people. The next day he arranged for me to go to another family. But first there's the story of how I came to Bochove's; it's not a nice story.

A few months before I was married I received a letter from the German authorities telling me to report to the train station; it gave all the details including what I should bring. I went to see Ans, to talk it over.

"I'm not going," I told her.

"No, of course you are not going."

I simply left Rotterdam and pretended I never got the letter. The odd thing is I don't remember where I went or where I stayed before my wedding. There are plenty of things I don't remember about those times, because I pushed everything away. I suppose it was necessary for my survival.

My parents lived in the north of Holland. They came to our wedding in September '42. That was the last time I saw them. In October they were caught in one of the first big roundups of Jews and taken to Westerbork concentration camp. We only learned about it when Henny got Father's letter from Westerbork. He wrote that he knew this was the end. He must have really believed that, because he also wrote that he now accepted my brother marrying his non-Jewish girlfriend, which, being a religious man, he had been very much against. This was the first such marriage in our family, and it was very hard for him.

Then we found out that my eldest sister and brother, together with their children and families, were also caught and sent to Westerbork. My brother Max corresponded with us from Westerbork for a very long time, but finally he was taken with the rest, in one of the very last transports to Poland. None of them came back.

By the end of the year the Germans ordered the entire Jewish old-age home where we were living to pack up and move from The Hague to the

Amsterdam ghetto—all of us together. I don't think we recognized the danger. I didn't; I thought we'd come through. At the time, what else could you think?

Living in the Amsterdam ghetto was terrible. I didn't know a single person. No one talked to me—it was too dangerous. By then, no one in the ghetto was actually from Amsterdam; those people were all gone. We lived in the house of Jewish people who had been taken away—it was their furniture, their kitchen, their plates, their everything. It was horrible.

Yettie Mendels, 1949

Before very long, the elderly people from our old-age home were taken away to Westerbork, but we were allowed to stay on because Bob, being an electrician, had special papers. The Joodsche Raad [Jewish Council], who ran things in the ghetto, gave special identity papers to people who were useful, to protect them from being sent to Westerbork. But you never knew: sometimes the next day the Germans would say, no, that paper is worthless, and they would pick you up. You could never feel safe, not even for one hour.

In May '43, Corrie Zondervan, my brother's non-Jewish fiancée, came to see us from The Hague. I was pregnant.

"It's not good for you to be here any longer. They will empty out the ghetto very soon and you will end up like the others. I'm going to take you out, but it's better if you don't go together. I'll take Yettie today and come back tomorrow for Bob."

I went with her that same afternoon. But before she could return the next day there was a big raid—no one had expected it—and my husband was picked up, right in the street. For two or three months Bob wrote to me from Westerbork, then he was sent to Sobibor, in Poland, where his life ended. But I didn't learn about that until much later.

Corrie took me to her home in The Hague where she was living with her parents and sisters; my youngest brother, John, was there too. A few months later the Gestapo came to their house looking for my brother. As they were coming in the front door, he ran out the back way, and all they found was me, with no papers—just a very big belly. I was so big, I couldn't run. So instead I put on a grand performance for them, pretending I was in labor. I had no idea I was capable of such a thing, but it scared them. They left me alone.

That same evening Corrie found somebody in the underground who brought me to a hospital. Giving me her own identity papers, she registered me as an unwed mother. Five days later my son Bobbie was born. I stayed in the hospital a few more weeks until the underground could arrange for new papers—which was not so easy—and find a home for me and the child. We stayed with a family of Communists for the next three months, until one day one of their sons was arrested and shot by the Germans, for working in the underground. Then it was too dangerous to stay there any longer.

Finding another family where Bobbie and I could be together was very, very hard, in fact, impossible. The underground people took away my three-and-a-half-month-old baby and sent him to the north of Holland. I didn't see him again until he was two and a half years old. In the meantime I waltzed from one place to another, here one night, there one night—fourteen places altogether—and all that time I never knew where my child was.

It was a funny life. I was young then, only twenty-three, and without much experience. I was alone. I lived day by day, very superficially; I didn't think too much—the time was like that. I didn't know what had happened to my parents, to my brothers and sisters, to my husband. You can't imagine what it's like—utterly impossible.

At last I came to a place where a friend of one of my sisters lived. She was too afraid to keep me for even a couple of days, but she knew where Ans and Henny were; I hadn't seen them since before I left the Amsterdam ghetto. She gave me the Bochoves' address.

Yettie Mendels newly reunited with her son Bobbie, 1945

When I arrived at the Bochoves' house it was full. I stayed only one night, but Bert found a very good place for me in Huizen, with a woman whose husband and son were in a concentration camp because they had helped Jews.

One day while I was living with this woman, the Germans encircled Huizen and began a *razzia*—a raid to find Jews in hiding. They visited every house in Huizen that day. I knew that my sisters and brother-in-law and other Jewish families were at Bert's, but I also knew that he had a good hiding place for them that was nearly impossible to find. The house where I was staying was on the edge of town, so the Germans were in our garden almost immediately. I was upstairs when they came inside. The lady called up to me, "Yettie, come down here. They're taking something that belongs to my husband." She couldn't speak German and wanted me to help. When I went down I saw that one of the men had opened a drawer and taken out a pair of binoculars.

I shouted at him, "You can't take that! It's forbidden! I'll report you to your officer!" He put the binoculars down and left. I wasn't at all afraid. I felt very secure. I don't know why, but I didn't believe that anything more could happen to me after that horrible night when I was nine months pregnant and the Germans tried to take me away. From that moment I had lost my fear. Later I would become afraid again, but at that point I had no fear.

They did pick up some people, but most of the Jews in Huizen came through that day. At Bert Bochove's they didn't find anyone.

THE NSB

Yettie stayed with this family several more months until the woman's husband and son returned from the concentration camp and there was no longer room for her. She took a job as a live-in maid with another family for the next four months. A few days after she settled in with this family, while cleaning a bedside table drawer, she discovered she was living with Dutch National Socialists—Nazis. She asked a clergyman who knew her situation what she should do. "Stay there!" he told her. "It's the safest place you could be."

I stayed with that family, knowing that they were NSB'ers, until late in September 1944. I wasn't too nervous about the situation. However, after the Battle of Arnhem, on the seventeenth of September, they began to be nervous themselves. One day the son-in-law came to me.

Dr. Van den Berg and his family, 1945

"I know you are in the underground. I have something I want to give you," he said, and he showed me a gun and two hand grenades. "If you want more, I can get them."

"No, I don't want these things. I wouldn't know what to do with them." I denied being in the underground, which was the truth.

"It doesn't matter. I'll leave them under the shrubs in the garden, and you can do whatever you want." Later I took them out and brought them to a church where I knew the priest. I soon left that family.

I left because the doctor in Huizen, Dr. Van den Berg, asked me to work for him in a little hospital he had opened for the Dutch refugees coming up from the south after the Battle of Arnhem. Before the war I had studied nursing and I much preferred doing that to being a maid. I lived at the hospital with a refugee couple from the south. The wife did the cooking and her husband was the handyman. I was the nurse.

It was both a clinic and a hospital, but only for childbirths. The people from the south of Holland were all Catholics so there was plenty of business; I think we had about ten beds. Dr. Van den Berg had his own private practice, but he came to the hospital every day, and if there was a birth, then he came for that, too. We had no electricity, only gas lamps. During a birth it was my job to hold up the carbide lamp. Dr. Van den Berg always said, "Look! The child is coming out now. He wants to see the light." He had a wonderful sense of humor.

Dr. Van den Berg's whole attitude was special. I never felt that he was doing me a favor. As a doctor he had plenty of responsibilities besides helping Jews and doing other forbidden things, but he was always friendly; I never heard a cross word. He and Bert Bochove, who was his good friend, had many things in common: they were both outgoing men. Like Dr. Van den Berg, Bert never gave you the feeling that you were a burden to him. When I think of Bert, I always remember a big smile. I'm sure he had quite a bit to not smile about. I don't think his life has been easy.

The hospital was quite near to Bochove's store, on the same street. I didn't visit too often because I was very busy, but I did walk past the

The Mendels children: Henny, John, and Yettie, 1938

pharmacy every day and would stop to say hello to Bert, Annie, Ans, and Henny, while Henny was still there. When Henny and Pam moved to the little house in the woods I could visit her much more often. Because of my hospital work, I had a bicycle, and even a pass to go out after the eight o'clock curfew.

Henny and I were always very close. She was already twelve years old when I was born, so she became my role model of how I thought I should be. I didn't resent her because of that; on the contrary, I admired her very much.

During the war I think she wanted to help me more than circumstances allowed. Her daughter Marion was born only four months after I gave birth to my boy, but Marion was never separated from her parents. They had their child and I did not have mine. I felt that Henny understood me, that she felt my pain even more than I felt it myself, because I am very good at pushing away the things that hurt. Henny wasn't like that. I think her character was much stronger than mine.

BUILDING A NEW LIFE

Yettie stayed at Dr. Van den Berg's hospital until the end of the war in May 1945, after which she remained in Huizen for another year, attempting to make her life normal again. It took several months of searching to trace the whereabouts of her son, who was by then two-and-a-half years old. As time went by, she learned the sad fate of her husband and the other family members.

My way to learn about something, to understand it, is to read about it in a book. You know, I have plenty of books about the Holocaust, but no matter how much you read about it, you still can't understand it—you can't understand what people went through; you can't have their experiences. I went through a lot, but to not make it through, that horror I have not experienced. My family members who died in the camps have gone through it; I have not.

I have talked these things over with Henny, but never with Ans. She can't. I always want to hear about it, to read about it, to talk, but Ans is exactly the opposite. She doesn't want to hear about it. Never, never, never. If I start to say something like, "You know, Father . . . ," she says, "No! Don't tell me, don't speak!" Henny and I often talk about Father, about his sense of humor, about his wisdom, about things he did or said. We remember him. I told Ans, "I don't understand why you can't talk about him. They had to live through this. They had to endure it to the end. The least we can do is identify with them."

I came to Israel because I couldn't live in Holland anymore; I was living among ghosts. Everywhere I went I imagined I saw this one, or that one, or that one. Many of my friends married during the war, as I did, but none of them survived. Of my friends, of my family, not one is alive; I have no friends from my childhood. I didn't find out all at once. Slowly, over the years you find out who didn't come back.

3 ⌒ A Child Just Like You

Born in Holland in 1916, to a Jewish family of comfortable means, Mirjam Waterman became a schoolteacher at the age of twenty-two. Soon after, she found herself deeply involved with the Youth Aliyah movement, an offshoot of the Zionist movement.

Youth Aliyah was organized in 1933 to save Jewish children from Nazi Germany and Austria by helping them emigrate to Palestine. After Kristallnacht, November 9, 1938, when many German Jews understood for the first time the seriousness of their situation, the number of parents turning for help to Youth Aliyah greatly increased.

Because the demand for Palestine immigration certificates soon exceeded their availability, Youth Aliyah brought thousands of the refugee children to "safe" European countries, especially Holland and Britain.

By the outbreak of World War II in September 1939, Youth Aliyah had arranged for the immigration to Palestine of over five thousand German and Austrian Jewish children and the safe transport of fifteen thousand others to as yet unoccupied European countries. The children called themselves Young Palestine Pioneers.

Mirjam Waterman Pinkhof was instrumental in forming a group led by the charismatic resistance worker Joop Westerweel, which rescued approximately 320 of the 821 Young Pioneers living in Holland after 1938. Although Jewish herself, and in constant danger of detection and deportation, Mirjam passed up opportunities to rescue herself to save the German children. The group worked tirelessly to find refuge for the children in Holland. Eventually they established underground routes to smuggle many of them to France, which was safer than Holland. From France, 70

Young Pioneers managed to reach Spain and Palestine before the war ended. Of the 48 teenagers living in Loosdrecht, 34—about 70 percent—survived the war. In comparison, only 20 percent of all the Jewish people living in Holland during the war survived the Nazi occupation.

Next to the North Sea and close by the Dutch border, Sophie Yaari was born Sophie Nussbaum in 1925, in Emden, Germany. Her father owned a small grocery shop. Twice widowed in childless marriages, he married a third time, to a woman twenty-six years younger than he. That marriage produced three daughters; Sophie was the middle child.

Sophie's entire family lived in Emden, a town of thirty-four thousand people in the 1930s. The Jewish community of Emden numbered about one thousand, comprised of families whose ancestors settled in Emden in the fifteenth century, following their expulsion from Spain.

The shock of Kristallnacht galvanized Sophie's parents to send her and her younger sister alone to Holland just days after the official pogrom throughout Germany. Soon after, Sophie found her way to the Youth Ali-yah home in Loosdrecht, whose youthful idealistic leaders were organized by their friend Mirjam Pinkhof into the group that saved Sophie and most of the other teenagers at the home.

Joseph Heinrich was one of ten children born to a middle-class Jewish family in Frankfurt am Main, Germany. His father, who ran a small grocery shop, was sympathetic to the Zionist movement. By 1937, when Joseph was thirteen years old, his four older brothers and sisters had already left Germany to settle in Palestine.

Like Sophie, he was sent for safety to a Youth Aliyah home in Holland after Kristallnacht. He first met Mirjam Waterman when the progressive school where she and Joop Westerweel were teaching invited the Youth Aliyah foreign refugee children to attend their classes. Several years later, when the Jewish children were told to report to the German occupiers for deportation, Joseph was saved by Mirjam and her Westerweel group. Smuggled into France, through a series of improbable adventures, Joseph illegally crossed the Pyrenees in the winter of 1944 and sailed for

Palestine before the war ended. He remained in Israel until the end of his life.

Joseph Heinrich related his story in his home in Ajanot, Israel, April 10, 1988. He passed away in 1992, at the age of sixty-eight.

Sophie Yaari emigrated to Palestine directly after the war ended. Today she and her husband run an innovative dairy farm, part of a cooperative that has been studied and emulated by agriculturalists from many countries. She gave this interview in her home in Beer Tuvia, on April 11, 1988.

Mirjam and Menachem Pinkhof also emigrated to Israel shortly after the war. Menachem died there in 1969. Today Mirjam lives in Haifa, where she gave this interview on April 7, 1988.

Mirjam Pinkhof

I grew up in an environment of very advanced liberal and humanistic ideas, but knowing nothing about Jewish subjects. We were a completely assimilated family.

Mirjam Pinkhof,
Haifa, 1987

My mother's family was Portuguese Jewish; her name was Lopes Cardozo. As a young woman she entered a utopian society for better living: the Frederik van Eeden Community, something like Walden in America. After her marriage she remained active in humanistic, antimilitary, and antifascist organizations.

My entire family was assimilated, except for my father, who came from the poor Jewish quarter in Amsterdam. He worked his way up in the world by leaving the unpromising conditions in Amsterdam and moving to the countryside, where he bought land to start a nursery for fruit trees and roses. But the times were not right for it. It was around the beginning of World War I, and there was a boom in the diamond trade but problems in the nursery business. So for the rest of his life my father earned his living in the diamond trade, while the farm and fruit trees became his hobby. He always stayed in contact with the Jewish community in Amsterdam and with many of the Jewish refugees coming to Holland in those days from Russia and Poland. He was a very "Jewish" man.

But my father was also a vegetarian and an active participant in many socialistic activities, which is how he met my mother. This is why we five children grew up in Loosdrecht—far from Jewish life—in an enormous garden, surrounded by people who were trying to build a better world.

TEACHING

There was a school in Bilthoven called the Werkplaats Kinder Gemeenschap [Children's Community Workshop]. The founder was Kees Boeke, who was well known at the time in educational circles all over western Europe for his progressive ideas. Boeke was a Quaker, and his school was notable for its idealistic principles. It was run somewhat like a kibbutz, forming its own community and growing its own food. The people who taught there did so out of moral conviction and idealism rather than to make money, because the school paid its staff very little. The head teacher was Joop Westerweel, who later became famous in Holland for his resistance against the Germans. I was a teacher at this school.

One of the principles of the school was that the pupils could have a say about our teaching and how we ran the school's daily life. In this spirit, a student stood up one day in 1939 and told us that when he came to school in the mornings he passed a house where he saw teenagers hanging around, some up in the trees—all of them very bored. That day he got off his bicycle to talk with them. They told him they were Jewish refugees from Germany who had been brought to Holland by the Youth Aliyah movement. They had a nice place to live, but they had no books, no school, and nothing much to do. Our student asked us, "Could we possibly arrange to bring these children to the Werkplaats for school?"

Joop Westerweel said, "Of course! They must come!" Kees Boeke rented a special classroom building for these twenty-five Jewish children, and pretty soon they were coming to our school every morning, returning to their Youth Aliyah house only late in the afternoon.

Because of my Jewish origins, the school appointed me to teach this group. Out of this contact Joop Westerweel and I became very good friends. I learned at first hand about his enthusiasm for helping the Jewish children, and his anti-Nazi, anti-German feelings. He was 100 percent on the Jewish side, wanting to enrich the lives of these children and do everything possible to help them. We both worked extremely hard, trying to show that we wouldn't collaborate with the Germans and that we were against everything the Nazis represented.

DISMISSED

In mid-1941, bowing to German pressure, Kees Boeke asked Mirjam to resign from teaching at the Children's Werkplaats, because she was Jewish.

After her dismissal from the Werkplaats, Mirjam returned to her parents' home in Loosdrecht, where, in the fall of 1941, she opened a school for the local

*Jewish children who, by German decree, could no longer attend their public
school. Sixty students came to her house every day.*

THE SECOND YOUTH ALIYAH GROUP

Not far from my parents' house in Loosdrecht was a place called Pavil-
joen Loosdrechtse Rade. About seventy teenagers, aged twelve to sixteen,
were living there with their leaders, all members of another Youth Aliyah
group. Most of them were German Jewish refugees, although there were
also a few Dutch people among them. The boys worked with the local
Dutch farmers, studying agricultural practices, while the girls worked with
the farmers' wives, learning how to milk cows, perform household tasks,
and everything else a farmer's wife needs to know. Some of the boys were
learning other skills, such as carpentry or blacksmithing. All of the Young
Pioneers were devoted to preparing themselves for a new life in Palestine.

I had never given much thought to Zionism before the war, but when
Hitler invaded Poland in '39, I began to think about it. When the Germans
occupied Holland in '40, I became a Zionist. It was only then that sud-

denly something inside told me I belonged to the Jewish people, to the Jewish side of the whole thing. I joined the Zionist youth movement. Like most people starting something new, I entered into it with a great deal of enthusiasm.

Being so close, I had a lot of contact with the Loosdrecht Youth Aliyah house—I became very involved in their cultural life. For every Jewish subject, for a Jewish holiday, or the Friday evening Sabbath, for instance, I invited the Palestine Pioneer leaders to come and talk to my pupils. As I became more deeply involved with the Zionist youth movement, I sought the advice of the Youth Aliyah house leaders on those matters as well. This was in 1940.

By 1942 the school at my parents' home was finished. The Germans opened a school just for Jewish pupils, but they soon deported all the students to Westerbork via Amsterdam, including most of the children who had attended my Loosdrecht school.

As the roundups of Jews became more and more frequent, the Loosdrecht leaders and I started to think about what to do with all the Young Pioneers in their care. You might ask, why was it your business to worry about those kids? Well, we were trying so hard to resist the Nazis, it was just understood that we would attempt to protect those kids.

Even so, most of the leaders thought that hiding them would be completely impossible. In the first place, it was not very easy to find families who were willing to save people, especially teenage children who could barely speak Dutch. Living together in a closed, isolated world, they had had virtually no experience with the gentile world. They were very Jewish.

One of the leaders was Joachim Simon—everyone called him Shushu. He was an exceptionally fine man who had a great influence on all the children, but he was very pessimistic about what Jewish people could do to save themselves from the Nazis. He was German and had already been in a concentration camp in '38, after Kristallnacht. Believing he understood the German mentality very well, he had no hope that anything good would come out of it for the Jews. He was completely convinced that the Nazis were all-powerful and we could never hope to win—it was absolutely useless to resist.

Another leader was a Dutchman, Menachem Pinkhof. He was also completely pessimistic about what was happening in Germany, although at that time no one in Holland knew anything about death camps or gas chambers. I must say we Dutch people were very naive; we couldn't even imagine all the things that had actually happened already.

One day a man who knew much more about the situation than we did came to Loosdrecht. The Germans had sent this man, Edelstein, from Prague to help set up the Jewish Council in Amsterdam. Edelstein warned us that we could expect only the very worst for people sent east to camps in Poland or Germany. This was actually the first time that I heard about these things— not gas chambers yet, but that we could expect nothing but death.

Menachem was the only one of the four leaders who had made up his mind that we should never give ourselves up to the Germans. He was the one who finally persuaded Shushu that we must try to find safe hiding places for all these children. Shushu thought it was impossible. But he changed his mind when I approached Joop Westerweel, asking if he was willing to help us. I knew his personality and felt confident of his answer. I also knew that he had connections with a large group of people who wanted to rescue Jews.

THE WESTERWEEL GROUP

From the moment Joop Westerweel came to help us, everything changed. We began to work. We set up a small group—most of them were Gentiles, but it also included Jews like myself, Menachem, and Shushu. We started by making a list with the names of all the children to be rescued, and tried to place opposite each child's name the name of a family that was willing to accept them. We made photographs of each child for false identity cards. Trying to find more than fifty places, the work went very slowly. We searched all over Holland.

From our effort of working to save this group of children grew a resistance movement of Jews and non-Jews laboring equally, one next to the other, until the end. The end for some of them was death. Many were caught.

Joop Westerweel was shot to death in August '44. Shushu was caught in January '43. When he was in prison he committed suicide—he was

Joop Westerweel, c. 1942

afraid he would break down under interrogation and betray his friends. So that was the end for them. In 1944, Menachem and I fell into a traitor's trap and were caught. We went through prisons and ended up in Bergen-Belsen, but we lived. We were very thin and weak at the end, but I'm here, able to tell you the story.

Keeping our fifty Young Palestine Pioneers underground meant finding safe places for them to stay, ration cards for food, money, books, making frequent visits to keep up their morale, and passing on to them letters from their friends and sometimes from their relatives. The need for places to hide was never-ending. People who were hiding one of our children were asked by a neighbor if they had a Jew in the house. They became afraid to keep the child any longer, and we had to look for a new address. It was an enormous job.

Our group grew in numbers. We made contact with other groups that worked on different levels, with different aims. You got to know people who could help you with ration cards or identity cards: we looked for clerks or officials who were willing to collaborate. When somebody died we tried to get his identity card and prevent the death from being recorded, so the card would still be valid. We did all kinds of things, but the most difficult was finding hiding places.

When I came to a house, I never knew if I could trust the people or not. The only way to figure it out was to have a talk with them. I always looked them straight in the eye and asked myself, can I trust you? It was a hard decision every time, but I dare say I never found traitors. This was the particular strength of Westerweel. Even people who were collaborating with the Nazis would start to feel guilty when he talked with them. He had an extraordinary gift for touching that good part in everyone; he went straight to it. When he went to a house to ask if they would take a boy or a girl, he never came back with a no.

We were a very close group. While Joop Westerweel was still teaching, we had meetings in his school. After he went underground, we met in other places. Each person had their own contacts. When we came together, we exchanged information and planned how to work together.

In March '43 my family had to leave our home in Loosdrecht to go underground. Actually, my parents were taken off to prison first. The Germans came to our house looking for my sister and me, and not finding us at home, they took our parents as well as a younger sister and brother and sent them to Westerbork. I managed to get them free. There were people you could bribe—Germans, Gestapo. I made contact with them—which was very dangerous—but I was able to bribe them. My parents, sister, and brother were all sent back to Amsterdam.

A few days later the Gestapo came to fetch them again, but in the meantime I had found a hiding place for them, where they stayed safely until the end of the war. From that day on I slept every night in a different place. I never stayed long at one address because it was too dangerous. That's how it worked.

THE GREEN BORDER

As time went by the situation grew worse: more and more people wanted a hiding place, and hiding places became increasingly harder to find. At a certain point our group decided to simply try to get the children out of Holland altogether. It was safer for them to live in the south of France than in Holland. Belgium was a little safer, but France was even better because

Loosdrecht school for Young Pioneers, where Mirjam Pinkhof taught, c. 1941

the French had only a military occupation, while in Holland we had a much more oppressive civil occupation.

Shushu found the first contacts into France; eventually we developed three routes. We discovered people—mostly smugglers—who could help you across the Belgian border. We called it going over the "green border" because you did not go on a road, or past a regular border post, but crept through the bushes and across farmers' fields—a route where there was no route. Westerweel himself took many of the kids through this border.

From Belgium they went to France, and in France there was another illegal group—all Jewish Young Pioneers—with an organization that had been set up first in Paris and afterwards in the south of France. It worked so well that seventy of our Young Pioneers managed to cross the Pyrenees during the German occupation. They reached Spain, and from there set off on ships bound for Palestine. That was our greatest success: seventy kids reached Palestine in '44, before the war even ended.

One day Joop and another man—who, by the way, is still alive today—were taking two girls across the "green border" into Belgium. They were caught right at the border. Joop, of course, was underground, using the false identification papers of a Belgian tobacco smuggler. By that time the Gestapo knew a lot about Joop and were looking for him. What Joop didn't know was that the man whose identity papers he was using was also being sought by the Germans. When Joop was caught on the border with the two girls, the German police looked at his papers and said, "Ah hah! We've got Le Lievre!"

Too late, Joop discovered that this Le Lievre had a record of crimes against the Nazis a mile long, including killing a German policeman. He thought they might treat him better if he told them who he really was, so he confessed to being Westerweel. But it didn't help him, and soon enough his situation became quite serious. First they took him to the local police station, then to the police station in Rotterdam, after that to the Rotterdam prison, and finally to Vught, the second transit camp in Holland after Westerbork. In Vught he was imprisoned in a concrete bunker with no hope of escape.

BETRAYAL

We were able to make contact with him through another prisoner in Vught, a Dr. Steyns. Dr. Steyns, who was not Jewish, was being held for somewhat unimportant things. Because of their lack of medical personnel, the Germans allowed him certain privileges. He was scheduled to finish his sentence in just a few months, but while he was still in Vught he tried to help us as much as he could. With his help, Westerweel concocted an escape plan.

Young Pioneers at Youth Aliyah home, Loosdrecht, c. 1942

He would take special pills provided by Dr. Steyns which would make it appear that he was hemorrhaging. If, as he hoped, the Germans transferred him to the prison hospital, where security was more lax, he would try to escape from there. The first part of the plan worked, and Westerweel found himself in the prison hospital. While there he gave Dr. Steyns a letter to smuggle out to us, giving us the details of his planned escape. But somehow the Germans sniffed out something suspicious and unexpectedly searched Dr. Steyns. They found Joop's letter and proceeded to set a trap. They had a Dutch traitor deliver Joop's letter to the addressee Joop had written on it—a member of our group. So this Dutchman came to us with a genuine letter from our friend Joop saying, "I'm going to help you get him out," and telling us exactly what he was going to do. That's how he infiltrated our group.

On the day we expected Westerweel to come out of prison, the traitor came to the address where I was staying, bringing the Gestapo with him. They rounded us up and put us all in prison. At the same moment, they arrested Menachem at the railway station, where, according to the plan, he was waiting with a suitcase full of clothes for Westerweel. Menachem and I were kept handcuffed, under very heavy guard, with no possibility

Jewish man being arrested by the SS, Amsterdam, c. 1942

of escape. When we were brought to Westerbork they immediately put us in the camp prison.

Even in prison, Menachem and I always had some contact with each other. We had good friends in Westerbork who tried to do whatever was possible to help us, but the only thing they could do was to have our names put illegally on the list of people being sent to Bergen-Belsen instead of Auschwitz. This may have saved us, who knows? Bergen-Belsen was a death camp, too, but a certain number of Bergen-Belsen inmates were set aside for possible exchange with German POWs in Palestine, and we were on the list of people who had certificates for Palestine. Such an exchange of prisoners actually did happen once: 222 prisoners left Bergen-Belsen by train bound for Palestine.

This traitor who betrayed us is still alive, living in Amsterdam today. I had a very bad feeling about him from the beginning—I didn't trust him, although the others did. That's why I always told him my whole made-up story—he never knew I was Jewish. I was living as a non-Jew with a false identity card, so it was easy. When I came to the Westerbork prison, they didn't know I was Jewish.

The prison interrogations were very, very difficult. In the end, I thought I would have an easier time as a Jewish woman and just be sent to a camp. As a resistance worker I was afraid they would shoot me, like Joop. I had a very hard time convincing them of the fact, but finally they accepted that I was a Jew. They sent me to Bergen-Belsen, where I remained exactly one year, from April '44 until we were freed in April '45. It was a terrible, terrible year, but that's another subject. Menachem was never really healthy again after the camp. We were married in Holland when we both came back from Bergen-Belsen. That was how we ended the war.

We both knew that we could have easily saved ourselves quite early in the game. Before the resistance group was formed, Joop Westerweel said to me, "I want you both to come to me. I will help you and look after you." I told Menachem we had a chance to be saved.

He said, "No, I need to stay here. I'm responsible for these children."

He was one of the leaders and couldn't leave them. Soon after that the idea was formed to save the whole group. We didn't want to save only ourselves; we wanted to save as many children and Jews as possible.

THE JEWISH CHILDREN AFTER THE WAR

Once I had to take two little children away from their parents, to deliver them to a young woman at one of the stations in Amsterdam. The arrangement was for her to take them to a hiding place, I had no idea where. This was always terribly hard. The little girl was only two years old, and her baby brother less than two weeks old.

Sometime later I was in Hilversum, visiting one of our pioneer girls who was hiding in a home to rehabilitate juvenile delinquents. The director of that home was very helpful and took in many Jews.

Our pioneer girl said, "Come here. I must show you something. I have two little children to look after now."

She showed me the same two children I had brought to the station in Amsterdam. I was so happy to know where they were and to have contact with them again. Although there were two German raids on that house, when the war ended the children were safe. But their parents didn't come back. We had their names and birthdates and were able to trace them. We learned in exactly what camp and on what day they were gassed, only a few days after they had given their children to me.

Immediately after the war there was quite a bitter fight in Holland about the Jewish children who were rescued by non-Jews, who had no surviving family members to come back for them. The non-Jews had no understanding of the Jews' feeling that these children should come back to the Jewish community. They felt, as good humanistic people do, that all the people in the world are one big family and it made no difference whether or not they were raised as Jews. The non-Jews who hid them had very close ties to these children; they loved them and they wanted to keep them. With the two children I was concerned about it was a different situation, be-

Mirjam Pinkhof with Tsuika Araten Hamerslag, the "baby" she took to Israel after the war, Haifa, 1987

cause they were not with a family but in a home, and it was not a good place for them to stay.

So in the context of this fight to get Jewish children back into Jewish families, I said that I wanted to adopt those two children, knowing that I did not really want to adopt them myself. I wanted to take them to Palestine, and that's what I did. They were adopted by a family in Haifa, and now this boy who was a tiny baby when I first saw him is married and has a family with four children. He is very involved at the moment in learning about his family, in finding his roots. He lives five minutes from here and we see each other often.

Today we are all very close—the Zionist pioneer children and all those non-Jews who helped. We share a past together. It was not only the experiences of the war, but also coming to Palestine—as many of us did—and trying to build a new country here together. I feel as close to them as to my own family.

Sophie Yaari

There was a very nice Jewish life in Emden. We had our own school and a very beautiful synagogue. Emden had a *real* Jewish community—very close and warm—not assimilated like the Jews in Berlin. Some of the families were Orthodox, but not all. My family was kosher and religious but not strict Orthodox; my father closed his shop on the sabbath and on Sunday too. Most Jews did not do that.

All the Christian people shopped in our store, and we did business with the hotels as well; Emden was a harbor town and there were many hotels. Then in January 1933, Hitler took over, and right away the boycott of Jewish businesses began. People stopped speaking to us—not everyone, but most. I was only seven years old, but I remember this very well. Children who played with us one day the next day did not. We were Jewish.

So it began. SS men waited in front of the Jewish shops to take photos of any non-Jews who went in. They printed the pictures in the SS paper,

Sophie Yaari, Beer Tuvia, Israel, 1988

Der Sturm, to make everyone afraid and to be against the Jews, even if they didn't feel it in their hearts.

Some of our customers told us they didn't think too highly of Hitler; they wanted to buy in our shop but were afraid to be seen entering. So I delivered the groceries to their homes in my doll carriage, or in my school rucksack. Sometimes I had to make three trips to a house in one day because I couldn't fit all the groceries in the carriage and still have room for the dolls.

Life began to be very hard for the Jewish people. Slowly more and more things changed. It didn't all happen in '33, but in '34, '35, every few months there were new prohibitions, and we felt them deeply. Then they started taking people to concentration camps. They began with the Communists and political people, next were the Jews.

The life of our Jewish community was very important and warm, but even so, many people were leaving for America, Holland, Belgium, and other countries. But most German Jews were saying to each other, "This is our country, our home. Hitler won't last. In a few years things will be better. We will stay here." They felt themselves to be not only very Jewish, but also very German. It was terribly sad, and not very clever.

My sisters and I grew up in this kind of atmosphere—we heard everything, saw everything, knew everything. But we could not understand how people who came to our house, gave parties for us, went with us on picnics, whose daughters we played with in our house, suddenly were not our friends.

Our hairdresser lived on our street; my sister and I played with his daughters. Our two families had been friends since around World War I, when my father had helped them out quite substantially with food. Being in the grocery business, my father knew many farmers, and he could get eggs, cheese, and butter when they were scarce—he always helped everyone.

Now it was 1933, and my mother and I went to the hairdresser to have our hair cut—I remember it very clearly, even the wicker chairs we sat in while we waited. Mother had heard that he had stopped cutting the hair of Jewish clients, but he was our friend—she was certain he would treat us differently. We waited quite a long time while he attended to another client. When he finished at last, he looked over at us and shrugged his shoulders.

Mother said, "I don't understand. When the other people leave, then you can cut our hair."

"I'm very sorry," he said, "but I'm no longer cutting Jewish people's hair." We had to go somewhere else.

That was merely sad. As time went by, our situation grew worse. There was always some new thing forbidden to us, and always more and more Jewish people leaving Germany. My father was afraid to emigrate; he was much older than my mother and had three small children to look after.

KRISTALLNACHT

Then Hitler ordered the pogrom on the ninth of November 1938—Kristallnacht. I was thirteen years old. We were all in bed sound asleep when we were suddenly woken by a loud knocking on the door—it was one or two o'clock in the morning.

"Open up! We're taking all of you to Palestine," they shouted.

We never believed that, of course. They broke our windowpanes, and the house became very cold. Quickly, my mother tried to gather up some valuables—some gold things—but one of the men hit her on the arm with his gun, making her drop them. They made us leave everything behind when they took us away—to a Christian school. We were standing there, outside in the cold, still in our night clothes, with only a coat thrown over. They kept bringing more and more Jewish people from all over the neighborhood. Babies were crying.

The horse butcher and his family were there. He was Jewish, but his wife was not, and they had not raised their children as Jews. I can still hear the daughter crying, "But Mommy, we are not Jewish!"

"You are not here because of your religion, but because of your blood!" said the SS.

Then they made everyone lie face down on the ground. It was quite cold. "Now, they will shoot us," we thought. We were very afraid.

Then, abruptly, "Get up!"

They kept us there until the sky was light, and then they took us into the gymnasium and called out everyone's name. They had lists—wonderfully organized. After that, we were allowed to go home. But they kept the men.

When we got home, we found an SS man with a gun walking up and down our street. Everything was smashed up, but we were not allowed to go into our shop—it was forbidden. He said that it wasn't ours any longer, that we owned nothing, we were nothing, our lives were nothing. When the SS got to the furthest corner, I ran inside and took out what I could.

My mother was afraid they might come back to our house that night, so she sent my younger sister, Ruth, and me to sleep at our Aunt Lena's house—somehow they had forgotten about Aunt Lena. My mother and grandmother, who was living with us, went upstairs to the flat above ours, to stay with Mrs. Ludenstein. About four o'clock in the morning they

Sophie Yaari at
Loosdrecht, c. 1941

heard heavy footsteps, then nothing—everything was quiet. My mother was afraid to go down, but my grandmother said, "I'll go." She found my father sitting there, making himself a cup of coffee.

The SS had sent Father home because he had influential Christian friends who had interceded on his behalf. The other men were not so lucky. When Ruth and I came back the next morning, we overheard the street cleaners saying, "Oh, during the night they brought all the Jewish men to the train station and took them away." They sent them to Sachsenhausen and Oranienburg concentration camps.

But my father was free, and we were so happy. We cleaned up the mess, and they let us open the shop. On the fifteenth of November the SS came to our house again.

"Mr. Nussbaum, come with us to visit Mrs. Ludenstein," they said. "Her husband has died."

My father had to go with the Gestapo to tell Mrs. Ludenstein that her husband was the first to die in the concentration camp. Everyone in the Jewish community was afraid when they heard about it. So soon. He had only been there two days.

After a few weeks, they let the men out of the concentration camp, but now they had to work for the Gestapo, cleaning the streets. We saw lawyers and scholars out in the cold, with no hats, repairing the roads—it was a terrible sight. My mother told me it was not important what your work was as long as it did not harm another person. I was getting an education: I saw my uncles working very hard all day long and still not earn enough money to feed their families. My father helped them a lot. We still had our shop, but now we were allowed to sell to Jewish people only between five and six o'clock in the evening.

Then on a certain date we had to close the shop. My parents had to leave our house and move all six of us—grandmother too—into one room in the house of three Jewish old maids who lived on another street.

After Kristallnacht, the Dutch government began giving visas to German and Austrian children who had relatives in Holland. Ruth and I had an aunt there who applied for us. When our visas arrived a few months later, we immediately packed up and went with our mother by train to the border. My father stayed at home because only one parent was allowed to accompany the children.

I'll never forget how she said goodbye, crying. Everything was terrible. My mother told me I was responsible for my sister, who was ten years old. She walked with us to the border; we said goodbye and walked across—it was only a few meters. It was January 25, 1939. I never saw my parents again.

On the other side there was a Nazi woman in uniform.

"Take off all your clothes!" she ordered.

We took off our clothes. She looked us over to see if we were hiding money, because Jewish people were not allowed to bring out more than ten marks—about ten dollars. They put us on a train to Rotterdam. When we arrived, we were met by ladies from a Jewish committee, who took us that same evening to a place that in normal times was a summer camp for poor Dutch Jewish children. They had opened it up that winter for the German refugees.

Ruth and I stayed in this home with about forty other refugee children until April. I'm sorry to say that the Jewish woman in charge of the place was not good for us. She didn't understand what we needed and made us feel very bad. We were not allowed to write home whenever we wanted, only once a week. We could phone just once a month, and then we would do nothing but cry on the phone. I was at the age of puberty and had no one to speak to about it. It was a hard time. Then we learned about the Zionist Youth homes that were opening for children our age, and I asked to go.

LOOSDRECHT YOUTH ALIYAH

One month later Ruth and I came to Loosdrecht. Then it was our happy time. The leaders were only four or five years older than us, and they treated us like people, not like stupid children. They understood us. Menachem

*Mehta Roethler,
Young Pioneer,
dancing at
Loosdrecht, c. 1941*

was very good; Shushu was wonderful, someone very special. There was also Hanna for the girls, and a teacher named Lodi. We learned all about Palestine. They taught us Hebrew. Menachem was crazy about classical music—especially Bach—and he taught us to love music. We worked there, we studied there, we learned there; we were free. I was very happy.

In May 1940, we were evacuated for a few days while the Dutch army tried to fight the German invasion. Then it was all over, and the Germans ruled Holland. We went back to Loosdrecht and went on with our lives. We lived in a protected world—as if in a hothouse—without feeling what was going on around us. The Germans started with their decrees and prohibitions; we did not feel it. They knew it would not be so easy to do the things in Holland they had done in Germany, so they began slowly. They had lists with every name and address, just as they did in Germany. In the summer of '42 they began with the transports, taking the Jews away to Westerbork and to Poland.

One day that summer I went to Amsterdam to meet a Jewish family I had heard about; they were from Emden, my home town. The woman couldn't do housework because she suffered from eczema; she asked if I could help her out. The leaders at Loosdrecht said it was all right, so I left my Youth Aliyah home to live with her for a few months.

On July 7, while I was still living with her family, I received a letter telling me to report to the train station in three days. I asked Mrs. Bloot what to do. Mrs. Erika Bloot was a very nice Jewish lady from Amsterdam who came every week to Loosdrecht to give us lessons in classical history. She did so much for us, she was almost like our mother. She was able to arrange permission from the Germans for me to stay on with the family from Emden, but it was only for the time being. They said I would be getting another letter in the future.

The woman I was helping wanted me to stay on with her and not go

Menachem Pinkhof listening to music, Loosdrecht, c. 1941

back to Loosdrecht. About the next letter I was assured of receiving she said, "If we have to go, we will go. God willed it. If we hide with Christian families, we won't have kosher food. At least in Westerbork the food will be kosher." She really said that! There was even a Christian family that offered to hide her and her family, but she said no.

Nobody could believe what was happening. But in every Jewish house there was a rucksack ready for each person, with warm clothes, a scarf, and vitamins. Although we didn't know what was actually happening, in some sense we knew. We felt it. I think we knew people were not coming back.

"I'm sorry," I told her, "but I want to be with my family, and my friends are my family." I went back to Loosdrecht the next day.

Mrs. Bloot had good connections with the Joodsche Raad in Amsterdam. She told the Loosdrecht leaders that if any of us were on the transport list she would give them warning. At the time, however, we children didn't know anything about this—only Menachem, Shushu, and Mirjam Waterman; they kept it very, very secret.

Mirjam was not one of our leaders, but she lived close by and was Menachem's friend—that was the connection. We saw them together all the time. It was Mirjam who had the idea how to help us young people in Loosdrecht. If it were not for her we would not be alive. I can tell you that's really true. She had connections with non-Jewish people in the Socialist movement, and she used them very well.

At some point early in August, Mrs. Bloot telephoned our Loosdrecht leaders, saying that on the fifteenth or sixteenth—I don't remember exactly—we would all have to report to the station in Amsterdam. But they didn't tell us young people about it—we never knew about any of our leaders' troubles or worries. We never felt anything was wrong, and we never asked.

Then on the evening of August 13 they called us together for a special meeting. We gathered in what we called our "learning room," our study room. Menachem began to speak.

"Pioneers, we have received notice that we are to report to the train station in Amsterdam. We have decided not to go. We have found many good Christian friends who will help you for the duration of the war. How long it will be, nobody knows. You must do what these people ask of you, even if it is not always pleasant. There may not always be enough to eat, but they are helping you, and saving your lives. Be good." That was his speech.

Shushu spoke too: "In half an hour people will be coming to take some of you away, but not everyone, since we still haven't found enough places. Some of you may be at your first addresses only temporarily until a better place is found. We won't forget you. We will be working for you."

That same evening Shushu took me, my sister, and our friend Paul Zonderman by train to Amsterdam. It wasn't as simple as it sounds. We didn't have the proper identification, and Shushu looked very Jewish—if we were stopped we could be arrested. In Amsterdam we came to a street of very old, tall houses. He took us up three or four flights, to the attic in one of these houses. There were two very dirty rooms, and no toilet or shower. We were told to use a flower vase for a toilet and empty it out of the window onto the roof—there was no other way. The other rooms in the house were rented to students, two or three to a room. We were in the flat of a writer who was away on a two-week holiday. We could stay until he came back, but the woman who owned the house was not supposed to know we were there.

Shushu stayed with us that first night because it was already past the twelve o'clock curfew and too dangerous to leave. The Germans imposed the curfew so they could come for Jewish families in the middle of the night, when the neighbors wouldn't see them. In the morning everyone in the neighborhood would find a seal on the doors of the Jewish houses. Then they knew that the people were gone.

That night Shushu told us, "I will not go to the concentration camp again. You should know that we won't all be alive when the war is over."

Early the next morning he said, "Shalom," and that was the last time I saw him. When he was caught by the Germans, he took his own life.

Mirjam knew Leo, the man who had the key to this place. He came the next day to ask us if we needed anything. Leo didn't have any food coupons for us, but he brought whatever he could buy without ration cards—endive, cucumbers, and other vegetables. He told us we were not to leave the flat, not even to go downstairs. We did what he said, and stayed there. The conditions were terrible, but we knew it was for only a short time. "People will help you," they had told us, and it was true. Sometimes you had the feeling that they forgot you, but they never did.

We had been there about nine days when, without saying a word, Paul went down to another floor. He had a dark complexion—immediately recognizable in Holland as Jewish. Somebody must have seen him and told the landlady, because at ten o'clock that evening she came up to our flat, with her broom. "I'm very sorry, but you will have to leave this house immediately. If you don't, I will phone the police. This is a war, after all."

We picked up our rucksacks and left the house. We were in the center of Amsterdam and didn't know what to do. We were speaking rather poor Dutch, with a strong German accent that Dutch people immediately recognized. They hated Germans and the German language, and that made our situation doubly dangerous. We had an address of a cousin but didn't know if it was safe to go to him, or even if he could help us—he was Jewish too.

Everything was forbidden. We couldn't stay on the street after midnight. I looked less Jewish than Ruth or Paul, so I volunteered to go to one of the ships in the harbor, to ask if we could spend the night. The captain said no, I must go to the police station. "Oh, that's a good idea," I said, "why didn't I think of that before?"

Then Paul said, "It's not good for us to stay together. Everyone must go on their own. If we're alive tomorrow we will meet at the train station." He knew the emergency address where we could make contact with

SS removing household goods from home of deported Jewish family, Amsterdam,
April 17, 1945

someone from the Loosdrecht group. We were told that only one of us in a group should know it, and since Paul was the oldest and a boy, he was the one. He left us, taking the secret with him. It was nearly midnight.

I said to my sister, "Look, if we stay on the streets they will pick us up. Let's hide under the bridge." We crept under the railroad bridge next to the Amstel river. All through the night we heard the church clock strike, every half hour, and trains rumble by overhead; babies cried, and the sound of soldiers seemed to be everywhere. We were sure in the morning it would be our turn.

But in the morning the station was crowded with ordinary workers in work clothes, and we didn't stand out too much. We waited and waited there for a long time, looking for Paul, but he didn't come. Finally we decided to go by tram to find Hanna, one of our Loosdrecht leaders; she had left several months before we went underground. My sister remembered her address, but we didn't know if she was part of the underground network. With our dark hair, we felt conspicuous among the Dutch people on the tram; it seemed as if everyone was looking at us.

When we found her address, Hanna opened the door, saw it was us, and immediately said, "Come in!" We began to cry—we were still kids. She put us in a room upstairs and brought us food. She was living with her husband, Harry, and her parents.

"You can't stay here," she said. "Yesterday they took my brother, and my father has had a heart attack. He must not know that you are here, even for a few hours. Harry will bring you to another address." We found out later that Harry was very actively working with our Loosdrecht leaders.

From that day in August 1942, until the end of the war, I was hidden in eighteen different homes in Amsterdam, Rotterdam, Doorn, and other towns and villages in Holland. Some places I could stay for a month or two, others for only a few days. Throughout that time I was always protected and looked after by the group formed by Mirjam, Menachem, Shushu, and Joop Westerweel.

One Sunday Ruth and I were at home alone—everyone else was gone for the day. The doorbell rang. We didn't answer it; we were strictly forbidden to open the door to anyone. The front door of this house had a window from which we could see out, but no one could see in. Looking through the curtain, we saw a man with a child standing there. He rang again and again. Finally, he put a letter under the door and went away. I opened the letter—that was not very polite, but I did it anyway.

He wrote, "I will send you food coupons. I was here. Joop." That's all.

"I'm going to go and find this Joop" I told my sister. "He can help us."

"Don't go," Ruth begged me. She was afraid.

I left anyway and walked and walked a long way, looking for him. It was a Sunday afternoon and the streets were full of people, mostly families on outings. But there were too many people, and I couldn't find him. I was very unhappy; I lost all hope. But then, as I walked back through the park, suddenly I saw him sitting on a bench, watching his son play.

He was unusual. If you saw him once you would always recognize him again. I had seen him only through the curtain, but I immediately knew it was him. I went over to the bench and looked at him. He looked back at me and said, "You are Sophie. Go home and I will follow you." At home, he sat with us for a while. He told us everything would be all right, that he would be like a father and help us, and that we shouldn't be afraid. He gave us food cards, which we put in the envelope with his letter, to make it look as if he had never been there. He said someone would come for us in a few days to take us to another address.

Some time later, when I had been with a family in Rotterdam for a few months, I discovered that I was living on the same street as Joop Westerweel. Then I began to see Joop and his family quite often. All their telephone messages came to us because they didn't have a telephone. So I brought them the messages. Usually they were in some kind of code, and I couldn't understand them. His wife, Willie, was also very busy with the

Posters advertising Nazi anti-semitic propaganda film, The Eternal Jew, Amsterdam, c. 1942

underground, often working late into the night. On weekends Joop was helping people go over the border to Belgium on their way to France.

Joop was not an ordinary person: he was something special. He was a pacifist; before the war, he refused to serve in the army. He did not pay taxes; he was against it. His brilliant word was "free." People must be free. Before the war he had gone to Indonesia to help people there, and in Indonesia he lived in the same houses with the poorest native people, not in the big houses where the rich Dutch were living, like the whites in South Africa. He was a fighter. He often said to us, "It's not important how long you live, but how you live." He said he would die on the barricades, not in a bed, and he did. He was happy doing that work.

MIRJAM WATERMAN

It was Mirjam who asked Joop Westerweel if he would help us. He wanted to do something against the Germans, but not because he hated them. I can't say that he hated Germans—I don't know. His idea was that no one had the right to tell anyone else what they could or couldn't do. Everyone should be free to choose his own way. He wanted to help us not because we were Jewish people, but because of the injustice of the German policies against us. If we had been Hottentots he would have done the same—he would give his life. Mirjam would too, although Mirjam is the daughter of our people, the Jewish people.

It was a very good organization; there were people in the group who always knew where everyone was. At Doorn, where I spent several months, Mirjam sometimes came to visit and bring us things. She brought us life and hope; she was like a friend, even though we didn't know her too well. She wanted to know how the people were treating us, if it was all right staying there. Mirjam came, and her sister Ellie, too. I'll never forget it.

Mirjam was blond and didn't look Jewish. She had so many non-Jewish friends, she could have easily left and made a life for herself. But she didn't do that. She did not want us to fall into the hands of the Germans. She worked with the non-Jewish organizers as if she were not a Jew—with false papers. It greatly endangered her life, but she took on a big job, a great work, and she did it very well—she, her future husband, and her sister. We don't even know all the things that she and Menachem did, but they did a lot.

I have not had a normal life—sometimes I think I'm still like a child. I feel that I have lost many years, from the time when I left my house and parents in Emden. I always wanted to go back. I was searching for something I knew I couldn't find here in Israel. The first time I returned was in April 1965. I gave a talk in the grade school in Emden.

I told the children, "I was a child just like you. I laughed here, I cried here, just like you. I loved this town. And then, suddenly from one day to the next, it was over. Girls who played with me, who came to my house and ate at our table, suddenly said, 'I'm not playing with you anymore. You are Jewish.' That was so strange."

I invited the children to ask me questions. I found out that their parents had not told them that there had been a thousand Jewish people living in their town, that they had been an important part of the community, and that many non-Jewish people had worked for their businesses and in their homes. They didn't tell that generation anything—they knew nothing. Only one child asked me a lot of questions. Then he said, "The Fuhrer also

did many good things. He gave people work and he built the autobahn."
That's what those children had been taught. That made me very angry.

Sophie was liberated on November 23, 1944, in the south of Holland. The German occupation continued in the north for nearly six more months. It was not until the following May that her sister Ruth also came safely through the long years of war. Their parents and most of their relatives in Germany perished in concentration camps.

Sophie's friend Paul, who decided to leave Sophie and her sister to go off on his own, had spent the night in a bunker near the train station. Jews escaping from roundups frequently hid in these bunkers, so it was a place where the Germans often looked. He was picked up and arrested, sent first to Westerbork, then to Auschwitz, where he died.

Joseph Heinrich

On November 9, 1938, we stood by the window of our house—the house where I was born—and watched while they burned down the big synagogue across the street. The Börneplatz Square was crowded with thousands of spectators; they made a circus out of it. We saw it all. Suddenly they burst into our rooms with axes and bars and smashed everything up.

We ran to the neighborhood police station for help. They looked at us and just laughed. We fled from them to find shelter with a family my father knew. Then in the evening we took a taxi to my aunt's house. That was Thursday. On Friday we saw them arresting Jewish people all day long. Friday evening, we were still with my aunt. We heard a knock on the door; they had come to arrest my uncle, my father's brother.

My father said to them, "I won't let him go alone."

"Fine. You can come too," they said, took them both away.

A few hours later my sister and I went to the police station asking for our father. They told us to get lost. Several days after, on the fifteenth of Novem-

Joseph Heinrich,
Ajanot, Israel, 1988

ber, my mother sent my little sister Lorle, my younger brother Asher, and me to Holland. We went together with a group of about twenty-five children, organized by some Jewish women; I don't know who they were.

When we arrived at the Dutch border, two SS men took us off the train, into a waiting room. All the Germans had to leave the room because they couldn't have Germans and Jews in one place together—we were very dangerous people, you know; I was fourteen, Lorle was eight, Asher was twelve, and there was another child of three or four. They told us there was no toilet, no water fountain, no nothing, and don't cry. Right away the little ones started crying.

We weren't allowed to leave the room until evening when they put us aboard another train, the Rheingold Express—I remember it very well. We crossed the border into Holland. When we arrived, a committee was waiting to greet us. There were journalists and photographers; everyone was asking how things were in Germany. We told them about the burning and arrests.

Kristallnacht fire destroys Börneplatz synagogue, Frankfurt am Main, November 8–9, 1938

I don't know if I can tell you how I felt; as a young child, maybe it was like some kind of adventure; I know I wasn't afraid. Even when I saw the synagogue burning and how they broke up our flat, I'm certain I was not afraid—really not.

But when we arrived in Holland, that moment was very hard for me. I think I realized all at once that something was irreversibly broken. It was only at that moment that I understood what was going on, or maybe more, I started to think about what might be in store in the future.

The next day the people looking after us told us to write letters home letting our parents know that we had arrived safely. They made sure we stayed in contact with our families by writing every week. I found out that my father was imprisoned in Buchenwald concentration camp. But then he was set free because he managed, through a cousin, to get an affidavit for England. In 1938 Buchenwald was not yet a death camp, although there were plenty of people who never left the place. If you could show you had an affidavit to emigrate, they would set you free and let you leave the country, but it was very, very hard to do. There was practically no country in the world that would take Jews—not America, not England, none. Ships were leaving for America, but if you were Jewish you couldn't go, even if you had the money. The only place you could go to easily was Shanghai, and who had enough money to go there? Very, very few. When the Germans invaded Poland on the first of September 1939, my mother said to my father, "You must leave, otherwise they will arrest you again." But there was no affidavit for my mother. I never saw her again.

My father was on the last civilian train to cross the Holland border, and then on the last boat from Holland to England. In England he was arrested right away for being German—an enemy alien—and put in a detention camp on the Isle of Mann with Nazis! He was there for a long time.

In Holland, Lorle, Asher, and I were put in a home for refugee children in Den Dolder, near Bilthoven. Nearby was a school called the Children's Werkplaats. The Werkplaats was a very special place, a private school managed by Kees Boeke, somewhat along the principles of Montessori in

Market on the Börne-platz with view of Börneplatz synagogue and the Heinrich family's bedroom window (arrow), Frankfurt am Main, 1925

Switzerland. Children began in kindergarten and stayed there until they were eighteen years old. Mirjam Waterman was a teacher there. Once one of the pupils told her, "Mirjam, do you know there is a group of young people—refugees—who have nothing to do? Do you think they could come to us?" It was her students who made the connection between our refugee home and their school.

Boeke rented a special house for all of us Jewish refugees from Germany—about forty-five or fifty children. At fourteen, I was the oldest; the youngest was only four years old. Because we didn't know the Dutch language yet, they put us apart from the other children, to make it easier for them to teach us. That was how I met Mirjam: she was my Dutch-language teacher.

Mirjam was very patient as a teacher; I think she felt sympathy for the little children who had to leave their families. In the beginning I think she just felt sorry for us, but later on she became really involved, with all her heart.

We became very close; if there was anything I needed to talk about, I went to Mirjam, not to any of the male teachers. There was only about five or six years difference in our ages and she was like a big sister to me.

One time she brought me home to her parents. "Mother, this is Joseph" was all she said. It was that easy. Her mother became like a mother to me—really.

My impression was that her father was a very rich man; I think he was a diamond merchant. He had some land, and orchards with apple and plum trees. He was an easygoing man. Mirjam made me a present of a bicycle; between Bilthoven and Loosdrecht, where they lived, it was only a twenty-minute ride. I went to their house very often—in fact, every moment I could.

Other children in the refugee group were friendly with them, but none were as close as I was; I was like their child; I was at home there. I could go to her mother if I felt sick. Her father had a library with a lot of books, which he took great pride in and carefully protected. No one was allowed to touch the books, but he made an exception for me.

Then in 1939, before Hitler started the war, the children at our Den Dolder refugee house were sent to live with families all over Holland. My sister Lorle went to a family in Friesland, in the north, where she stayed safely until the end of the war. Asher went to a family in Bilthoven, and I was sent to an orphanage in Utrecht.

When the war in Holland broke out on May 10, 1940, the director of the orphanage sent me to a Youth Aliyah group in Zeeland. I stayed there for only two or three weeks until the Germans decided to evacuate all the Jewish people from the province. They sent me to another Youth Aliyah House, this one in Loosdrecht, in the neighborhood of Mirjam's parents. That was the connection: Mirjam knew us and our leaders, who were all young people her age. Officially, she was not part of the Loosdrecht Youth House, but she came over all the time; it was only two hundred meters from her house. Now I was at home at two places: Loosdrecht and Mirjam's.

At Loosdrecht there were about fifty boys and girls my age, between fifteen and seventeen. On a certain day we got an order that we had to go to Westerbork concentration camp, the whole group together. The leaders decided to hide us instead, although they had only a few days to make the arrangements.

THE WESTERWEEL GROUP

Mirjam was the link between our Loosdrecht leaders and several teachers from the Werkplaats school in Bilthoven. They formed a group headed by Joop Westerweel, a non-Jew. I was in his home quite often before all the troubles began. He was a really special person, a very strong man. For Joop there were only two sides: something was either right or it was wrong.

He said, "It's wrong to persecute people for their religion or race. It's wrong, and you must fight wrong without compromise."

The Dutch government had prepared identity cards for everyone in Holland before the war even started; there was nothing like it in any oth-

*Asher, Lorle, and
Joseph Heinrich, 1941*

er western European country, not even in Germany. So when the Germans
came in, they found the whole Dutch population registered and accounted
for. That made it easy for them, and difficult and dangerous for underground work.

But Joop had refused to take an identity card for himself or his family.
"I'm not a sheep to be herded," he said, "I'm a human being." When he
began to work in the underground, however, he took an identity card
then—a false one, of course. He and his wife, Willie, went into the war
without any compromise, even though they had four children, and Willie was pregnant. A Christian person risked everything by helping Jews—
his whole family. When Joop and Willie were caught they had to hide their
children, including their baby less than a year old.

Joop left his teaching job, and Mirjam became 100 percent involved after we went into hiding. It was not the kind of work you could do part time. They had to go around to all the places where we were hiding and bring money, false identity papers, and ration stamps to the families looking after us. They also had to travel all over Holland, constantly looking for new families that would take us in. It's a small country, but in those days travel was not so easy. Even if you had a car, there was no gasoline. There were curfews, raids all the time, and German guards at every station checking identity papers on the trains. It was a full-time job.

GOING UNDERGROUND

The first underground place I was sent to was the home of a painter in Arnhem. I was in a group of eight or nine boys there; the time had been too short to find a place for each of us. This artist had a Jewish girlfriend who was caught by the Germans after we had been with him for only two or three days. We had to leave quickly, in case they decided to search his place. Within a few hours we were taken to another address in Arnhem. A few days later, my brother and I and a young Dutch student, not a Jew, moved again, to a place near Appeldorn. This man's name was Urban, and he was known far and wide as a Communist. Whenever something bad happened in the neighborhood, they called on Urban first.

German refugee boys' sprint race at Loosdrecht Youth Aliyah home, c. 1941

One night the Dutch police came yet again to arrest Urban for something or other. We were sound asleep and didn't hear them coming. Suddenly I heard a policeman asking me, "Where's your identity card?"

"I'm only fourteen years old. I don't need an identity card."

"You are only fourteen?"

"Yes."

"Get dressed then. You have to get out of here."

It was two o'clock in the morning. My brother and I and this Dutch boy, who had false papers, left the house, out into the cold and rain. We went around to the neighbors to ask for shelter, but nobody would open their door. They didn't know who we were, but they knew we had been staying with Urban—we had his stigma.

All night long we stood in the rain, waiting for daylight. Then, soaked through, we took a bus to Amsterdam and made a connection with some members of our Westerweel group; they found another place for us. That's how it went: you had to change places all the time.

So many things happened, you couldn't stop to think too much about any of it. You just knew you had to go from point A to point B, and that's all. You could go straight or go around; you had to figure it out for yourself. Nobody told you how to behave—only the newcomers didn't know. One thing you learned was that when you see a German, don't step off the pavement, but walk straight ahead; it's your right to walk on the sidewalk. Don't act afraid, or cross the street, or they'll look at you. Don't look over your shoulder. Behave like other people. Coming from Germany, our language was German, of course, but if a German speaks to you in German, don't answer. Sometimes they would be standing right behind you and say, "Come here!" You couldn't turn your head. We spoke in Dutch and the Germans couldn't detect whether or not it was with a German accent.

I didn't see Mirjam again until after the war, but Menachem, our Loosdrecht leader who became Mirjam's husband, I saw very often. I was also in frequent contact with Jan Smith, a teacher from the Bilthoven Werkplaats, and he saw Mirjam frequently. He brought me her greetings and news; I always knew what was going on with her and her family. I knew when they went into hiding, but I didn't know where. No one wanted to know more than was necessary.

Menachem was an intellectual. He worked at the Youth Aliyah house as a teacher and a leader, but by profession he was an engineer. A man named Lodi Cohen was the head of the Loosdrecht leaders, and Menachem was second. There were four altogether—Cohen, Menachem, Hanna Asher, and Adina Simon, who was married to Shushu.

It was not easy for these leaders to work with us. We were children who had left our families, there was the war, and on top of that all these German decrees on how we were to behave, such as Jews having to wear the star—I think I wore it only twice. We were a group of youngsters—fourteen, fifteen, sixteen years old—and our leaders were only twenty-two or twenty-four years old themselves, yet they were completely responsible for us. They worked very hard.

I don't think I was an especially good boy. One time my brother and I and another boy, Dov Ascheim, decided to run away from Loosdrecht to be on our own. We made a connection with the secretary of the village to provide us identity cards without the incriminating "J" stamp. But then he went to our leaders, telling them that three of their boys might be planning something. Menachem took me aside and said, "Joseph, we will all go into hiding together. Give me your identity card, and don't make trouble." It was a very hard responsibility for a young man like him to take on; he couldn't know whether he would succeed in hiding us.

Every one of them could have saved themselves. But if all the leaders went away, who would take care of the children in hiding? Somebody had to stay in Holland to go on working. The shepherd cannot leave the flock. I think they had to be very, very brave and courageous to take on this task. What they did was a very great deed. And they paid the price.

Shushu, for example, brought his wife to Switzerland and on the way back he was caught. Afraid that he would say too much, he asked for a razor blade from the policeman in the prison and committed suicide.

At a certain point they started to bring the Pioneer children to France, reasoning that if they brought a lot of them to France, it would make conditions easier for the others in Holland.

I left Holland in April '43, with my brother. My little sister stayed behind, safe with the family in Friesland. Our plan was to go to Spain, to the American army, but we were caught on the way.

UNDERGROUND IN FRANCE

We had made our way to Antwerp, where we were staying in a pub called Julia's Anchor, waiting for our guide to Spain—he was the husband of the woman who was hiding us. At first it was just my brother Asher and me, then two other boys showed up, four of us now waiting for this man.

Twice he had made the trip to Spain with Jewish boys from our Dutch Pioneer group. We didn't know that on the second trip the Germans caught him. So we were waiting, and meanwhile more and more boys showed up. Now there were ten. One day a neighborhood woman who was

friendly with a German soldier told him, "You know, I think there are a lot of Dutchmen hiding in that place." He came to see for himself. Fortunately, we had work papers and identity papers bearing the swastika stamp—printed by our organization in Holland—saying we were Dutch students working for the Germans in France.

The German police and soldiers were very brutal, but when they saw the swastika stamp, you could tell them just about anything and they would believe it—everything was all right. With the Gestapo, however, it was different; you had to be more careful with them.

Joseph Heinrich, 1943

We told the soldier we were homesick and had gone home for a visit, but now we wanted to come back to work. He never suspected we were Jews.

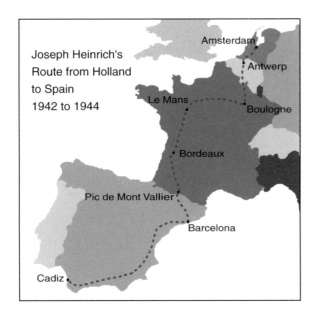

Map showing Joseph Heinrich's route from Holland to Spain, 1942–44

Joseph Heinrich's Route from Holland to Spain 1942 to 1944

Amsterdam
Antwerp
Le Mans
Boulogne
Bordeaux
Pic de Mont Vallier
Barcelona
Cadiz

"So you ran away from work? Well, now you have to go back!" He gave us an escort of soldiers and put us on a train to France. Well, okay, we thought. France was all right for us; we wanted to be there. They brought us to La Manche, about twenty miles south of Boulogne.

For eight months we worked in France, first in the north at Le Mans, later in the south near Bordeaux. Living in France was safer for us: it was easier to disappear into the crowd. Throughout that whole time we stayed in contact with the Westerweel group in Holland. Someone was always going back to bring more kids over the border, one or two at a time.

But how can I explain some of the things that happened? They make no sense. When they took us from the pub to "go back" to work, we had to undergo a medical exam by a German doctor; it was not so nice. There were fourteen Jewish boys in the work transport with twenty-five or so non-Jewish Belgians. The doctor was an officer. He checked us from head to foot. But he did not say one word about what he saw—he said nothing, we said nothing.

"You want to work?" was all he asked.

We were very pleased. Our morale was very high. We went to work for the Todt Organization in France. We were paid wages and were free to come and go as we wished. It wasn't forced labor.

By then it was very difficult for civilians to buy a train ticket, so we traveled on military trains. We told them, "Look, we are working for you; we are Aryan; we can travel on your trains." They considered the Dutch to be Aryan, so it was all right. We traveled for free. We could never have done that in Holland, but in France we did it several times. Even when we went to the Spanish border, it was on a military train.

When I thought about it afterward, I realized that sometimes we did very stupid things. For example, if we were hungry we took what we called an "order paper"—printed with all the proper stamps by our organization in Holland—and wrote in my false name: "Jaap So-and-So is traveling from Paris to Lille." We showed the pass to the camp supply commandant. It said I had to travel for twelve hours so I must have bread and sausage for the journey. We signed these passes to each other; sometimes we put four or five names on one, and then we could get food for ten men.

There was a Todt Organization man who was very, very tough; we called him "Stucka," after the fighter plane. One time he said to one of our men, "I am sure you are a Jew." We went to the camp commandant to make a complaint: "Why was he calling us Jews?" After that a car was sent to pick us up and take us to work every day. Everyone else had to walk, but we got a car! The Yiddish word is *chutzpah*.

When we ran away from Holland we took only what we were wearing. September came and we had no warm clothing, so we wrote ourselves passes and went south, by military trains, of course. We wanted to be close to Spain, but from the Spanish border north for about eighty or one hundred kilometers was a restricted military zone. So we stopped about sixty kilometers south of Bordeaux, and there split into two groups.

One day when we met with the other group, they told us they had noticed two young men living in little wooden houses, one right up against the other. They were pretty sure they were Jews. The problem was how to make contact without giving anything away; we couldn't figure it out. Finally one day, when he was within earshot, one of our men whistled "Hatikvah." They whistled "Hatikvah" back! It turned out that the two men were brothers, Hungarian Jews named Greenbaum, who had run away from Paris. We became friends, and later they came with us to Spain.

TO SPAIN

Joop Westerweel and his group arranged for us to cross over the Pyrenees into Spain in February '44. He made connections with a Jewish group in

Valle de Arán (Lérida) in the Pyrenees, Spain

the French Maquis, and they had connections with smugglers who knew the mountains. Joop's Dutch organization paid the smugglers so much for every head. As in all the underground groups, you only knew what you needed to. They told you on a certain day, at a certain hour, you have to be here. You didn't ask questions. So many things we only learned about afterward. Joop came all the way to the Pyrenees to say goodbye to us. On the way back he was caught, because of a false name; he had the papers of a man the Germans were looking for. It was very stupid. Why did they catch him and not me?

We crossed at the highest point in the Pyrenees—about three thousand meters—near a point called Pic de Mont Vallier. The smuggler guides brought us halfway, pointed out the direction to Spain, and left us there. Then the thirty-four men in our group had to climb the mountain. The snow was so high, when my little brother took a step he sank up to his chest—he almost disappeared. Another group crossed over the next summer and found the track we had made in February; the snow was so deep it was still there five months later.

We had a French police officer with us, a non-Jew who was in trouble and had to run away, I don't know why. Nobody asked anybody anything. If you were part of the group, fine; we all went together. Fortunately, this man was experienced in the mountains. During the day the marching kept us from freezing, but when night came, we were on top of the mountain: it was snowing and very cold. He showed us how to bury ourselves in the snow to stay warm through the night. Some people didn't trust him at first because he was a policeman, but we were lucky to have him: we were wearing only light clothes and might have frozen to death otherwise. We didn't have much food; each man had eight or ten cubes of sugar and a little bit of raw meat. For water we had snow. When we were hungry we put a little bit of meat in our mouth and chewed on it.

We marched for three days, but—it's amazing—I didn't feel real hunger. I knew I was climbing the mountain; I saw the clouds, and they were beneath me! There was ice and snow, snow and ice everywhere; the sun was shining. How did I feel? I don't know!

It was a very hard thing to do, but once we started there was no other choice. We were thirty-four, and we all made it. There was one old man with us—he was about sixty—and the rest were all boys of nineteen or twenty. Before we began the march they told us, "Don't expect help along the way. If you fall down, you cannot expect help." At a certain moment the older man and a young Dutchman, who was very heavy, fell behind. We had stopped for a rest, sitting down for half an hour or so, when far, far behind us we saw these two men crawling on all fours. We talked it over and said, no, we won't let them die in the mountains. We sent a few of the strongest back to get them. After that, we pulled and pushed them all the way for two more days, and they made it.

In the evening of the third day we came to Mohgarri, on the Spanish side of the border. We spent the night with a man who was very kind: he cooked soup for us; we gave him watches and fountain pens. People in the village asked where we were coming from. When we told them Pic de Mont Vallier, they said, "No, that's impossible! No one could come from there in February." But we did.

The next day, two boys whose feet were bad stayed behind, while the rest of us went on to Esterri. As we left, we saw fresh ski tracks pointing away from the village; we knew that someone went off to warn the Spanish police about us. By then we were so exhausted we didn't even care; whatever would happen would happen.

We walked all day—ten hours—until we came to Esterri. The police were waiting for us. They locked us up for the night. The next day four or five policemen were asking our names—things like that—but only one of them could even write. Well, he didn't so much write as paint the letters. We had thrown away our papers before we crossed the border, of course. Later they gave us a meal at a little restaurant. There was not much food available, but the wine was plentiful.

Young Pioneers about to emigrate to Israel from Spain (Joseph Heinrich is third from right, top row), 1944

TO PALESTINE

At that time the Spanish government was accepting refugees from Nazi-occupied countries who made their way into Spain. My group went first to Lérida, then to Barcelona, where we hoped to sail immediately. But we had just missed the Portuguese ship *Nyassa,* which departed at the end of January, carrying 750 immigrants to Palestine. We waited eight months for the next opportunity. From time to time, small groups of French and Dutch Young Pioneers who crossed the Pyrenees in subsequent treks joined us. We were supported with funds provided by the American Joint Distribution Committee and the Jewish Agency. Finally, in October 1944, the SS *Guine* sailed from Cadiz for Palestine carrying 175 young Jewish refugees who had illegally crossed the Pyrenees. I was among them.

We landed in Haifa on November 4, 1944. Since I have been here, there has always been war, more or less. C'est la vie.

PART 2 ～ Czechoslovakia

To save one life is as if you have saved

the world.—THE TALMUD

Before the outbreak of World War II, Hitler destroyed the liberal and democratic Czechoslovakian Republic with virtually no resistance from the Czechs or other European powers.

The first step was the infamous Munich Agreement, signed on September 30, 1938, by Germany, Great Britain, France, and Italy, which turned over to Germany the western Czechoslovakian territory known as the Sudetenland. The excuse for the takeover was the complaint of the German minority living in the region that they were mistreated by the Czech majority. Great Britain and France viewed the treaty as a peaceful means to appease Hitler's appetite for territory.

With the Sudetenland annexation, the Czech army, which had its main fortifications within the Sudeten area, was eliminated without a fight; its arms and ammunition were appropriated by the German army. Six months later Hitler pressured pro-German Slovakian fascists to declare Slovakia's independence; in actuality it became a puppet of the German Reich, and Czechoslovakia ceased to exist as an independent state. Two weeks later Hitler invaded the western Czech provinces of Moravia and Bohemia. Meeting no resistance, the area was declared to be a German protectorate under the rule of the German-appointed Reich Protector, Konstantin von Neurath.

Before the German takeover, approximately 350,000 Jews lived in Czechoslovakia, one-third in Bohemia and Moravia. They enjoyed the same civil rights and religious freedom as all other Czech citizens. On June 21, 1939, von Neurath issued a long list of anti-Jewish decrees, essentially identical

Map of
Czechoslovakia

 SUDETENLAND: Czech territory ceded to
Germany at Munich, September 30, 1938

 Czech territory given to Hungary by Germany
and Italy at Vienna, October 2, 1938

 Czech territory annexed by Poland, November 1, 1938

to those in effect in Germany, designed to destroy the economic viability
of the Jewish population and confiscate all Jewish property. In October
1939, the first Czech Jews were deported to concentration camps in Poland. By October 1942, 75 percent of Czechoslovakian Jews had been deported, most dying at Auschwitz.

German power in Czechoslovakia finally ended on May 11, 1945, when
Russian soldiers liberated Prague. Only twenty thousand Czechoslovakian Jews survived.

4 ∿ I Saw Something Terrible

Anna and Jaruslav Chlup were born in Czechoslovakia in 1910 and 1911, respectively, and grew up in small villages close to the Sudetenland. When Anna was twenty-two her parents built a new house just outside the village of Sedlice, near the border town of Zihle. Her father owned a small grocery store that supplied the farming families in the area.

Anna met Jerry at the start of World War II, when she was twenty-eight years old. They were married the same year. In the early years of their marriage they lived with Anna's parents in the family home. Jerry commuted about thirty miles each day to a factory near Pilsen where he worked as a cabinetmaker. Anna helped her father run his store.

One day in the last year of the war, Jerry Chlup brought home to his wife's care the emaciated and wounded Herman Feder. Unknown to Anna, Jerry had been a member of a resistance group for three years. When the group blew up a bridge, they inadvertently forced a German train full of prisoners bound for a death camp to make an unscheduled halt of several days. Many of the prisoners seized the opportunity to escape, Herman Feder among them. Unstintingly sharing their modest resources, Anna and Jerry devoted themselves over the next three years to nursing Herman back to physical health. They provided a safe haven that helped to heal the deep psychological wounds resulting from Herman's harrowing concentration camp experiences.

Herman Feder was born in 1904 in Galicia, a region of Poland then under Austrian rule. By the age of six he spoke Polish, German, and Ukrainian, later in his youth acquiring fluency in Russian and Czech as well. His mother's death when he was ten years old was a devastating event. His father, unable to care for his four children, sent each one to live with a different relative. Herman went to Germany to live with a Berlin cousin. When his father died ten years later, the financial support Herman had hoped would see him through law school came to an end. He married and settled down, opening a store selling linens, blankets, and sheets, in the German city of Hirschberg, close to the Czechoslovakian border. Postwar borders placed Hirschberg in southwestern Poland. Today it is called Jelenia Gora.

Like so many others, Herman did not perceive the seriousness of the Nazi threat soon enough. Defrauded of his money and possessions when he attempted emigration with his young family, Herman soon shared the fate of most European Jews: he and his family were separated and deported to Nazi concentration camps. But unlike most Jews in this situation, through a combination of sharp wits, strong spirit, and sheer luck, he managed to survive five years in six different camps. Late in the war Herman found himself on the Auschwitz-bound transport that was intercepted by Jerry Chlup and his friends.

He stayed with Anna and Jerry Chlup until 1948, when the Communists took over Czechoslovakia, making it a Soviet satellite. First he moved to the spa town of Marienbad, about an hour's train ride from Sedlice. He visited the Chlups frequently. A year later he met and married his second wife, Blanka. They soon emigrated to Venezuela where Herman, taking advantage of his concentration camp experiences, went into the shoe business and eventually owned a small shoe factory. When Fidel Castro came to power in Cuba, the possibility of Communist rule in Venezuela prompted the Feders to emigrate again, to the United States. They settled in Los Angeles in 1961. Every Sunday morning for nearly thirty years they talked to Anna and Jerry Chlup on the telephone, carrying on the tradition with Anna after Jerry's death.

Herman Feder told his story in his West Los Angeles home on June 4, 1987. On January 17, 1992, he passed away at the age of eighty-seven.

In 1949 Jerry Chlup made some derogatory remarks in public about the local Communist regime. In short order the Chlups found the door to their grocery store locked and Jerry under arrest. The sentence would be hard labor in the uranium mines. Between Jerry's two trials Anna arranged for them to make an abrupt escape in the night, with no baggage, across the border to Germany. They expected to spend about six months there, waiting for the Communists to be ousted from power in Czechoslovakia. Eighteen months later, still living in a German camp for displaced persons, they despaired of ever returning to their native country and applied for Canadian visas. They eventually settled in San Francisco, where Anna lives today.

Anna Chlup spoke for herself and Jerry in their San Francisco home on May 20, 1987. Jerry died in the spring of 1988, at the age of seventy-seven.

Anna and Jaruslav Chlup

I was afraid to marry; I don't know why. I liked my mother and father and didn't want to leave them. I used to tell my mother that I would never get

Anna and Jerry Chlup, San Francisco, 1987

married because I didn't want to wash some strange guy's underwear. I'm not sure what made me change my mind. It may have been my age, or because I saw that all my friends were married while I was still single.

I got married in 1938. In 1939 Hitler came—we were afraid to have children. We heard that Hitler was going to move the entire Czechoslovak population to Morocco and take our country for himself. He wanted our beer hops and uranium mines. Because the times were so uncertain, it seemed better to wait until after the war to have children. But after the war the Communists came in, and again we were afraid. We never had children.

My father was a businessman and a very smart guy. He always took care of all of us. We never went hungry. Sedlice was a farming community, with no poor or working-class people. If a family had a cow, a chicken, and a pig, they had milk, butter, and eggs and meat. Everyone could eat.

Every morning my father and I went to work in the village. Every evening we closed up the store and went home again. We heard very little about the war because there was no foreign news in our newspapers. Of course, we knew about it when Pilsen was attacked, but that was the Americans, and it was only two or three times. The Gestapo and SS stayed over in Kralovice on their army base. They left us alone in Sedlice.

I remember one trip to Pilsen just before Christmas. My father and I had gone there to do some shopping for the store. While we were in the city the American planes came over and bombed. We went into the underground shelters with everyone else until it was over. Afterwards we tried to take the train back home, but the bombs had destroyed the railroad station and we had to walk all the way back to Sedlice—about ten hours.

We didn't know what was going on over in Germany. We didn't even know what was happening in Terezin [site of Theresienstadt concentration camp near Prague]. I saw it for the first time after the war. In our little village there were no Jews, although before the war I think quite a few lived in Kralovice. I don't remember a synagogue, but I know they had a Jewish cemetery there. We never thought there was anything different about the Jewish people; they were like the Czechs and the Slovaks. Some were married to Catholics; they stayed at home and wore the star, and didn't go to concentration camps. I remember one person I always used to see with this star. We knew that the rest of them were taken to the camps. Oh, yes, we did know that—none of them came back to Kralovice. When they took away all the Jewish people—that was about '42 or '43—some of them tried to run away, but they didn't know where to go.

I remember one evening in 1942, about seven o'clock, a policeman—a family friend—brought an older couple to our house. They were maybe thirty-five or thirty-six years old. The policeman had caught them as they were trying to cross the border to Sudetenland, on their way to Pilsen. Why they were running to Pilsen, I don't know—there were so many Germans there. The policeman took the woman to my room and told me to look her over to see if she had some gold. These people didn't even have a suitcase, just handbags. He checked the man, but I didn't search her. Then he took them back to where they had come from. Around eleven or twelve o'clock that same night there was a knock on my parents' bedroom window. They had come back. Would someone please show them the way to Pilsen? My father got up from his bed and walked with them for a long, long way—more than two hours—far across the forest, and put them on the highway. What happened to them after that, I never knew.

I'll tell you something we did know about—forced labor. The Germans took all the young men and women from Sedlice who were born in 1922, to work in Germany. Married, or not, everybody had to go. Luckily I was too old, and so was Jerry. Our village was not big so it didn't concern too many people, but my sister's son was born in 1922, and he had to go. He wrote to my mother from the camp in Germany, "Grandma, please send a letter saying you are very sick so they will let me come home to take care of you." My mother sent the letter, but they didn't let him go. They didn't care. He tried to escape, but they caught him and beat him. Then they put him on a train that went around and around, back and forth all over Germany, because by then it was 1944, and the Americans had started bombing.

My nephew had been a big, tall man like Jerry, but when he came back from Germany in 1945, he looked very bad—only skin and bones. When we went to visit him in the hospital, it was terrible: the hospital was full

Anna Chlup, 1932

of young people from the labor camp, and they all had these big lice—even after they bathed them. I think they were coming out of their wounds. He asked my mother to bring him home with her, which she did, but he was very sick. My mother told my sister that she had to come and take him. He died just a short time later—only twenty-four years old. My sister became a Communist later on; I think losing her son pushed her into it. I don't know why she thought the Communists would help; her son was already dead.

The first time I ever saw the Gestapo was in 1943. I was at home by myself when two men came to the door. I knew they were Gestapo because they had badges on their caps with the skull and crossbones. They searched the whole house. I didn't know what to think. When I asked what they wanted, they spoke in German, which I didn't understand. I didn't know what they were looking for, or if they would do something to me to find out what I knew. Nobody had told me anything—not Jerry, not them.

They wanted to talk to Jerry. Luckily our good friend the policeman found out what was happening and was waiting for him at the station where he changed trains. He warned him not to go home. The Gestapo waited all afternoon. About six o'clock, when Jerry didn't come, they left. Finally, about nine o'clock, Jerry came home. I told him what had happened.

"Oh, it's a big complicated story. I cannot tell you about it," he said.

And he didn't. I didn't find out about the things Jerry had done until the war was over, when everyone started telling these stories. Only then did I learn that he had been part of the guerrillas for three years, from 1942 until the end of the war.

Jerry always took the train to work, from Kralovice to Pilsen. A Luft-waffe general from Kralovice usually took the same train, because there was a big military base in Pilsen. That day in 1943, the general was on the train, in the same car with Jerry. He put his briefcase on the seat next to him and fell asleep. While he slept, Jerry picked up the briefcase and threw it out of the window. Of course, there was a big investigation right away to find out who had been in that coach, and that's why they came to search our house.

One night near the end of the war, Jerry and his guerrilla friends blew up the bridge between Zihle and Pilsen. As a result, a train trying to get to Pilsen, in German territory, was forced back to Zihle. Inside this train were Russian, Yugoslav, Belgian, and French prisoners, packed into cattle cars like animals. Mr. Feder was one of the prisoners.

The night of April 19–20, 1945—it was still winter, snowing and cold—

about forty-five people escaped from that train, running off in every direction. But they didn't know where they were and some ran back toward Germany and were killed. A few days later three of them were found in the Czech forest, dead.

Our policeman friend called Jerry that night. "Come over here and I'll give you a coupon for a pair of shoes."

That was special because during the war we had ration coupons for everything—shoes, clothing, salt, sugar, flour. Jerry went off on his bicycle to Potvorov, a village just before Zihle. The policeman told him about the escapees. When he came back home Jerry said to me, "I saw something terrible tonight. Tomorrow morning I have to hire a wagon from the farmer."

Instead of going to work the next morning, he hired the wagon and a pair of horses and filled it with a lot of straw. Then he went back to Potvorov. He came back with Mr. Feder, carrying him into the house in his arms like a baby, he was so weak—he only weighed about eighty pounds. He was wearing a striped suit from the concentration camp with a number on it, the same number that he had on his arm. His arm was broken, his leg was broken, his body was covered with lice.

I'll tell you something about how I felt. If somebody needs help, you have to help, so you do. I don't think everybody does that.

But you don't know what it's like during a war: one family is okay—you can trust them—another family maybe is not. We were afraid to call the doctor because you never knew who might betray you. So many people were traitors. We bandaged his wounded leg ourselves. Jerry made crutches for him. I fed him dumplings, chicken soup, and roast pork. It was a mistake. He liked it, but it made him sick. After that, I was more careful.

We didn't know who he was or anything about him, but he said he was Polish, so we decided to call him Pavel (Paul) Plotzk. To me he is Paul, still today.

Jerry gave him his new shoes. He really needed them himself, but he felt that Paul needed them more. Before Jerry picked him up, the priest had given Paul a beautiful red wool turtleneck sweater. When I saw all the lice I knew I would have to burn it. Still, I thought what a shame to throw away such a beautiful sweater. I threw it in a bucket and covered it over with slivovitz and soaked the sweater in it. Pretty soon the lice were dead and I could wash it. Slivovitz is something like vodka. We made our own during the war.

The second time I ever saw the Gestapo was a few days after Paul came to our house. As if from heaven, our policeman again came to warn us that the Gestapo was looking for the escaped prisoners. The SS in Kralovice was sending a big truck to Sedlice to find them. We had to get him out of the house.

Near our house was a big farm with its own little park, a small forest they kept for hunting rabbits and other game. Quickly I helped Paul get dressed, checking his clothes to make sure there was no address, nothing in his pockets. I gave him a sandwich and told him to run over there as fast as he could, lay down in the woods, and cover himself with leaves. He hopped away on his crutches across the fields.

But some of the "nation-guests" who lived in the house across the road saw him. "Nation-guests" were what we had to call the high-class German people who had been evacuated to Czechoslovakia when the Americans started bombing Germany. We were not allowed to call them Germans. The Czech people were required to take them in, give them a room, and feed them.

The Gestapo were already in Sedlice. Everybody in the village was standing in the square while they searched the houses. Those "nation-guests" went straight to the square and told the SS what they had seen. We knew what was happening because my mother had sent my brother to the village to find out. When he realized that the Gestapo were at the entrance to the village and on every road, he ran back to a big meadow where he

Game park where Herman Feder hid from Nazi search, 1987

could see what was going on. The Germans saw him there and screamed, "Stop! Or we will shoot!" They put him on their truck. Meanwhile we were waiting and waiting. Finally my mother said, "I have to find out what's happened." As soon as she left the house she saw the truck coming down the road with her son on it.

She screamed at them, "What are you doing? Where are you taking him? He's my son!"

He didn't have the right identification card for Sedlice because he was only visiting us. My mother explained to them that he came every month to help her with the house, and they let him go. But one of the SS got off the truck with his machine gun and went over to look in the little woods where Paul was laying on the ground. It was snowing.

The others searched our house. They didn't find Paul. They didn't find anyone else either, because our policeman friend, who knew where all the escaped prisoners were, had gone from house to house to warn everyone. Finally they left. Jerry ran to the forest and brought Paul home, but it was too late; he was sick with a fever.

He was already in bad shape with his broken arm and wounded leg, and weighing so little. Now he had a constant fever over one hundred degrees. I went out to the deep well across the road to soak a bedsheet. You had to pull the water up with ropes. Every two hours, even through the night, I covered him with a fresh cold, wet bedsheet—on his head, too. I could have used the water in the house, but the well water was colder. We didn't have a refrigerator in those days.

Everyone said that the best thing to bring down a high fever was cottage cheese, but cottage cheese was a luxury, and the farmers wouldn't sell it. Normally we never could get it, but people knew we had him at home and now when I asked the farmers, they gave it to me. And we couldn't eat any! I soaked the cottage cheese in cold water and then covered Paul's feet with it, along with the wet sheet, every two hours, day and night, for about eight or ten days. Jerry had to go to work, so I spent the time with

Deep well Anna used to cool Paul's fever; her house is in background; Sedlice, 1987

Paul, running here, running there. A bedsheet is large; wringing it out with your hands—it's work.

We were living by ourselves in a small house at that time. Jerry and I gave him our bed. Since Jerry had to go to work, he slept on a little couch we kept in our bedroom. I put three chairs together with some blankets close to the couch and slept on that. Jerry really helped. In another family the man might not allow his wife to wash a strange man and be there with him twenty-four hours a day, but Jerry never complained.

It was dangerous, but we called the doctor twice. He gave him a little medicine—not much—because he only had a little. On the second visit he said it looked like typhus, and Paul shouldn't stay with us any longer. He needed some injections the doctor didn't have; he needed a hospital.

Paul was crying; he was afraid to go to the hospital. He knew the war was not really over. The Russians were pushing hard, but the Germans were still in charge. The hospital Jerry took him to in Kralovice was a temporary one, set up in a school building to care for the wounded people coming back from the Sudetenland. A very good doctor there gave Paul the injections he needed. When he left him at the hospital, Jerry gave Paul one hundred crowns and said, "Paul, when the barber comes, ask for a haircut."

Anna's brother, father, Paul on crutches Jerry made for him, Anna, and Jerry, Sedlice, 1945

Jerry and Anna Chlup, 1949

One hundred crowns is what Jerry got for six days work. Later, when he was all right, the money was still there under his pillow.

We went to see him every day. When they went to Kralovice my mother and father went to see him too. One day I asked him, "Paul, could you tell me your wife's name?" and he said, "Oh, it doesn't matter. I will die."

I think maybe it was a mistake for him to go to the hospital. While he was in our house he was conscious, but when he went to the hospital, they didn't have the wet bedsheets and towels, and after two or three days he went into a coma.

When Paul had been unconscious for about eight days, the doctor said to Jerry, "I won't give him any more injections. I need to save our medicine for people I know will get through. This one is dying." My husband begged the doctor to give him just one more. He didn't want to do it, but finally he agreed. Jerry didn't leave the hospital until he saw the doctor give him this last injection. Later that night Paul woke up! Jerry really saved his life.

A few days after Paul was conscious again, we had a call telling us the hospital was going to close. Those who could take care of themselves had to leave, the very sick would be moved to a hospital in a bigger town. They asked would we take Paul home or should they send him to the bigger hospital? We didn't know how long it would be for, or what would happen when the Russians came, but Jerry brought him home.

Paul was still afraid when he came back to our house after the hospital. He was always afraid, but then we were, too—the Gestapo and SS men were still around. When the Russians and the Americans came, the Germans ran off, but even though the war was over, if they met you in the forest or some other place, they would kill you. I remember Jerry telling him, "Paul, in this drawer there is fifty thousand crowns. If we don't come back, take the money."

Paul got better pretty fast. At first he couldn't do anything; he was very weak, and underweight. Then when he could walk again, he worked in our store. He and Jerry became almost like brothers. Paul was quiet; he never drank or smoked. He was good company. We talked a lot. You know what he always thought? That I had Jewish parents!

"Panni (he called me Panni—it means 'Mrs.'), your parents are Jewish," he would say.

"Why?"

"Because you are like a Jew." He meant because I liked business, like my father. Paul was a businessman.

We never asked him if he was a Jew or not, and he never talked about it. Maybe he was afraid. We never thought about it. He had told us he was Polish, that's all. After he had been with us about a year, he decided to go back to Poland to see if anyone in his family had survived. When he found out that everyone had died he came back to live with us. About two or three weeks after he returned, he got a letter from a Jewish organization telling him that because he didn't return to Poland his business had been confiscated. He cried when he got this letter.

"Paul, why are you crying?" we asked. "For your business? You should be happy that you are alive. You can always make more money."

"Oh, Panni, it's not about the business. I am crying because I received this letter from the Jewish Committee—because I didn't tell you I am a Jew."

I said to him, "So what?"

We always helped somebody. Sometimes people are good to us, and remember, and sometimes they forget. Paul never forgot us. We are country people—simple people. Maybe if people our age had everything and never suffered, maybe they wouldn't do what we did. No, we didn't suffer either, but we were never rich. We are glad, of course, that we could save him, and that he could enjoy life, because so many died when they came back—like my nephew.

When I go back to Czechoslovakia and see our old house again, I always think about Paul running across the fields, and the SS and Gestapo looking for him. I remember a lot. I was afraid then. Of course.

Herman Feder,
Los Angeles, 1987

Herman Feder

I was thirty-five years old when they took me. It was already after the Kristallnacht, the black night when the Germans burned all the synagogues. Naturally, I was aware of the danger. I tried to get out, but there was no place to go. Europe was already taken by the Germans, so I tried for South America. I heard that a visa for Chile could be obtained from a certain person for five thousand dollars. I went to have a talk with this man, who, as I found out, came from a very rich family. To raise the money I sold the business—everything. My wife and I filled four crates with all our remaining possessions, sending the two with the important things to the port at Hamburg from where we were supposed to be leaving for Chile. The other two we stored with a family we felt was safe—a Jewish husband

and Christian wife. I paid the five thousand dollars to this man, and he vanished! I never saw him again. We didn't know where he went or even if he was alive. And I wasn't the only one. A whole group of "investors" had paid him huge sums. We never found out what happened to him.

The crates we sent to Hamburg were lost, and my business was gone. There was not even enough left to pay the rent. We had to move in with a German-Jewish family. The Germans conscripted me for manual labor, digging sand, but I lasted only one day. I had never done hard physical work before, and I couldn't fill the quota. They sent me home without pay.

I could see that they were arresting Jews and sending them away. I assumed they would come for me too, but I didn't think it would be so soon. I was at home with the German-Jewish couple when they came for me. Because he was German, they didn't take the man of the house. They had come only for me; my wife, Sabina; and our two-year-old son, Freddie, because we were Polish Jews. They took us directly to the station and put us on a train. A few hours later the train stopped, I don't remember the name of the place. We saw thousands and thousands of people sitting on their luggage, on boxes, whatever they had. We did the same. It was a concentration point for deporting Polish Jews who were living in Germany.

By nine o'clock in the evening, we were still sitting there. My boy was crying. We had no milk, no water—nothing. I was becoming desperate. Finally I said to my wife, "Let's just go." We walked back about a kilometer to the railroad station and boarded the next train returning to Hirschberg; nobody stopped us. When the train pulled into Hirschberg about two o'clock in the morning, we walked back to our friend's apartment. Luckily nobody saw us, nobody knew.

Five or six weeks went by without anything happening, and then one day a police detective came to the door. I knew him as a friend—I had dated his daughter some years before. He said, "Herman, I'm very sorry but you are a Jew, and I have to take you to the police station." He took just me, not my wife or son. At the police station there was a new man in charge, a Nazi whom I also knew—his son and I were good friends. He also apologized, "I'm so sorry, Herman, but I can't manage to keep you free any longer. I knew all the time that you were here, but I held back. I can't do that any longer. I have to send you away." Because he knew me I was treated well. Instead of jail, he put me in a bedroom in a police apartment and closed the door. I was there for two days.

They sent me by train to a jail in another town where I was put in a cell by myself. The straw in the cell seemed to be moving, it was crawling with so many lice; I stood up the whole night. In the morning they put me on another train to the Alexanderplatz in Berlin. There I was put in a jail for the very worst criminals and murderers—maybe two hundred men, sitting on the floor together, without food or water.

The next morning they read off a long list of names—about eighty people, including me. We were destined for Sachsenhausen concentration camp. It was the first of many camps where I was to spend the next sixty-seven months and three days: Sachsenhausen, from 1939 until 1941; Gross-Rosen, the worst; Buchenwald; Dachau; Auschwitz; Buna; and Dora. The Nazis knew from experience at Auschwitz and other camps that when a prisoner was in one place for very long he became known to the SS and could sometimes take advantage of the situation. To prevent prisoners from getting friendly with their SS guards, they shifted them from camp to camp.

The atrocities I endured in the camps were incredible, impossible to describe. Whenever there was a big beating, it was for me, but I was strong when I was young—they couldn't kill me. Naturally, I always prayed. In the morning, in the evening, at work—I prayed. I knew that my mother was near me. I was beaten, buried alive, my arm was broken. I was in hell, alive.

The first day in Sachsenhausen I had to get up during the night to go to the bathroom. To my horror, I found a corpse in the bathroom—a young boy, twenty years old, who had died of meningitis. I held back and returned to the bunk until they took him away. A few months later I routinely walked over corpses to relieve myself. The place was full of corpses.

Map showing concentration camps where Herman Feder was imprisoned

During that entire time in the camps I got one letter from my wife—when I was at Sachsenhausen. She wrote, "I am well. Freddie is well. I signed all our possessions over to the German government. They told me I will get a visa for Holland." It was from Treblinka. So at least I knew where they were. I had a deal with an SS man: he gave me a piece of bread, I gave him a diamond in exchange; we got a lot of diamonds from the Belgian Jews. When he told me he was going to Treblinka, I asked him to look in their records for the names of Sabina and Alfred Feder. A week later he came back and told me, "They are on the list. They were in the gas chamber."

I never felt like giving up. I told myself that my mother was at my side and God was with me—I won't give up. I could have done the same thing that hundreds of Jews did: grab the electric wire at the fence. Every morning when we came out of the barracks we saw corpses hanging from the wire.

One day my luck turned. They were asking for shoemakers. I raised my hand.

"Are you a shoemaker?"

"No, I am a master shoemaker," I said.

They took twenty-five of us shoemakers to the depot where they issued the new clothes we would need to work in the town of Auschwitz. As we were standing there all in a row, the SS man took out his pistol and said, "Anyone who lied to me about being a shoemaker, I will shoot you on the spot!" I was the tallest and first to be asked, "Who are you?" I said again I was a master shoemaker. I got my new clothes, shoes, and a hat. The next morning I went out of the camp to work.

That moment marked the end of my suffering, of my beatings, but even so, I had some difficulties. We were in barracks with forced laborers: twenty-five Germans, twenty-five Italians, twenty-five Poles, and our twenty-five prisoners—one hundred people working on shoes. Between eight o'clock in the morning and five o'clock in the afternoon we each had to repair six pairs of shoes. Four of us sat together at a little table. The one to my right said, "I know you're not a shoemaker, you close your eyes when you hit the nail." He already had three pairs, and I had nothing; I nailed on two soles and they both fell off. I asked him to show me how to do it.

"Why should I help you?," he said. "What can you give me?"

"My finger, my arm, my soul, what do you want? All I have is a spoon and a bowl."

"Give me your soup in the evening, and I will show you how to repair shoes."

I gathered up all the materials and brought them to him, and he taught me. By five o'clock when the boss came in, I was ready with the shoes.

In the evening when I got my soup, my mentor—the whole camp called him Mickey Mouse because he had such big ears—said from behind me, "Give me your soup." I gave it to him, went off to my bed, covering myself with the blanket. I hadn't eaten the whole day and couldn't bear to look at them with their soup. But I had the chance to go out of the camp to repair shoes again. The next day we marched the eight kilometers to town in snow and mud. I was so hungry, I had very little strength. All of a sudden I saw something in the road, and even though it was not allowed—the guard had the right to shoot if someone bent down—I bent down and picked a potato out of the mud. I ate it raw. No cake in the world could have tasted as sweet or as good as that dirty potato. It was delicious!

Later, as I was working on my six pairs of shoes, the boss came in asking, "Who knows how to read and write?" I was the only one to raise his hand. The others were Polish Jews from little towns and villages, and they didn't know how to read or write in German.

Herman Feder, 1947

"You can read and write?"

"Yes. I had my schooling in Berlin." I told him which gymnasium I had attended.

"Come with me!" He took me into the office and showed me a little window where civilian customers came in with shoes for repair. He showed me how they accounted for each pair with three slips of paper: white, blue, and yellow—one to put in the shoe, one for the books, and one for the customer as a receipt. I got the job, and life became a little easier.

One day a fat man came to the window. I had on a white coat and my hair was completely shaved off; he didn't know I was a prisoner.

"Heil Hitler! Here are my shoes. Put leather soles on them."

"Mr. Schultz, I'm sorry," I said. "We have no leather, only rubber."

"No, I can't use rubber! It's impossible! I want leather!" He got a little bit too loud, so I called in the boss.

"The gentleman here is insisting he wants leather soles, and I told him we don't have them."

The boss turned and said to him, "We don't have leather!" Schultz took his shoes and went away.

The next day this Schultz came again, with a red stamp from the camp commandant authorizing him to have leather soles.

"Mr. Schultz," I said, "I told you I have no leather. I have to give you rubber."

"Listen, I work in the kitchen on a wet concrete floor. It's slippery and I'm afraid I'll break my neck."

"Oh, you work in the kitchen?"

"I'm the head chef."

"In that case, I would like to help you. I'll have to steal it for you (which wasn't true), but I will find you leather. In exchange, I would like to have something to eat. We have twenty-five prisoners here and we are all nearly starved to death."

"Sure. Send two men with a kettle, and we'll fill it up."

But how to do it? I went to have a talk with the guard who was watching over us.

"We can get a kettle of food and a special plate just for you," I told him. "Would you go with two men to bring it back?"

"Are you crazy? How can I leave you here?"

"You can. Don't worry. If one of us runs away, you can shoot me. I guarantee it with my life—no one will run away."

He took the two strongest men and in ten minutes they came back with a full kettle of mashed potatoes. This was really special. After that, little by little we got everything—we could eat our fill. We even took a kettle home to the barracks to feed the others, marching eight kilometers with this heavy thing—it must have weighed seventy-five pounds. You took five or ten steps, put it down, then someone else picked it up. We had to be careful because sometimes the commandant came down the road in his car.

In 1945, near the end of the war, I was put in a transport with about a thousand other people, for Bergen-Belsen—for the gas chamber. We were in closed cattle cars, standing back to back, with no room to even sit down. Sixty or seventy people were in each car, with nothing to eat, without water. People were dying like flies; every morning there were no less than ten corpses. I and another guy volunteered to carry the dead bodies from our wagon—one took the hands, the other the feet—to the two open cars they kept at the end of the train for the purpose. The next day, the same thing. But at least I could be outdoors, and it gave me the chance to steal a sharp-edged stone from the railway bed. Later I used it to cut my tongue; with this little bit of blood I got through four or five days without food or water. I think that's what kept me alive.

In our wagon was a small window with bars, blocked with a piece of wood. We broke off the wood for a little air and light. One night the transport stopped. Looking out we saw a sign: "Zihle." I knew from the way the "Z" was written—with a mark over it—that we were in Czechoslovakia. A Russian soldier was put in our wagon then; he found a space next to me. I could speak Russian, so we started to talk. He was an officer who had been captured, escaped, and then was caught again. As we talked, a locomotive came along, and suddenly our train was underway again, traveling the whole night. I fell asleep. By morning the train had stopped. I opened my eyes, looked out of the window, and saw the sign for Zihle again. I thought I had lost my mind; I couldn't understand it. Later, I learned that Jerry and his friends had blown up the bridge to Pilsen the night before and the train couldn't get through. It was forced back to Zihle, where it stayed.

All day long we heard thunder. Hoping for rain, we put our spoons through the bars to try to catch a drop of water. But the rain didn't come.

That night I was standing next to the window and could hear the conversation of three or four SS men sitting around a little fire they had made just below us. I overheard one say, "I only have three bullets left. If these prisoners get the doors open they'll kill us."

"I have only one bullet," the second one said.

Then the third said, "I have none. Tomorrow morning I'm running away."

They pushed their fire away and left. I translated their conversation to the Russian soldier. He thought about it and then told me, "Tonight I'm going to break out."

*Zihle train station,
view from the tracks,
1987*

Outside of our little window was a big pile of wood. Sometime in the
night—I had fallen asleep—the Russian apparently reached through the
bars and managed to pull in a piece of wood from the stack outside. He
used it to break out the bars. Then he crawled out of the window, came
around, and opened the door to our wagon and all the other wagons as
well. When I opened my eyes, the moon was shining in through the open
door. I looked around and saw that the wagon was nearly empty, just five
or six were lying there—those who couldn't run. I thought, "My God, what
should I do? If I stay and they find me here with the others gone, they will
kill me." I went over to the edge of the wagon and looked out. In the bright

moonlight I saw people running away, like rabbits in a field. I didn't see anyone who might stop me, so I jumped out and ran, too.

I heard gunfire, and suddenly I realized I was hit in my left ankle, but I didn't stop; I kept on running. Then I couldn't run any more and fell down. A German and a Pole—friends from the concentration camp—picked me up and dragged me away to a little forest. They left me and ran off. I wrapped up my foot with my shirt and lay down. Then two other prisoners turned up. I went with them about a kilometer further when we saw a little hut—it was really an old railroad car—next to a cemetery, surrounded by barbed wire. I crawled under the wire and knocked on the window. The other two guys were scared and ran away.

"Who is there?" someone called out. When I heard the Czech language, I kissed the ground—I knew I was saved. I started crying. A man came out and took me inside. It was the home of the gravedigger.

His wife was upset about me being there. She had heard the guns and was afraid the Germans would come. Her husband just said to her, "Mother, bring some soup and bread!" and he put me on the sofa. I begged him, "Please! Hide me under the sofa," and he did. Before he could even give me something to eat, I heard the rattling of pistols and machine guns. I lay there, shaking and very frightened. Jerry came in the door.

"Did you see some prisoners?"

"I have one here. He's wounded," the gravedigger said to him.

Jerry was also speaking in Czech, but I was still shaking.

"Come out from there," he said. "Don't worry. Nothing will happen to you. I already have twenty others in the church tower. Stay here and I will bring a doctor."

About a half an hour later he came back with a doctor. They put me on a chair. Someone held my hands, someone else held my feet while the doctor took the bullet out of my ankle, without anesthetic or anything. When Jerry left he said he would come back for me the next day, but I didn't really think he would; I was still afraid.

But he did come the next day, with a big horse-drawn wagon, some

Cemetery where Paul was found by Jerry Chlup, Potvorov, 1987

pillows, and a pair of pants he got from the priest; they were so big I could put them around me twice. When we got to Jerry's road, a Czech policeman was waiting in front of the house. He started asking me a lot of questions. I couldn't even speak, I was so frightened of everybody.

"Don't worry. I'm a policeman, but I work for the Czechoslovakians." He was speaking in Czech. Then he took out some papers.

"Listen, forget about your real name. From now on you are Pavel Plotzk," and he gave me the identity papers of a Polish peasant, a prisoner who had run away.

When they brought me inside, Jerry's wife didn't say anything, although I had the feeling she was against the idea of having me in their house. But Jerry had brought me home and she accepted the situation. Then when she realized how far gone I was, no one worked harder than Anna to help me.

For the next few days they took care of me. I tried to clean myself, but I was so full of lice, it was impossible. They had to take off all my clothes until I was completely naked. Jerry held up a strong light, while Anna picked off the lice with a tweezers. Then Jerry made me a pair of crutches— he was very good at woodworking. I was beginning to recuperate a little bit. On the third day Anna's brother suddenly came running in from the village, crying, "The SS is here! They are looking for you!"

Very fast, Anna gave me two big pieces of bread, a piece of chicken, and the crutches, and I ran off to a little forest about three hundred feet away. I was barely hidden when the SS pulled up to the house in their truck. From where I was lying I could see them on the road. One of them took a bicycle and entered the woods, coming straight toward me. He was within ten or fifteen feet when he laid down the bicycle. He aimed his pistol directly at my eyes. I was looking down the barrel of his gun. I stopped breathing. You can't imagine what it's like when you see that. How can I explain it? My feelings stopped, my heart stopped, my thinking stopped; everything stopped.

But, he didn't see me, or maybe he didn't want to see me. He turned to

Game park where Paul hid from Nazi search, Sedlice, 1987

the right and went along the edge of the woods. He turned to the left, went around the other side, and came back to the place he started. He picked up his bicycle and went away.

In a minute or two I heard the truck leaving. I just lay there catching my breath. Five minutes later I heard Jerry whistling, and I stood up. Jerry took me down to the house again, in his arms. The next day I had a very high fever.

The fever persisted for many days. Finally one morning Jerry left to look for a doctor. He went all the way to Pilsen on a motorbike the SS had abandoned in the woods. He found a doctor's sign, walked into the office, and demanded, "Doctor, come with me. I need you for a patient at Sedlice."

"Oh, no. I'm not going that far," the doctor said.

Jerry took out his pistol and threatened him, "You will go or else!"

The doctor came back with him on the motorcycle. He examined me in the bedroom, then went to talk to Jerry and Anna. I couldn't hear what he was saying, but I imagined it was typhus. When they came back I said, "Listen, Anna and Jerry, please take me away. I can't stay here and infect you."

They denied it and kept me a few more days. Then they heard about a temporary hospital set up in a school building nearby in Kralovice, and they took me there, promising to visit everyday. In the hospital I fell unconscious and didn't wake up for many days. About a week after I woke up, they closed the hospital; the war was over and they needed the space for the Russian military.

The Chlups took me back to their house, where I stayed for three more years. It was a quiet life. Jerry and Anna had a little grocery store; after I got better I helped them out. I did my job the whole day, waiting on people, selling flour, bread, beans, whatever we had. I sold, I did the books, I did the buying. Anna would sit there knitting or doing some other work. I became used to them and was comfortable; it was like home. They were my parents, my brother, my sister, my whole family. There was no problem with my being Jewish; nobody besides them knew about it. I never told anybody, but Anna knew because I was naked when she picked off the lice.

One day I said to Jerry and Anna, "I'm going back to Poland to see what is left. Maybe I will find someone." In my mind I thought I would find somebody from my family. They gave me a rucksack full of food and I set off for Hirschberg, which by then was part of Poland. I found the house where my wife and I had left our two crates when we thought we were going to emigrate to Chile. The wife of this family was German and had been able to save her Jewish husband's life. They told me that only Polish people lived in Hirschberg now. Of all the Jewish people who once lived in that city, this man was the only one spared.

They gave me the key to the cellar and I went down. The crates were still there, but they were open and all my clothes, my suits, nearly everything was gone. They told me that the SS had searched their house, looking for somebody one time. They found the crates and took everything away.

I did find two things I had hidden: my father's watch and a ring. I put them in the rucksack, went outside to sit on the steps, and wept. They were crying too. I had lost my whole family. Not one person was left from 188 relatives—not my wife, my child, my brothers, or sister. The lady wanted to give me something to eat, but I still had food that Anna had given me. I said no and started back the same day. It was a sad encounter.

I went back to the Chlups, but now I had the desire to go far away, to emigrate. I wasn't accustomed to living in a little village; I had always lived in big towns. The year before I left for good, I took a job as the manager of a little store in Marienbad, about sixty miles away. Anna came to visit every week, bringing fresh food and clean laundry. She still looked after me.

If it wasn't for the Chlups I wouldn't be alive. There isn't another pair of people in the whole world who would have done what they did for me. When Jerry brought me to his home the first day, he opened the closet and showed me a shoebox with a lot of money in it, more than a hundred

View of Anna and Jerry's house from woods where Paul hid, Sedlice, 1987

thousand crowns. He said, "Pavel, take as much as you want. Don't ask me. Take what you want." Another day he came home with a nice pair of shoes. I had boots from the concentration camp, but they were not a pair.

"What nice shoes you bought," I said. "Try them on so I can see."

"Oh, no, I brought them for you."

Whatever they could do, they did for me. What Anna went through to help me, no one else would have, not my mother, not my wife, nobody. They did the utmost possible. So many died. I was on the verge of dying too. They really saved my life.

PART 3 〜 Poland

People are far stronger than one can ever imagine.

Horses are weaker.—BARBARA MAKUCH

Before World War II, 3,300,000 Jewish people lived in Poland, 10 percent of the general population of 33,000,000. Located mostly in urban areas, large Jewish communities had flourished in Poland since the Middle Ages, maintaining their own language, culture, and religious and social institutions, distinct and separate from the Polish culture around them. Despite their long history on Polish soil, many Poles regarded Jews as foreigners living in their midst.

By the 1920s and '30s the majority of Polish Jews were living in varying degrees of poverty, the result of the overall poor economy of the newly independent Polish state, which was compounded by government-sanctioned anti-Jewish measures such as a 1938 law revoking the citizenship of Polish Jews living abroad. Jews had limited access to Polish universities and professions. They lived in a general climate of anti-Semitism that not infrequently flared into violent pogroms. Even before the Nazi occupation, Jews in Poland were isolated from the mainstream and in a poor position to defend themselves against the extremely severe measures that were to follow.

Hitler's army invaded Poland on September 1, 1939, the start of World War II. On September 17, following the agreement of the Molotov-Ribbentrop Treaty, the Soviet army invaded Poland from the east. The ill-prepared Polish army soon succumbed, surrendering to Germany's vastly superior forces on September 27. The Polish government fled into exile in Romania. Re-forming with new leadership, it eventually operated from Lon-

don, coordinating and sending support to the various underground resistance groups in Poland.

On September 28, Germany and the Soviet Union partitioned Poland into three major areas. The western territories were annexed into Germany, eastern areas into the Soviet Union, and the central portion, named the General Gouvernement, became a German protectorate, governed by German civil authorities under the autocratic leadership of Hans Frank.

German-directed upheavals to the Polish population were immediate and drastic. In the first months of the war, tens of thousands of Polish intellectuals, particularly teachers and religious leaders, were killed. The Germans forcibly expelled Poles residing in the annexed western territories, sending them to resettle in the General Gouvernement, while many others living in what became the Soviet territories were equally displaced. The Germans regarded Poles as "subhuman" and Polish Jews as somewhere beneath that level, treating both groups with extreme and brutal harshness.

The German program for Polish Jews was one of concentration, isolation, and, eventually, annihilation. Initially they forced the Polish Jews from the annexed territories and from all rural and smaller urban areas into large, overcrowded urban centers. Now in large concentrations, they isolated them from Polish society into sealed ghettos—walled-off cities within cities—where they had to endure appalling living conditions. Governing the ghettos were the Nazi-mandated Jewish Councils, whose members were former Jewish community leaders. While aspiring to alleviate the tremendous suffering of ghetto inhabitants, they unintentionally played into the hands of the Nazis, making their job of annihilation easier. Eventually the German authorities deported the debilitated ghetto populations to concentration camps specifically built to kill people on an unprecedented scale.

By 1942, Poland was the Nazi regime's dumping ground for Jews from all over Europe; first the Polish ghettos and then the concentration camps were the destinations for Jews rounded up in every Nazi-occupied country. By the end of the war, over 3,000,000 Polish Jews were dead, with only 50,000 to 70,000 surviving.

The chronology below lists the course of some of the anti-Jewish measures in Poland.

October 1939	Jews are liable for forced labor. They can be picked up off the streets for work at manual labor jobs such as digging ditches, shoveling snow, and cleaning streets. Synagogues destroyed throughout General Gouvernement.
	Jews forbidden from certain areas of major cities in General Gouvernement.

November 1939	Jews must wear identifying star on their clothing. Every Jewish community must elect a Jewish Council. After the formation of the ghettos, the Jewish Councils became the governing bodies, trying to provide social services, but also serving the German authorities by delivering Jews for forced labor and for deportations to the death camps.
	All Jewish bank deposits frozen. Jews can withdraw only the equivalent of fifty dollars per week.
December 1939	Jews can not change residence. Curfew for Jews enforced from 9:00 P.M. to 5:00 A.M.
January 1940	Jews can not travel by train without special permission.
	Jews are required to register ownership of all property, including clothing, furniture, and jewelry.
April 1940	First major ghetto built, at Lodz. Curfews in the ghettos are enforced from 7:00 P.M. to 7:00 A.M.
October 1940	Warsaw ghetto built. The city's Jewish population is sealed inside.
	Mass deportations of Jews, Gypsies, and Poles from other Nazi-occupied countries to the General Gouvernement area of Poland begins. Since the death camps are not built yet, the deportees are first sent to the overcrowded ghettos.
March 1941	Cracow ghetto built.
October 1941	Jews forbidden to leave ghettos on pain of death. Gentiles who knowingly help Jews are subject to the death penalty.
December 1941	Lvov ghetto formed, the third largest in Poland. Most of the ghettos in Poland were established by the beginning of 1942.
	Death camps begin operations. Poland is the site of six

	major concentration camps set up to kill Jews: Lublin, Kulmhof, Treblinka, Sobibor, Belzec, and Auschwitz.
March 1942	Jews from Lublin ghetto deported to Belzec death camp.
July–December 1942	Three hundred thousand people deported from the Warsaw ghetto to Treblinka death camp.
March 1943	Cracow ghetto liquidated.
April 1943	Attempt to liquidate Warsaw ghetto is met with unexpected armed resistance.
May 1943	The Warsaw ghetto is liquidated.
June 1943	The Lvov ghetto is liquidated.
Late 1943 until liberation in 1945	In every city with a ghetto population, a pattern is repeated: Those able to work are organized into slave-labor battalions to produce goods for the German military. Everyone else must fend for themselves. Food supplies are at starvation levels. Lack of sanitation and overcrowding promote the rapid spread of disease, especially typhus, resulting in an extremely high mortality rate. Periodic mass deportations from the ghettos to the death camps are followed by an influx of newly arrived Jews from all areas of the German Reich.

5 ∿ Another Side of the Story

Barbara Szymanska first saw Poland when she was eight months old. It was then that her parents, Janina and Franciszek, returned to their native land after several years in Russia, where they had gone to avoid Franciszek's conscription into the German army. It was 1918, and Poland was an independent state for the first time in nearly 150 years; it seemed a propitious time to start a new life. Within a few years of their return, Barbara, or Basha, as her family called her, had two new sisters, Halina and Hanka. But in post–World War I Poland the young family's prospects continued to be very poor, forcing the couple to send their three-year-old middle daughter, Halina, to live with a childless uncle, with the hope that she might be raised in more comfortable circumstances.

Growing up in the north of Poland, Barbara briefly attended a well-known progressive school, but she eventually graduated from an agricultural school in Wilno. Then early in September 1939, just as she was making her application to a Warsaw university, Hitler's army invaded Poland, and all Polish education ceased. In the chaotic days that followed, her father was shot dead by a German soldier in broad daylight on a Warsaw street. Janina Szymanska gathered up her daughters Barbara and Hanka and took them to live with her at her sister's home in Sandomierz, in the southeast of Poland, close to the Ukrainian border. Barbara soon found work teaching at an agricultural boarding school for boys in the nearby village of Tarnobrzeg. Her mother moved from Sandomierz to be with her.

Although reared in the home of her uncle, Barbara's younger sister Halina often visited with her parents and sisters. Halina remembers her most important early experiences being the times spent with her mother and her years at the Liceum Krzemienieckie, a school in eastern Poland famous since the nineteenth century for its enlightened intellectual attitudes.

On October 17, 1939, as a result of the secret and infamous Molotov-Ribbentrop Treaty between Germany and Russia, eastern Poland overnight became Russian territory. Feeling unsafe, Halina and her classmate Olla left Krzemieniec to live with Olla's aunt, Dr. Olga Lilien, in Lvov, near the Ukraine.

In Lvov, following a six-month training course, Halina found employment as a laboratory technician, initially at the State Institute of Hygiene run by Dr. Henryk Meisel, and subsequently at the Weigl Institute, presided over by Rudolf Weigl. Both men were renowned bacteriologists who worked on the discovery of the typhus vaccine.

Halina soon became involved with the Polish Socialist Party, where she also met her future husband, Slawek Ogrodzinski, an active member of the party since his university days. Before the war there were many political groups with overlapping membership in Lvov; during the Nazi occupation each had its counterpart in the Polish resistance movement. Thus, from the Lvov Polish Socialist Party evolved the local branch of Zegota, a Warsaw group founded in October 1942 specifically to funnel money and give other aid to Polish Jews. Zegota was the only formal organization to directly help thousands of Jews in Nazi-occupied Poland. Slawek was second-in-command of the Lvov branch. Working for Zegota, Halina arranged for Jewish people to be smuggled out of the Lvov ghetto, to receive medicine, false identity papers, and money.

Barbara was even more deeply involved in helping Jewish people, activities for which she paid a steep price. While living with her mother in Tarnobrzeg, she helped two Jewish people find protection in the boys' boarding school where she was teaching. One was a young boy who successfully passed himself off as a Christian Polish student. The second was Dr. Olga Lilien, Halina's former classmate's aunt, who became the school cook. Although they lived on minimal means in a tiny apartment, Barbara and her mother also accepted responsibility for a little Jewish girl, unexpectedly brought to them one day by the girl's desperate mother, Rachel Litowitz. Fearing detection in such a small community, Barbara took the girl on a dangerous journey to Lvov, to the relatively greater safety of a convent school.

In Lvov, Barbara joined Halina in her work for Zegota. On a Zegota courier mission, Barbara was caught and subsequently imprisoned, first in a notorious jail, later at Ravensbruck concentration camp in Germany. During her years in prison and camp, Barbara faced the harshest tests of her courage and endurance. Remarkably, she not only survived but even managed to help save the lives of fellow inmates, including Dr. Henryk Meisel, Halina's former employer.

Dr. Olga Lilien was born in 1904 in Lvov, to an assimilated Jewish family. When she was a young adult finishing her medical studies, she interned for one year in the United States at a hospital in Terre Haute, Indiana. She practiced pediatric medicine for the next year and a half in Berlin, followed by a year in Paris, finally returning to Lvov. Olga then began teaching hygiene at the same high school she had attended as a girl. By the start of World War II, she was also assisting in the bacteriological research laboratory of Dr. Henryk Meisel.

Dr. Olga's self-deprecating sense of humor and strong spirit of independence were important factors in her survival of the Nazi occupation of Poland. When Barbara helped her secure a position in the kitchen of the boarding school where Barbara was employed, Dr. Olga successfully passed herself off as a simple Polish peasant, on one occasion serving an especially fine meal to a contingent of Nazi SS visitors.

Situated on the Vistula River, Sandomierz was a commercial town with a large Jewish population. Its history dates back to the Middle Ages. By the 1930s, one-third of the population of ten thousand was Jewish, including Rachel Litowitz and her family.

Rachel owned a shop selling clothing for men and women; her husband was a tailor. They had one child. As the Jewish situation in Sandomierz rapidly deteriorated, Rachel, realistic and fearing the worst, abruptly left her seven-year-old daughter in the care of strangers—Barbara Szymanska and her mother—known to her by only the vaguest recommendation. Mother and daughter did not meet again until after the war's end, when Rachel, who had survived Auschwitz, discovered her daughter living well-protected in the Lvov convent where Barbara had taken her.

In the aftermath of the war, Rachel learned that her husband and most other family members had died in the camps. Finding life in Poland untenable, she and her daughter emigrated to Canada, where, like so many other survivors, they built a new life. She gave this interview on July 26, 1987, in Montreal, Canada, where she makes her home today.

After the war Barbara also emigrated to Canada, where she lived with her husband, Stanley Makuch. Barbara told her story at her home in Montreal on June 23, 1986. Returning to Poland after Stanley's death in 1993, in order to bury her husband in his native land, Barbara decided to remain with her family in Sandomierz, where she lives today.

Halina Szymanska Ogrodzinska remained in her native Poland. Her husband became a member of the diplomatic corps. She lives in Warsaw, where she gave this interview at her home on July 2, 1987.

When the war ended, Dr. Olga chose to remain in Tarnobrzeg, where she returned to the practice of pediatric medicine. She lived there until the end, on close terms with the Szymanska family. She related her account in Sandomierz on July 4, 1987. She died in 1996, at the age of ninety-two.

Barbara Szymanska Makuch

My mother was a special person. Not educated in a formal way, she was certainly intelligent; she had an open mind and was always reading. She helped anybody who asked, not only Jews. Whenever my mother saw a real need she would just do it. I grew up in this kind of home, in this kind of atmosphere. Her attitude was, don't say no, we can't do it. We will try. If it's *really* impossible, then we can say no.

When the Germans first occupied Warsaw, my father began working for the underground, helping to prepare hiding places. They shot him, leaving my mother a widow with three daughters. Even in this position, she accepted our underground work. Not every mother would do this.

Our apartment in Tarnobrzeg was very small—only one room and a kitchen. Since this was my first teaching job, the pay was quite low, and from that my mother and I had to squeeze the rent money. But we managed. It was enough.

It was late in the afternoon, one day in 1942, when a woman named Rachel Litowitz and her child came to our door, saying she came because somebody had told her I was a good person. I had never seen her before. She had nowhere else to go—she was desperate. She wanted me to take her child. I knew that in Sandomierz that day the Germans were "cleaning" the town. A very bad raid had been going on all day. I had seen them shoot Jews right in the streets.

We all felt very scared. By law, the penalty was death if you offered so much as one glass of water to a Jewish person. The Germans killed us exactly the same as they killed the Jews. My mother and I knew that, but how could we refuse this woman's plea? We didn't even talk it over, we just invited her inside.

We talked with her for a few hours, and then she left the child with us and returned to her husband in Sandomierz, where he was working in a camp the Germans had set up for people who could still do useful work. I didn't set eyes on Rachel again until after the war. I learned that she went to Auschwitz, but I knew she was very strong. Twice she escaped from the gas chambers.

So seven-year-old Rebecca stayed with us: we called her Marysia. I slept in the kitchen, and my mother slept with her in the other room. In the beginning everything was okay because she was blond, with a pale complexion and freckles, and slightly curly hair, which I would straighten by making her little braids. We told people she was my niece. At home her family spoke Yiddish, although fortunately Marysia had linguistic talent and could speak Polish quite well. But like all children in this situation, she was shy and frightened. Her mother had said to her, "I'm leaving you now. After today, Basha will be your mother." How can a little child understand this? She grew close to my mother because my mother was staying at home while I was away every day at work. Right from the beginning my mother became her "aunt."

Later on I discovered how Marysia came to us. Mrs. Litowitz ran a small clothing store in Sandomierz and my aunt was a customer. She asked my aunt to help her, but my aunt had two young daughters and was afraid. She told her to go instead to Tarnobrzeg where I lived with my mother, and that maybe we would help.

One evening after curfew, when my mother and I were visiting my aunt in Sandomierz, Marysia's father showed up. He was standing by the fence, very frightened. When he saw me he threw over a hat saying, "This is what I have. Take it and the child, and go to Switzerland. I have a brother there who will help you." But he had no address to give me.

"Everybody in Zurich can tell you who Litowitz is," he said.

When we went back in the house I found sewn inside the hat five Russian rubles. I cried when I saw this, because I knew it was everything the poor man had.

STEFAN

The news that we were helping a Jew traveled fast among the many people needing help. Soon after Marysia arrived, a girl came to the house asking me to help her younger brother. But with Marysia already there, I couldn't do it; there was absolutely no room for him. So I went to the director of my school and asked him if he could accept this boy, "Stefan," as a student. Dr. Polowicz took a look at Stefan and accepted him into the school without a single question. But, he knew.

From time to time a priest came to our school to give lessons in religion. Stefan paid close attention; he was a fine student. The priest would sometimes wonder why he knew so much about some things and next to nothing about others, occasionally just asking him outright whether he was really a Catholic or not. Stefan never gave a straight answer. He became adept at dodging the questions, so everything went all right for him. He finished school and later got a job. I never saw him or his sister again, but I know for sure that he survived.

DR. POLOWICZ

Our director, Dr. Polowicz, was a brilliant and special person, perceptive and willing to help however he could. He had come from western Poland, near the German border, and spoke perfect idiomatic German. In fact, many people thought he was Polish-Deutsch, a Polish person who sympathized with the Germans. He never objected to this idea because it was useful. When the Germans came to his office threatening, "We hear you are harboring Jews here!" he would yell right back at them, "What are you talking about?! You think I don't know who the Jews are?! I have a lot of people here, but no Jews!" He was so strong.

DR. OLGA

Then another person turned up on our doorstep, a woman of around forty. I didn't know her personally, but she knew all my family, especially my sister Halina, who had even stayed in her home in Lvov. Olga looked very Jewish, like so many of the Jews who lived in Poland, with full long hair and very big eyes. And she was afraid for her life. Again I went to my

Jewish women being deported, Poland, 1942

school director, Dr. Polowicz, and asked him if she could stay in the school kitchen and wash dishes. He agreed to it.

We knew from Halina that Olga Lilien was a pediatrician. She had been working at a girls' school in Lvov, teaching hygiene and health. As luck would have it, not more than a month after she came to us, the director's fifteen-year-old niece came for a visit from Lvov, where she was a student at the same girls' school. One evening she happened to spot Dr. Olga in the kitchen and immediately she headed indignantly straight off to her uncle.

"Do you know who this lady is?"

"She is a kitchen worker," Dr. Polowicz replied.

"No, no. Do you know who she *really* is?"

"No."

"She is a Jewish lady doctor!"

Dr. Polowicz became very angry with his niece and started to yell at her, "If I hear one more word about her being a Jew, you will leave this house!"

Then he went to Olga and asked if there was any truth in what his niece had said. Dr. Olga answered, yes, and from that moment on she was appointed physician to the director's family of five children. The niece never told anyone, and Olga continued to work in the school kitchen until the end of the war, all the while becoming a close friend of the whole Polowicz family.

She looked Jewish. Oh, yes, she knew very well that she looked Jewish, even though she never mentioned it to me. Her sister was completely different—completely; she looked almost like an Egyptian painting. But Olga felt very strongly that she was Polish and this conviction gave her strength. It is important for her to think that Dr. Polowicz asked her to work for him, and not that I asked him to help her. I know how her mind works, or rather, how her mind prepares itself; it is a very flexible instrument. It's very good, because if she hadn't felt so strong perhaps she would have died. She was very proud. She was always working and she always had money. This is Olga.

After the war, Dr. Olga had many opportunities to take positions in big hospitals but she rejected them all. She said she'd stay until the end of her life with the people who had dared to help her during that very dangerous time. Today she's in her eighties, but she's still there, living in a small one-room apartment, taking care of the children all around. We write often, and my husband and I have visited her. I remember when my mother became very ill before her death. Dr. Olga was living in Tarnobrzeg, but she walked the fifteen or twenty kilometers to care for my mother in Sandomierz. She stayed with her until the very last moment. A very beautiful person, very beautiful.

SOPHIE

The only drugstore in town was owned by a Jewish family. They had a daughter named Sophie, about my age.

There was no particular schedule for the German raids on the Jews. One day they started in again "cleaning" the Jews from Tarnobrzeg, coming to each house yelling, "Dirty Jew! Get out! Get out! Get out! We need you to help in another town!" Somebody reported that they had seen Sophie's parents—old people—lined up in the street with the other Jews. One of the Germans started shooting and her father died right there in the street. In the next hour they killed her mother, too. People saw the bodies lying in the street. But when the raid began, Sophie had run out of her house by the back way and managed to escape. That evening she came to our door asking for help. What kind of help could we give her? Talking it over, we decided that she should leave immediately for the big city, Lvov. But she was well known in Tarnobrzeg, and it was too dangerous for her to buy a ticket.

We made a plan that my mother would buy the ticket—I couldn't because I was working—and I would go to the station immediately after I finished school to be with her when the train left. The station was three kilometers by the road, but we usually took a short-cut through the fields.

I was still at school when somebody ran in saying, "Did you hear? Sophie was killed in the field!" My heart leaped. I jumped up and ran to the station, very frightened. But when I got there, there they were, my mother and Sophie, safe, thank God. I was so relieved. Why someone started that false story I'll never know. I boarded the train with her and stayed with Sophie until the last possible moment, because there was always a chance the Germans might still come looking.

Many years later, after I was established in Canada, my uncle wrote to tell me that he had heard Sophie was working in a library somewhere in eastern Ontario. My husband tracked down her address, and I wrote her a very nice, warm letter, telling her how pleased and happy I was to learn that she was alive and well, and that I would be so happy to see her again. She wrote back, "I don't remember anything about that story. I don't make any money in Canada, so don't count on my giving you any." Something like that.

Germans supervising destruction of Jewish graveyard, Poland, 1943

Her words hit me like a thunderbolt; I felt deeply hurt. Never before, not when I sent the letter, and never since, have I ever once thought about asking for money. I didn't write to her again. She is one of those people who have obliterated their past, and doesn't want to know the truth.

LVOV

It wasn't long before the neighbors started to talk. Marysia came to us at the end of July 1942, and Olga and Stefan soon after. At first everything was okay. But when Stefan or Olga needed something, they would come to our house, and people began to notice.

Marysia was my "niece," but I thought to myself, how will I explain what kind of a niece she is when the Germans start searching for Jews in hiding? What would I do? They would ask, who is she? Why is she staying with you? Where are her other relatives? Where is she from? In fact, after she had been with us for a few months the neighbors were already asking each other these questions. I became frightened about what might happen to us if we remained in Tarnobrzeg.

My mother and I decided it would be best for me to take Marysia to a bigger city where nobody would know us. I would give up my job and we would go to Lvov to live with my sister Halina. My mother, who was not so adventurous, would go back to Sandomierz to live with my youngest sister and my aunt. So, late in September, Marysia and I left. Of course, the school director, Dr. Polowicz, knew why.

Our journey was extremely dangerous. The train was in poor condition, short of coal, and it was always stopping, making long delays for supplies or because of damaged bridges. Lvov is not so far from Tarnobrzeg; normally the train took only eight hours, but this time it was two days. All through the trip I was very, very frightened, even though I thought I was probably not the only one with a Jewish child. I prayed. What else could I do? In the night, Germans marched through the train with their dogs, looking at the children and the other people. Once, while we waited for another train to pass, I saw them take people—families with children—off the train, taking them behind a building, and then I heard shots. It was very frightening. At any moment it could happen to me, or Marysia—at any moment.

Marysia was small. She curled up in my arms and tried to sleep. I didn't sleep at all. I had brought food for the journey, but neither of us was hungry. The child understood so very well what was happening. It was as if she became an adult all at once, growing as much in one night as another does in a lifetime. She knew that a particular uniform meant danger and that she couldn't talk or walk anywhere without me. Each hour was dangerous. God must have helped me; they didn't look at us.

We arrived in Lvov and made our way to my sister's apartment only to discover that this too was a dangerous place. Unknown to me, Halina and my future brother-in-law, Slawek, belonged to an underground resistance group. It was a committee that organized the Lvov branch of Zegota, a Warsaw group that was bringing money to Polish Jews in hiding. I soon joined them, so from that point on I was helping not just one or two but a great many others.

This was not a good place for Marysia, so a few days later we found a safer place for her nearby in the Felician convent, where there were already thirty-five Jewish children in hiding. The Germans allowed convents to look after orphans—not Jews, but orphans. The nuns took in every orphan that needed help, which happened, of course, to be mostly Jewish children, and so Marysia survived the war in their care. When the war ended she found her mother, who survived Auschwitz. Her father died in Bergen-Belsen.

ZEGOTA

I became a Zegota courier, traveling often to Warsaw to bring back money from the Polish government-in-exile in London. The Warsaw group had an underground press for printing counterfeit documents and false identity papers for Jews, and I brought these back to Lvov, too. Another job we had was contact with Janowicka, the big work camp for Jews in Lvov. On one visit we would deliver false papers to certain people, and then on the next, help them prepare to escape from the camp. If we learned that someone needed special medicine, we delivered it right to that person, not to the Germans. Sometimes we delivered money either to someone in the camp or perhaps to someone in hiding. Many people were hiding and they had to have money to give the person buying food for them. I did all these things.

At that time, each day in my country was dangerous. Each day. But Lvov was even more dangerous than other places because so many Ukrainians were living there who understood Polish very well. They might easily say, "Look at those two people walking over there. One of them is a Jew." You didn't have to wait long, either. They'd take you from the street, and that was that. Finished. You cannot imagine what it was like.

The Nazi intent was to destroy the Polish nation completely. They treated Poles as badly as Jews, although often the Jews don't recognize that: they say Jews were treated far worse. But to help just one Jew, you had to have the help of many other Poles. To get one loaf of bread one person must send another into the street, and already three people know about a Jew who needs to eat. If the Germans found out about this Jew, they'd kill not only him but the three other people as well. There were many Poles who hid Jewish people and went with them to the grave. It's another side of the story.

ARREST

Every few days I went to visit Marysia, but one day I did not arrive. I had been making frequent trips to Warsaw for Zegota, because I knew the city so well. This time on the return trip, approximately halfway back to Lvov, Germans came into the compartment and made a search, looking at baggage, papers, everything. They found all the Zegota papers in my bag on the overhead rack. There was no way to hide them. Not knowing whose bag it was, they arrested all twelve people in the compartment and took us to the Lublin jail.

At first I didn't tell them the bag was mine. One by one, they searched and interrogated each person, and of course, nobody knew anything about these papers or the organization. The others in the compartment were people carrying a little meat or fruit; none of them had papers. I was the only person without a good reason for coming from Warsaw to Lvov, so they concluded that it had to be me, and I had a very bad time.

I was kept in the Lublin jail one month. Every few days I was tortured. They put me in a chair and struck me with a belt. While one beat me, the other asked questions about the organization and who was working for it—a thousand questions like that. We had spoken many times in the underground about what to do if caught. I knew that I must talk, otherwise they would probably kill me. So I started telling them I knew some men, but I didn't know their names, only their first names.

"Where do they live?"

"In a store by a restaurant."

"What kind of restaurant?"

I told them about a restaurant where I'd never been. I built up a completely phony story. They asked me about this story every time they interrogated me and I repeated it over and over. The Germans made telephone calls to Lvov to confirm this story I had made up, but it was very hard in those days to telephone from one city to another—not like today when you dial and you're connected—so they weren't sure.

I was in very poor shape, completely black and blue. I was in a cell by myself, sleeping in my coat on the floor. There was no mattress. Nothing. At that point I gave up hope for my life. I knew that in the next day or two they would shoot me. I had carried documents for an illegal organization. They had to shoot me. There was no alternative. I even wrote a letter saying goodbye to my family.

One day in the jail infirmary where I was treated for the beatings, I met a lady with underground connections. The wife of a prominent person in the Polish government-in-exile, she had somehow learned that there were political prisoners in this place and had come especially to meet me, to try to help me. When I told her my story she said, "Okay, write this in a letter and I will get it out for you." I couldn't send it to my mother and sister in Sandomierz because I had told the Germans everybody was dead. So although it was for my sister Hanka, the letter was sent to my cousin's address, to let my family know where I had finished my life.

I didn't write that I was in jail, only that I was in Lublin. I told them not to look for me because I was near the end and this would be my last letter. Afterwards Hanka told me when she got my letter she was so scared she didn't say anything to our mother for two whole days. But then she told her everything and said, "I'm going to Lublin to find Basha." And she did.

Hanka came by herself to Lublin and started making enquiries about me at all the German offices. It was not a smart thing to do, but she was only fifteen years old and not so clever about these matters. After a whole day of going round from one place to another, somebody told her to try the jail. At the jail she asked a guard if there was someone there answering to my description. He was a lonely guy, so he said okay, he would take a look for her. He came back and said, "Yes, she is here." "May I see her?" He said no. God help us that we didn't meet then because she was in the jail at exactly the time when I was being tortured. I was downstairs and she was upstairs. If we had met by chance in the corridor she would probably have yelled to me, "Barbara! What are you doing here? It's a mistake!" giving away my whole story, and be jailed herself. I had told them she was dead.

Hanka Szymanska, Barbara Makuch's youngest sister, 1943

Instead, Hanka went away, returning later with a small package to leave for me. She packed up things I would know: her sweater, some stockings—the sweater I knew for sure—some bread, a piece of sugar, and butter. I recognized her handwriting on the wrapping paper and knew that she had been there and that now Halina would know where I was too; they would take precautions for their safety. Indeed, Hanka went straight from Lublin to Lvov to tell Halina about finding me in the Lublin jail. Then Halina immediately warned everyone in the organization, and they all moved to new quarters, to new addresses. I had not known every person in the group, but in Lvov alone I knew perhaps twenty-two people who were involved.

I was so relieved to realize that Halina would be warned and maybe everything would be okay for her; for myself, I never expected to leave that place. Never.

After my arrest, my sister and Slawek continued to work for Zegota, but Halina became more and more nervous and afraid. She always carried poison with her because she could not be sure what she might say if she was tortured. Thank God the Germans took me and not her, because if they had caught her she would be dead. Somehow I managed to stay alive.

After one month, they took me in handcuffs from the Lublin jail to Lvov. It was not until much later that I learned why, but it seems that at exactly the same time they caught me on the train, they also caught an entire resistance group in Lvov—not connected to Zegota: it was AKA, which means "Underground Soldiers." About thirty people were captured together at a meeting. The Germans couldn't figure out if I was connected with them, so I was brought to Lvov.

PRISON

Our train stopped at the big central station in Lvov; people were lined up as usual on the platform to meet the passengers. As we stepped down, the first person I saw was a young man I recognized from our organization; of course, he had come to meet someone else. He knew from Halina that I was in the Lublin jail, but he didn't know anything about my transfer to Lvov. Nobody knew. When he looked at me, I put my hand up to my head, to show him I was handcuffed. My German guards didn't notice. It was their first time in Lvov, and they were so confused they had to ask me for directions! All day that young man from Zegota followed us until at last

Guards at Loncki prison, where Barbara was incarcerated, Lvov, 1943

he saw us go into Loncki, a very large, dangerous, infamous prison, where many thousands of lives went down.

I was put in isolation, in a very small cell. The interrogations and beatings stopped.

The week of my name day—in Poland we celebrate name days, rather than birthdays, and I was going to be twenty—I received a beautiful little letter from Halina and Slawek. Somebody threw it into my cell. We called these letters *grypsy.* You used a very small piece of paper and rolled it up like a cigarette. Right away I recognized the handwriting. "My dear," she wrote, "we are so proud of you. Because of you we are all safe. We owe our organization to your strength. Thank you very much. We kiss you. Be good. Be brave." I was very touched and encouraged to receive this message. I had already been in their hands a whole month and no one else was arrested. The stories and names I had told them were completely false. Hope existed.

And now I knew for sure they knew I was in this jail, and I saw it was possible to have some kind of communication. This is how we did it. The prison didn't do any washing, but a charitable organization arranged it so that every week or two I could send out a small package of dirty laundry to my family and receive a few clean clothes back.

A real letter was impossible, so instead I pulled a little thread from a small place in the hem of my chemise, wrote a few very small words right on the cloth, and after sewing it up again with the same piece of thread, sent the chemise with the laundry. It could only be two or three words, not a real letter. When the clean laundry came back, or whenever somebody brought me anything, I always looked for a hidden little piece of paper; it was the only way to correspond. I knew Halina was receiving these messages because one day I asked for a certain ointment for some trouble I was having with my hand, and in the next package that came to me, the ointment was there. I never asked her how she discovered the message.

Still, I am amazed that I survived. There were moments when I felt I was already dead. No fresh air, no windows, only a very small piece of sky. I was completely alone in that cell for six weeks: it was the hardest test.

One day, sitting on the floor as usual, I heard someone in the next cell. Whoever was on the other side heard me, too. We discovered that the wall had bricks made with a hole in the middle of each one; the entire wall between us was built with this type of brick. With a spoon I dug out the mortar from the hole in one of the bricks on my side, and she did the same from her side. Pretty soon we had made a little hole in the wall and could just barely see each other.

"Now show me your nose."

"Show me your eye."

"Now, some more."

"What color is your hair?"

Her name was Eva. She told me her whole story and I told her mine. We promised each other that if one of us left Loncki prison, we would tell somebody the story of the other one. She was part of the AKA group of thirty arrested in Lvov the day I was taken to Lublin jail. She told me the Germans had already hung six of the men from lamp posts in the street.

*Dr. Henryk Meisel
and his wife, 1941*

Eva had studied German and spoke the language beautifully. One time when she was taken down to an interrogation, she told the Germans she was a professor of the German language. They started laughing, saying it was impossible. They had beaten her badly, and she was completely black. "When the Germans started laughing at me, saying, 'No, Eva, this is impossible, you don't know German,' I was in so much pain, I began to recite German poetry," she told me. You never know how you will react. If somebody had asked me what I would do if that had happened to me, I could not have said. It's very hard to prepare yourself.

A week passed. Then, in the early morning darkness someone opened her door. "Get out!" I heard through the hole. Then it was completely quiet. Previously when she went for an interview with the Germans, she would knock on the wall later and tell me about it. But this day and the next it was completely quiet. There was a very nice German guard who knew her—he didn't know about our talking. When he opened the small window in my cell door to give me food, he told me she was in the cellar and he didn't think she would come back. The next day she didn't return. The third day he told me they had killed her and another girl who I didn't know.

I had promised her I would pray if she died, but I couldn't do it. I can't even pray today, I absolutely cannot. From that moment on I became very depressed. There was a small toilet and wash basin in the cell, but I stopped washing myself. I stopped sleeping. I even stopped eating for a few weeks. I laid down on the floor and couldn't even go to the door to take my soup. I completely lost the strength to live. I felt that in a little while my life would end.

Maybe my mother was thinking especially strongly about me that day— she told me later she thought about me every day—because all at once I thought, "Wait. Am I going to let myself die here on the floor? No, not so easily. No." Suddenly I recognized that what I was doing was stupid. The Germans hadn't killed me, I was killing myself.

I tore a piece of cloth from my dress, took some water from the toilet and started to clean the cell, inch by inch, inch by inch. I was so weak, but I cleaned anyway, hour after hour, day after day—the floor, the walls—and when I finished I started all over again. This was very good exercise for me. After several weeks, somehow, my strength came back. Later, after I was transferred to another cell with companions, I saw how strong I was inside, and then I understood that the person most dangerous to me was myself.

DR. MEISEL

One day my German guard told me about a well-known doctor being held in the prison. When he said the name, I recognized who he was: a world-famous microbiologist who had discovered the vaccine for typhus. Halina had worked for his family in Lvov. He knew about my family and I knew about him, although we had never met. Dr. Meisel and his wife were in this same prison because they were Jews and the Germans wanted him to work for them. They were being kept in the basement, in a wet place. Everyone in this jail was sick, and for the doctor it was an especially terrible place; his morale was poor. The guard told me he was very close to breaking down. I made a package for him of half the medicine and ointment the prison doctor had given me for my injuries, along with what I had in the way of extra warm clothes. Maybe there was also a piece of bread from my ration, too. I asked the guard if he would deliver it to Dr. Meisel. A few days later the guard told me that Dr. Meisel was taken somewhere else and I forgot all about this incident.

After the war I was in Cracow visiting a close friend when she told me that Dr. Meisel, whom she knew, also happened to be in town. I told her I would be very glad to meet him. A few hours later he arrived at her apartment with several students. When I answered the door, he knelt down before me, this older man, kissed my hand, and said, "Please, I want to thank you. You were the first person who gave me help when I badly needed it. You saved my life." It turned out that from the jail he had been taken to a concentration camp, and somehow he had survived. Of course, I felt happy that I had been able to help him at that terrible time, but still, I was somewhat astonished and deeply moved by his touching gesture. He was a gentleman.

While I was in the Lvov prison, Slawek was working on my case, reporting my situation to people high up in Zegota, and they in turn were trying everything possible to save me, even giving bribes to various Germans. Finally, they had some success. Instead of execution, I was sent to Ravensbruck, the biggest concentration camp exclusively for women. It was the best they could do. At least there I had some hope of remaining alive.

RAVENSBRUCK

I arrived in the camp late in 1943 and did not come out until the war ended, May 1945, about two years altogether. Ravensbruck held nearly 150,000 women. I was number 36,000. If you have a really good imagination and can form the most vivid picture of hell—it won't even come close. You simply can not imagine how it was. Jail was nothing compared to the concentration camp. Nothing. In the camp, people destroyed themselves. They died like flies if they were not strong enough.

Some people who came to the camp, we called them "god-trees." They stayed in one place all day long, not moving, not eating, and slowly everything became mixed up in their heads. They had no feeling, no strength; they would ask others to do everything for them. You couldn't be that way and survive.

In our passports each nation had some symbol: "J" for Jews, a big "P" for Poles. For many Jews it was only "Thief," stamped in green. If you were homosexual or lesbian, they knew—your documents were stamped in lilac. But in the barracks we weren't separated. When you arrived you were sent wherever there was an empty place. There were only thirty-six barracks, and Ravensbruck was always full.

They were always counting us to make sure everyone was there. You had nothing to wear, only one dress, with nothing under it, and terrible shoes, made from two strips of cloth. Never any stockings or a sweater—nothing to keep you warm at five o'clock, four o'clock, sometimes three o'clock in the morning, when it was so very cold that you stood near one another to try to keep warm. Many people died there in the "street," as we called it.

Breakfast was one cup of black coffee and one piece of breadcrust. Later, soup, made with water, cabbage, sometimes one potato, and maybe a horse bone, but mostly cabbage, or turnips. In the evening again we had one little piece of bread, nothing else.

When the concentration camp was still small, each person had a bed: four pieces of wood, straw, and one blanket. Later, when more people came, two women shared a bed, then three.

I was very thin—all my bones stuck out—but inside I knew I was strong. My experience in jail taught me that. And again I was lucky, because I found somebody who knew my family: Mary Siweci, a Polish lady who

Work squad at Ravensbruck concentration camp, c. 1943

had been a pharmacist in Sandomierz. She was not exactly a political prisoner, but something like that. Whenever the Germans occupied a city, the first thing they did was arrest the prominent people, because they knew that they were the leaders. At first they filled the jails with these people, but soon they were sent to the concentration camps. In the little city of Sandomierz the prominent people were the doctor and the pharmacist. For six years Mrs. Siweci stayed in Ravensbruck—all through the war. She had made connections, used her wits, and survived.

In certain respects the concentration camp resembled the real world: there were good and bad people. And in the camp, as in the rest of the world, there were different classes. At the top were the survivors, who were strong and smart, who knew how to do business, you might say. When I came, Mary Siweci was working in the kitchen cutting bread, which made her a person of real importance. If a lady was working in the laundry, or with a sewing machine, or making sweaters for the German soldiers, she was already somebody important, but most important of all were the people working in the kitchen.

The class system meant that if you were in the kitchen, you were not hungry, and you could bring a piece of food to someone else. When Mrs. Siweci found me, she started to help in a significant way. The first day I received an onion, the most valuable present of all. Even a piece of bread was not as important as an onion, because an onion contained vitamins for health. If later on you received a piece of bread, you put the onion on the bread, and this was something truly special. When I received under-wear, and then warm stockings, I knew I was going to survive.

All the time, five crematoriums were operating before our eyes. Each morning we stood in line while the Germans looked us over. One day maybe someone's mouth didn't look right, or their eyes, or hair, or skin. They pulled the women out of line and sent them to the chimney. Just like that.

Each day, people I knew went to the chimneys. One day I was talking with my girlfriend from the same barrack. The next morning she was gone;

Crematoria at Ravensbruck concentration camp, c. 1945

the Germans took her. I knew that the next day they might send me to take out the ashes and put them in the fields. I did that only once, but many people did it every day. You started to become completely numb, like a stone, to feel nothing, absolutely nothing. You had no idea what would happen to you the next moment. You lived each day, each moment, one at a time.

I worked in many places in the camp. For a while I was working in the fields, then in the squad of twenty-five or thirty women who were working outside of the camp making airplane parts. In the morning we walked a few miles to the factory, worked the whole day, and walked back to the camp at night. I was transferred many times from one place to another until finally I was working in the kitchen with the lady from Sandomierz. There I had more bread, I could eat enough. When our workday finished, I took a small bottle of extra soup back to sick ladies in the barracks.

LIBERATION

We had a secret radio in the factory so we always had some news. And squads working outside the camp also brought us news. We knew very well how the war was going, where the Russians were, where the Germans were, and we knew when the end was near.

The last few months, as the end approached, the Germans grew very afraid of the Soviets. They began spreading rumors that they would burn the whole camp to ashes if the Russians came. They stepped up the selections. Those who were sick, who couldn't walk, or who didn't get up for the morning roll call were sent straight to the chimney.

In January or February 1945, the Germans accepted an agreement of the Geneva Convention which allowed the International Red Cross to take sick people from the camp, but only those whom the Germans allowed to go. Big school busses appeared to collect a few people. Again, you needed some connections or you had to be a prominent person. I remember they let out some Norwegians, a few professionals, and people of well-known families. This was very good because those people would survive and might say something after the war. I never thought I would live to tell this story myself. I never once dreamed I would be in the West telling this story. So it was very important that the people who understood the situation be the first to go out and tell the world how it was. I think maybe five hundred people left for Norway during February, March, and April of 1945.

Then the day came when the Germans told us that anyone who couldn't walk would be left behind, and they'd burn everything. Everyone who could walk would go with them. They agreed to leave the old and sick with a few people who said they would care for them, but those of us who were working didn't know about this. We started walking.

First, the officers and higher officials vanished—escaped altogether. Some of the others took off their uniforms and put on our camp clothes so they wouldn't be recognized. But this didn't help. Many of them now had to face the revenge of women they had mistreated, and it was very, very bad. The Russian women were the worst. I saw with my own eyes Russian women attack a Nazi officer. They took him into the bushes, tortured, and killed him right away. They knew nobody would say anything.

It was April 1945, and we were walking across Germany to the west. The only Germans with us were the low-ranking soldiers and their dogs. The entire highway was clogged with people; it was so crowded that you were in a line moving in one direction, impossible to change.

The Germans took us by military roads, past fields where there were frequent aerial attacks. It was the last days of the war. The earth rumbled and shook beneath our feet, like being on the ocean, and it all made such a big noise. We walked and walked, from maybe the twentieth of April until the third of May.

I remember that day very well. It was rainy and dark when we came to a small city not far from the ocean. We could go no further because night was coming on. I had a very big headache from my bad teeth and nothing warm to wear. I found a big warm shawl, dirty of course, but I picked it up and put it on. We were in one long line in the road, a thousand people, more or less. German people came, bringing us vegetables or fruit to eat, whatever they had. We asked where we were, what was happening. They told us that the Russian and American armies were about to meet here. And indeed during the night an historic moment occurred: the Germans surrendered. We could see and hear the weapons being thrown down. An enormous bonfire of these weapons burned until morning. Many people were crying, "Thank God, they are finished with this war." But others were not so happy about it, yelling, "We'll come back!" A few were like that, not giving up their weapons but shooting themselves, patriotically.

The German soldiers were still with us. They went over to the American officers saying to them, "We are bringing these people to you from jail."

"From jail?"

"We are political prisoners," replied some of the old women the Germans brought along because they could speak fluent English.

"All these women!" The Americans could hardly believe it. They prepared an empty school building for us with beautiful, nice, fresh straw all over the floor, and for the first time, we finally slept a night in warmth, under a roof. It felt wonderful.

Now we were free to go wherever we wished. Some women went directly to Hamburg, fifty kilometers to the north, where there were boats waiting and the passage was free. But I had my two sisters and mother at home. I had been away so long, I didn't know what had happened at Sandomierz. Were they all right? What had happened to the town? My father had been dead since the first year of the war; as the elder sister I felt responsible. I joined a group going to Poland.

I walked with them toward my home until the end of May. We had no money. For food, we went from house to house. One day we came to a house that looked empty, but in the dining room we found a family of six Germans sitting in their chairs. Everyone was dead; they had slit their wrists.

At first it was a large group of about fifteen women walking together to Poland. We had no leader. As we got closer to our homes we split off

into smaller and smaller groups going in different directions. Being women, walking at that time was very difficult because the territory we crossed was entirely under Russian occupation. Every afternoon we looked for a place to barricade ourselves in for the night.

I was not very brave. I was a chicken, really hiding, and nothing happened to me, but many were not so lucky. The Russian soldiers were just like animals when they were drunk, and they were always drunk.

My last ride into Sandomierz was on the evening of May 28, on the roof of a train filled with coal. The station is across the Vistula River from the town, and the bridge is very long, but I walked across as if I had wings on my arms.

For the previous six months I had heard nothing from my family. Before that, my mother had been allowed to send a small monthly food package to Ravensbruck. Sometimes I received it, sometimes I didn't. I also sent her a letter. Of course, the letter only said that everything was beautiful and nice, that I was working and healthy, which was all we were allowed to write. But at least they knew I was alive, and I knew they were alive. However, for half that year their area on the Vistula River had become the front, and I had heard nothing from them.

When I arrived at the house, my aunt and her two girls were there, but my mother was at evening Mass. I ran to meet her. You can imagine how it was, the first time we met. Of course, everybody was crying.

They washed me, fed me, gave me everything. I related my whole story from the time of my arrest. I told them everything. My mother looked at me. Later she came to the bathroom to help me wash my back, staying with me a long time. Finally she stood before me and said, "I know you are telling the truth. I know you were there, but nevertheless, it is unbelievable."

When I told the story again to everybody around the table—friends, neighbors, people coming and going, whoever would stop to listen—nobody could believe it. It was impossible to believe.

In Ottawa I was once asked to tell my story at a symposium. It was the first time in my life that I spoke before an audience, and with my poor English, I was trembling. When I finished, a young man asked: "Why did you help while so many other people from Poland did not?" "How can I answer for the whole nation?" I said, "I can only answer for myself." He and his parents were Polish Jews living now in Toronto who had had terrible experiences during the war. I told them that I cannot answer even for my closest neighbor, but I could say, thank God, my sister helped as I did.

Now I am able to tell this story, but during the war it was not so easy; it was very hard. I could always feel my heart squeezing, not knowing what was going to happen in the next five minutes. It was like being in a cage with vicious dogs. I never had time to analyze why I did these things, or that maybe I shouldn't. I had no time for that. I knew that more people should have been helping, but I realize that others may not have had as much strength, or as much help as I had from my mother. From the beginning, she told us that if we can, we must help others; we can't all hide under the pillow. If she had said no to what I was doing, or had started to cry, maybe I wouldn't have done it. I just don't know. But I didn't have that kind of situation. I was fortunate.

Halina Szymanska Ogrodzinska

DR. OLGA

Dr. Olga was perfect for us; she took us in and treated us like her daughters. The Lilien family was absolutely Polonized—completely assimilat-

Halina Szymanska Ogrodzinska, Sandomierz, 1987

ed. They are from Lvov, a family of doctors. Dr. Olga's father was a pediatrician and she is a pediatrician too. [My friend] Olla's mother was a mathematician, and Olla also was very clever in mathematics, so good that the Soviets at our school in Krzemieniec were urging her to study in Moscow. All of that family were intelligentsia. So it is very simple why we looked out for Dr. Olga later on—we had a debt. When the Germans came it was a great tragedy for the Jewish people. That's when I sent Olga to Basha.

I was surprised to hear her say recently that she was so brave and never afraid during the war, that everything was all right. This must be some kind of psychological process. She is against any idea that she must have been persecuted. This feeling was probably less so at the time of the war but has grown stronger over the years. She would like to confirm that that was not her question, that she was not Jewish looking, that everything was all right, and that she was running without danger. In fact, she *was* very brave.

Today Olga is still a very intelligent and quite clever person. She's always helpful to everyone, and always without money, because if she has something, she gives it away. During the war she lost her whole family.

DR. MEISEL

Typhus was epidemic in wartime, especially at the front, where it was a calamity; so naturally the Germans were quite attentive to Dr. Weigl's research. When they occupied Lvov they immediately asked him to set up a vaccine production plant at his institute. It was in a school taken over for the purpose, and about a thousand people worked there, including me.

Because the Weigl Institute employees had special identity cards printed with the words "Military Institute," they were protected from many of the repressive German measures, and so people from all the different underground organizations were working there—it was like Noah's ark. At the head of this institution was a Dr. Ayre, a military captain, I think. He was German, but quite liberal, and a good man; his only desire was that the work be done. I don't know when or under what circumstances Dr. Meisel arrived, but it was Dr. Ayre who arranged for him and his wife, both bacteriologists, to come and work at this institute. They equipped two big rooms with all the instruments needed to carry on their research. But they weren't working on typhus: Dr. Meisel's specialty was certain bacteria that grow without oxygen and are important for stopping infections in wounds, a subject the German military was very interested in. I had strong reason to think that the brilliant professional advance of Dr. Ayre had a little bit to do with Dr. Meisel's research.

The Meisels were living and working at the institute, and they were not allowed to leave. They were interned, a bit like prisoners. But it was much better for them there than living in the ghetto since they always had something to eat, and they could work. I was in sympathy with them and so were the other Poles working there, and the Meisels liked me, and were very good to me. So I thought it was necessary to speak to them—as a person coming from the outside—to tell them to be careful. But except for moral support it was impossible to help them in this situation.

During the months I was working in Dr. Meisel's laboratory, I was going very often to their home to give Polish literature lessons to their daughter, Felka. Each time, Dr. Meisel's mother, the old lady, would make scrambled eggs or an omelet, always urging me to "eat, eat, eat," which I did because I was still a teenager and always hungry. At this time Dr. Meisel was beginning to realize that the situation for the Jews had become quite intolerable, and he had to do something about his large family. He saw it would be impossible to save everyone. With the help of some friends he arranged to send Mrs. Meisel's sister, Nina, to Warsaw, and she survived. Felka went to the orphanage run by the nuns of the Felician convent. Then Dr. Meisel had a long discussion with the old lady. They decided that because she was so old, the best solution would be for her to take poison. Being a doctor he could give her something good that would cause no pain. They never spoke about this with the rest of the family, and one day she was dead—like that. I was still very young but Dr. Meisel liked to talk to me, and he badly needed to speak with someone. He told me he had a very heavy heart, but I already knew that.

One day the authorities asked Dr. Ayre to eliminate all the Jews working for him, no exceptions. Ayre explained to them that the work of these people was important for the German army, but it was of no use; Dr. Meisel and his wife had to go to Auschwitz. The Germans had some sort of laboratory arrangement in the concentration camp, a little bit similar to the Weigl Institute, with worse eating and living conditions certainly, but the Meisels could still work on their research there. In general, I think that family came through the war rather well. Today Felka is a doctor and her Polish husband is a doctor too.

ZEGOTA

Zegota began its work in Lvov in 1943, but we couldn't wait that long to start helping Jews. We were in the PPS, the Polish Socialist Party, and many of our members and comrades were Jewish. So when the Germans came to Lvov, we had a lot of people to help. Among the intelligentsia, everyone knew everyone else. It wasn't necessary to have meetings; it was enough to just meet someone on the street and tell them you must do this or that.

The need for help came in waves. The first wave was when the Germans arrived. We tried to do whatever was possible for the Jewish people, mostly hiding them or sending them to other cities. I was frequently going into the Jewish quarter, before the Germans closed it. I would come out looking very fat, because I was wearing layers of clothing belonging to someone preparing to leave. They couldn't go out carrying luggage.

When the ghetto was formed, that was the second wave. If someone decided to take the risk to leave, we would help them. Zegota was providing a certain amount of money for each Jewish person, but if you were preparing to escape you needed more. The Jews would give us some valuables, perhaps jewelry, to hide for them, or to sell outside of the ghetto where you could certainly get a better price. In those cases we hid the money for them. We even had specialists for selling these things. When someone was ready to leave—sometimes it was just one person, sometimes a whole family—we would escort them, usually to Warsaw, where it was easier for them. I did that only once, but I had friends who did it many times. The assimilated people were easier for us, especially if they weren't very Jewish-looking and spoke Polish or German well, but we had some who were very Jewish-looking and who spoke Polish very badly, and they were very difficult. For example, there was the local trade union of feathermakers, a group of very brave women, but it was absolutely impossible to do anything for them. We could send their men to the partisans, but for these women, nothing. They refused to leave their families or friends. It was simply impossible to hide twenty people in your home.

When Zegota was organized, it was primarily for the distribution of money; before that time there was no special fund for Jews. If somebody lived underground, as Jews had to, they needed money to live: to pay rent, to buy food. They couldn't earn it. Olga, of course, was a special case. Another thing we did was to bring the people in hiding newspapers from the underground press, to help raise morale. They were very happy to have them. It was also very significant in the moral sense to visit them while it was still possible. After the second wave the ghetto was closed and a social visit was out of the question.

The last wave was when the ghetto was liquidated; then there was much less work. Some people who were in the underground needed protection, but otherwise there was no new work.

THE LANDAU FAMILY

When I was working at the Weigl Institute I lived in a rented flat with a friend and comrade from PPS, Maryna. My most vivid memory of that whole period was the night we had the Landau family. Maryna knew them very well; they were eminent people. He was a well-known defense lawyer specializing in political trials. For many months the Landaus had been told that for their own safety they must leave the ghetto, but Mr. Landau was a member of the Judenrat [Jewish Council] and felt it was morally wrong to leave his people. Then, the last night before the liquidation of the ghetto, he decided to go. A woman I had never met before visited us saying there was no place for the Landaus except in our home. I told her it was all right, and that same evening they arrived. We put them in an

empty room, with only a mattress on the bare floor. It was winter and there was no running water. Maryna and I were very nervous; we stayed awake reading through the night, not even getting undressed. Suddenly there was a knock on the door, very loud. Everybody was frightened; we didn't know what to do. The flat was up several stories, impossible to jump, and those poor people didn't even have poison. There were a few underground newspapers lying about; we started to shove them into the fire. All of a sudden the door flew open—the police. It was clear they knew very well Landau was there. They pushed us aside and went straight to the other end of the apart-

Halina Szymanska Ogrodzinska, 1940

ment after them. I heard Mrs. Landau start to cry. Maryna grabbed my hand and we ran downstairs and out the front door. We saw a police car waiting on the street, but no guards around. We ran across the back garden, climbed over the wall, and hid in the bushes until dawn when the curfew was over. No one came after us. They didn't want us; it was the Landaus they were after.

When the Germans came for Jewish people it was a little bit different than for political people. When they took someone for political reasons it was more carefully done. For Jewish people it was quite simple; they just took them.

I felt terrible; I was unable to save people who were in my house, and I had the horrible feeling that somebody had betrayed us. And then the awful feeling that I had run away and left them: it wasn't polite, but I had no choice. Perhaps if I had been stupid enough to try to do something and not escape—but Maryna was energetic enough to push me into running away. That episode was very unpleasant, very uncomfortable.

I didn't go back to the Weigl Institute the next day. Somebody told Dr. Ayre what the situation was, and he told them to let me know that I could come back to work, he wouldn't object. He said I could work until the Gestapo officially asked him to fire me, but I was not willing to wait for the Gestapo. Dr. Ayre was a German. I want to be fair.

BARBARA (BASHA)

Basha was in Tarnobrzeg with Mama where she didn't have the opportunity to work for the underground. She was very happy there. In Lvov, in this Poland of terrorists, it was an altogether different world; the atmosphere was very unpleasant. When the situation in Lvov became very difficult we told Olga to go to Basha and Mama in Tarnobrzeg. Not long after, Basha came to Lvov with the little girl, Marysia.

When she arrived, Basha had never heard of Zegota, but we needed people and Slawek immediately took her in. She wasn't especially political; she joined us for private reasons, for family reasons. Certainly I was more political than she was.

Slawek arranged for Marysia to go to the orphanage run by the Felician convent, where she would be safer, the same place where Dr. Meisel's daughter, Felka, was staying.

We had quite a good time, Basha and I; it was very easy to be close with her. Sometimes she was a little bit authoritative; she liked to take charge of things. Since I had been independent for so many years, I didn't like that very much, but otherwise we got on very well together. She looked for nice things for me to wear. She could sew well and made me beautiful blouses, and helped me fix up my poor hair. We were young girls and those things were very important, even during the war. It was a small society in this Polish Socialist Party. I don't even know if she was officially a member; it wasn't necessary. She was working together with us. My friends accepted her very quickly; they all liked her. We were a group of friends and we did what was needed.

Living together in Lvov, Basha was so warm. I remember that she gave me a lot of love. But I think I had lived alone more than she had and I looked at life more realistically. She was always a great fantasist, always optimistic. If one fantasy didn't work out, she would easily substitute another. It made me nervous. I think I judged our possibilities or people's intentions more realistically. But Basha's whole life was like that. The work in Zegota was perhaps easier for her because she always had the idea that everything would be all right.

It was the only period in my life that I lived together with Basha. We had a two-room apartment on a nice, quiet street. Under the floor of one room was a very sophisticated storage place where every evening we carefully hid Basha's Zegota documents. We felt there was a good chance we wouldn't be found out; the Germans couldn't look everywhere, after all.

At times Basha's work was very nerve-wracking—it was hard for her. She had to help people going from one place to another: to buy them train tickets, or to look out for someone, very tense, who was going to the train station. She took it all to heart, and it was exhausting.

But then in Tarnobrzeg perhaps it was also a bit dangerous. In one room Basha had these two Jewish people, Olga and Marysia. I don't think Basha even knew Marysia before. It was characteristic of my mother and sister that they would have needed much more courage to turn them out than to give them shelter. It was very dangerous for everyone around. Olga was not always there, but often enough for people to notice. She looked very Jewish, everyone could see that.

It's not easy to say just what it was that made people look Jewish. Sometimes it was the bad pronunciation of Polish words. Other times it was their nervousness that gave them away. Some people had a certain look to their face, to their mouth. Perhaps it was something in their attitude. The police knew when someone was a Jew because they did not look at them directly and were nervous—they looked afraid. They could almost smell Jewish people. Well, the Polish people were nervous too. When the Germans began offering two hundred deutsche marks for turning in a Jew, some people started noticing these things—this one looks like this, that one is like that. It was a public madness.

I don't know how many trips Basha made for Zegota, but she didn't work very long before she was arrested, I'm sorry to say. She didn't go to Warsaw often because it was a dangerous route. People were always subject to searches by the German police—not the Gestapo, but the police. In the train they were always looking for people, sometimes more carefully, sometimes less so. One time they might arrest a woman carrying butter and sausages under her skirt, another time Jewish people, or people for political reasons.

Basha's arrest was somewhat the fault of the Zegota central office in Warsaw; they gave her too much to carry. She took this suitcase with a false bottom in which they hid a great many documents. She also had a thermos with the paper insulation between the inner and outer bottles replaced with money. She had a lot of things.

When Basha was arrested she was badly beaten, but somehow she remained optimistic and was able to send news of herself to our youngest sister, Hanka, in Sandomierz. Hanka was small, blond, and thin. She often wore a blue sports jacket and white knee socks, and looked a little bit like a Hitler Jugend. She came like that—a very brave girl—to the Lublin Gestapo asking for her sister and insisting that they deliver the food package she brought to Basha. Most likely expecting to frighten her, the Gestapo left this little girl alone in a room with a huge, fierce-looking dog trained to attack people. When he returned, Hanka and the dog were playing together—she liked animals. The Gestapo officer accepted her food package.

When I first found out about Basha's arrest I was afraid, and I was sorry.

I didn't know what to do. I thought even if we changed houses the Gestapo would still find us. Of course, we immediately changed every address. Later, the owner of the house where we had been living told me that the Gestapo had come. They forced the door and searched, but found nothing.

Some people in our group didn't believe Basha would be strong. She wasn't a member of the party and had been with us for only a short time. The organization tried to work through cells of five people, to protect us from knowing too much, but in actuality everybody knew everybody else very well—we were all friends. Barbara knew a lot of people and a lot about what everyone did. She could have endangered many lives. Somebody in the group said to me, "Oh, that girl will be beaten and then everything will become clear to the Gestapo." Another friend, a very strong woman, was convinced that only she was strong enough for such a situation and that small young girls like Basha are too delicate and not trustworthy.

But Basha was very good; she never said anything. She made up a crazy story about falling in love with a handsome young man she met in Maria Czujko's cafe—Maria Czujko was well known to be on good terms with the Gestapo. Basha only knew this young man's first name, but she was so much in love, she promised she would go to Warsaw as a favor for him. She didn't know his address or anything else about him because they always met in this "false-Deutsch" (Nazi-friendly) cafe. All she knew was that he was so handsome. Her story couldn't have been more stupid, but perhaps because it was so idiotic, and coming from a young girl, somehow they believed her.

Because Basha never revealed anything, Zegota continued to help people as before. I had seventy different addresses during this time; I moved all the time. But there were no complications. I was never arrested.

After Lublin they brought her to Lvov, and she wasn't beaten anymore. We had a way to communicate with the prison in Lvov. We sent her clean clothes, she sent us dirty clothes, and in the dirty clothes we learned to look very carefully in every seam and hem, because we might find something. She would carefully examine the bread or anything else we sent her

where we could hide a message. Slawek was very proud that she held up really well in prison. He sent her his compliments.

I visited Marysia in the convent several times. I couldn't tell her anything about her mother or father. She would ask me for news of Basha. She was a sad girl, never smiling, but she liked it very much when I came to visit. I don't have an especially clear memory of her now because I visited so many friends in the same situation at that time. There were a great many small things that needed to be done for these people and sometimes it was very difficult. Those in the convent were in a good situation and didn't need our help, so we only saw her occasionally, but we knew her life was safe.

Somebody in our group must have made contact with a Gestapo officer, and that enabled us to propose an exchange of money for Basha's life. My memory of this isn't clear. We hoped only that a bribe would pay for better treatment; we never expected her liberation.

The first time Hanka and I went to Warsaw looking for money for Basha, we were not successful. Everyone told us the same thing: there were so many people in prison, it was impossible to find enough money to help each one. Then the Polish government-in-exile in London gave its Lvov representative position to Adam Ostrowski, a member of our Polish Socialist Party. His job was to negotiate with the Soviets, if they came. I was transferred from the underground printing shop where I was working for a PPS paper, to be his assistant. He knew Basha and took it upon himself to try to find money for her. Since he was our new delegate, everybody in Warsaw wanted to be nice to him, and he was able to put together a very big sum. It was at the time when the Russian front was advancing, and the Germans were beginning to be uncertain about the war. They were starting to liquidate the prison, and we knew that sometimes to empty a prison they would simply kill all the prisoners. They took our money eagerly and put Basha on the transport to Ravensbruck concentration camp.

Again, I think Basha's character was very helpful to her. In the prison she was active and optimistic. She looked around and tried to help other people, so there was no time to think too much about herself. For example, I am perhaps the only person ever to have received a gift from this prison—from Basha, of course. One day in her package of dirty laundry I found a wonderfully warm sweater. A Ukrainian girl in her cell knew she was going to be killed and gave away her things to the other women; Basha got the sweater. Here was Basha in prison, thinking that probably I was the one who needed a warm sweater! It seemed natural for her to give me a present. It was the same in the concentration camp when she was working in the kitchen and finding a way to smuggle out food to people who were starving. Her optimistic attitude made her strong.

In Ravensbruck, Basha was always active. It was the small things that made her daily life bearable. Little things became very precious. For a while she was in a work squad of women who marched out of the camp every day to work somewhere. A girl who had been part of this squad told me that each woman wore a little rag on her head, like a small babushka. While they were in the forest cutting wood, they always washed these little cloths so they stayed very nice and white. When they returned to the camp everyone could see how fresh and wonderful they looked. The German guard couldn't oppose something like that because the women weren't breaking any rules. But that was something special, you see. Their lives were made up of these small gestures of solidarity. I understand that very well, how important these small things are. If someone gives you something—a piece of bread perhaps—it's like a bouquet of flowers.

I didn't see Basha immediately after she returned from Ravensbruck because I was still in Lvov. I don't remember the circumstances of our first meeting, but I do remember her face. She had no teeth, from being beaten, and from conditions in Ravensbruck. She had some female problems too. She was very thin and had very little hair. We all had poor, thin hair, but especially after this period, hers would fall out. But she was so happy to be with us again, and to be alive. She had been so determined not to allow the Germans to destroy her morale in this terrible situation. She was radiant.

Dr. Olga Lilien

The Bolsheviks—we called them Soviets—came on September 17, 1939. Some people thought they were coming to help us against the Germans.

Dr. Olga Lilien, 1940

They didn't know about the pact made with Ribbentrop. The Bolsheviks didn't ever say they were going to help the Germans, but they helped them for almost two years. A great many people came from the west of Poland thinking they could help against the Germans somehow, but they were all taken by the Bolsheviks and sent to Siberia, Jews and Poles alike. The Russians thought that because these people were from the west, they would be traitors, sympathetic to the Germans, or something like that. Another group they took was the wives of Polish officers. They were sent to Siberia, too, along with their children. This is why Halina and my niece Olla came to live with me. Their Polish school was in a Russian occupied area and it was too dangerous.

The Russians were somewhat against the Poles. They said that the territory around Lvov was Ukrainian, not Polish. But other than that, they were not too bad. They didn't make much of a fuss about Jews, although they did make us get new passports. They wanted to give us a Hebrew family name, but my family was never religious, and my father refused. He told the person at the passport office, "I've lived in Poland all my life. I don't want to be a Jew now." My father convinced him to write down that both of us were Polish, and so we had Polish identity papers. When the Germans came I only had to change the family name from Lilien to Mazur, because it sounded less Jewish, and I never went to the ghetto. My sister, however, did go to the ghetto and was killed there, along with her husband. And my father died when the Bolsheviks were there.

It was after the Germans came to Lvov that it became difficult for the Jews. They closed all the schools and I had no place to work. For a while I was still able to work for Dr. Meisel, but then they persecuted him, and he no longer had a laboratory. The Germans took him to the Weigl Institute, and I had nowhere to work. I simply had no work, and I couldn't apply for any.

Before the war, I was sent to a small village about one hundred kilometers from Lvov, to practice medicine. I lived there with a Ukrainian family who were very nice to me. After the Germans came, I went back to that village three times to buy food, because there was a great scarcity in Lvov. On one trip—it was in November, maybe four o'clock in the afternoon— I was standing in the town square looking for a ride back. A horse cart came along and offered me a ride, but then just a few miles down the road to Lvov the driver said, "Get out here. I am going in another direction now." I got off with all of my heavy things.

By then it was dark and the curfew was in effect; you weren't allowed to be walking around. The Gestapo in that area had a terrible reputation.

I was wondering where I was going to sleep. I saw a light, knocked on the door, and was let in by a maid who was at work cutting up a big pile of cabbage to make sauerkraut. I asked if I could help her. "You don't have to help, you can just sit." A little while later the lady of the house came in.

"Who is this?" she asked.

"I would like to spend the night. It's late and I can't get back to Lvov."

"Oh, no, absolutely not. You can't stay here. You can leave your things, but I don't want you here."

"All right. Thank you for keeping my things."

I went away. I knocked at another door, and heard someone call, "Who is that?" I explained to him that I wanted to stay overnight. He said that it would be very nice but he was a bachelor and didn't think it was such a good idea.

I went to another door; nobody answered. Finally, I tried another place where I saw a light—the German work office. A woman came to the door. Again I asked if she could put me up for the night, and she said of course she could. There were two beds in the room. She slept with her husband in one bed and gave me the other one. They were Polish. They helped me.

BARBARA (BASHA)

The Germans came in June. One day in January someone told me that a Jewish woman who worked with Dr. Meisel at the Institute had been taken by the Gestapo and killed, that it would be best if I left Lvov right away. Halina gave me the address of Basha and told me I could rely on her, that she would help me. But I went first to my relatives living in a village near Warsaw. They were absolutely safe; nobody thought they were of Jewish descent. I stayed there for a while, but I couldn't continue living at other people's expense. I needed to work.

So then I went to Basha's address in Tarnobrzeg. She asked what could she do for me. I said, "Maybe one of your aunts needs a cook. I could help her in the house." And so she arranged for her Aunt Lilka, who had a very

Sandomierz town square, c. 1938

nice house with a beautiful garden a few miles from Sandomierz, to take me as her servant. I stayed there for five months. I wasn't a very good cook, but I was an excellent maid. This aunt is the same one who sent Mrs. Litowitz and her little girl Marysia to Basha. She had been a high-school teacher until the Germans closed down all the schools. Now she was involved in teaching Polish-language courses underground. This was a great risk for her because it was absolutely forbidden; she could have been rounded up by the Gestapo and sent to Auschwitz for doing it.

Lilka let me stay with them, but I knew they were nervous about it. They were afraid there might be a complication some day, plus she was already worried about her underground teaching. I thought, well, no one should be at risk because of me. So I said thank you, I won't be your cook anymore, and I went away to Basha and her mother, Mrs. Szymanska, in Tarnobrzeg. Their home became a very steady place for me at that time, a place I could depend on.

Basha was wonderful. She was goodness itself. She was not only good to the child, Marysia, but she was very capable and heroic as well. Basha was so very nice, but Mrs. Szymanska was like honey, a little bit fantastic. Her life wasn't easy, but she was so terribly good. She was very intelligent, always thoughtful of people, and always optimistic; she was a warm person, good-hearted and wise, with the kind of wisdom that doesn't come from books, but from the heart.

THE POLOWICZ FAMILY

In Tarnobrzeg I was without work again. One day Dr. Polowicz, the director of the school where Basha was teaching, said to me, "What are you doing, really? You come and go, back and forth. It's not a good idea." He was from Poznan, in the west of Poland, and had been expelled when the Germans came and annexed that area to Germany. So he was a refugee, too. He told me school was starting soon and he had no one to cook. Would I like the job? I said very well, this is my specialty.

Sandomierz town square, 1987

So then I stayed at the school, cleaning and cooking. Another girl and I ran the kitchen during the school term. I was earning six hundred zlotys per month, plus room and board.

One time the Germans came to see the school. The lady who delivered our groceries took one look at their uniforms and was so frightened she had an epileptic seizure. I didn't even know she was an epileptic. Well, there was nothing to do; you just had to wait for the attack to end. I cooked a better dinner than usual for the Germans that night. They liked it.

After five months in the school kitchen, Dr. Polowicz said the term was over and the boys were going home, but if I wanted, I could work in the fields. I said all right, I'll help in the fields. After all, that was an opportunity to earn my money. I wouldn't have to eat bread divided in portions, taking it away from somebody else. So I went to the fields. Dr. Polowicz and I became good friends, and before long Mrs. Polowicz asked me to be her cook—a promotion. It was beginning to be a career. She took me into her house where I cooked and taught their three children, who had no school to go to. There was a school, but it only had the first three grades. The Germans said it was enough for the Poles to learn to read and write and count up to ten.

I stayed with the Polowicz family until the end of the war. They stayed on at the school for one more year, then when Dr. Polowicz was appointed director of another school, he hired me to teach anatomy. Later the whole family returned to Poznan. I visited and we always exchanged presents and letters at Easter and Christmas. Now they are both dead and I have no contact with the children.

During those war years I was caught by the Germans three different times, but I wasn't afraid. You see, I didn't feel Jewish. I felt Polish and I spoke Polish perfectly. I could speak German, too, but I never told them that.

The first incident, I was on a little ferry boat crossing the Vistula, on my way to Lvov with a package of flour. A German came on the ferry and said, "Show me your documents!" I showed him my documents, and he started to speak to me in German. I said I didn't understand. He was from Silesia and spoke Polish fluently. He asked me where was I going, what was I doing. Then he put his hand on my package and asked me what it was. A package of seeds. He gave me back my documents. I was perfectly calm.

Another time—it was Christmas, and I was pretty tired—I was going from Tarnobrzeg to Warsaw to visit my relatives. A German stopped me and said, "You are Jewish."

"No, I'm not Jewish."

"We'll see. We'll see. Come along with me."

We went to his commandant. He asked him, "Is she Jewish or not?"

"Oh, certainly she is Jewish. Put her in the ghetto where she belongs."

The commandant left, and I went along with the first one again. We were

Halina Ogrodzinska and Dr. Olga Lilien, Sandomierz, 1987

walking down a very poor street. "Where were you going?" he asked me. I told him, to a Mr. Toscinsky, which wasn't true. He took the address, smiled in a German way, and told me to go along. He never did anything about it.

The third incident involved a German who spoke very good Polish and was known to be pretty bad to everyone all around, Jews and Poles alike. You see, the Germans found very little difference between the Poles and the Jews. This German was looking for a man in Tarnobrzeg who he wanted to hang. They asked me to come to a meeting where they were questioning people about this man. Everyone was telling the German they didn't know where the man was, when suddenly he looked at me and said, "Oh, but this is a Jewess." The head of the village said, "Oh, no, she cooks at the school. She is a very good cook." Nobody said, "Oh, well, she is Jewish. Take her." He let me go.

The population of the village was about two thousand. They all knew there was something "wrong" with me. Any one of them could have sold me to the Germans for two hundred deutsche marks, but out of two thousand people nobody did it. Everybody in that village protected me. I had very good relations with them.

Rachel Litowitz

There is nothing good to say about Sandomierz. It is a subject I would be scared to talk about—it's not healthy. I can tell you that Basha and her family were good, but I can't speak about the rest of the population. She was not responsible for them. She was good. That's all.

For a few years I had a store, not too big. When the Germans came in, right away the business was finished. No Jews had stores after that. Who could keep anything? We just hid. We were afraid of them, and we were right.

Sandomierz is a little town where everyone knew everyone else very well. Basha's aunt, Mrs. Damagala, and her husband were my customers. During the wartime, Mr. Damagala's brother—he had once been a member

Rachel Litowitz,
Montreal, 1952

of the Polish parliament—came over to Sandomierz from the border area between Germany and Poland. For some reason, I didn't understand why—he really didn't know me—he used to come and talk to me a little. It was before we knew that they were killing Jews all around. One day he came in and said, "Rachel, I want to help you get out."

"Okay, if you can take my daughter, I think I can run away."

"I will come back with some information in two hours."

When he returned he gave me Basha's address. "They don't know anything about this," he said, "but go there right away. If they don't want to keep your daughter, leave her and run away."

There was no choice. There were not too many opportunities, and no time to think it over. Who would take a Jewish child? Who would be responsible? It was close to the end: two weeks later they killed all the Jews in Sandomierz. That was why I took her then.

Postwar monument constructed from Jewish tombstones Nazis had desecrated and used as paving stones, Sandomierz, 1987

I had never met Mrs. Szymanska before. She was Mrs. Damagala's sister, living with her daughter, Basha, in a little village a few miles from Sandomierz. When I came to their house they were like angels. They took my daughter. I told Rebecca, "If you want to be alive, stay here with Basha." She didn't hesitate.

The whole Szymanska family are angels; they are aristocrats. Basha's sister in Lvov hid Jews, too. There were two or three girls in that family, all working underground. You know what the mother said to her daughters? She told them it doesn't pay to die for a little piece of paper with big ideas written on it, but to save a life, a Jew, is different. This was an idea from that older woman.

You don't find many people like the Szymanskas. There are some, but very, very few. The rest are not like that. I knew when I gave my daughter away to them that she would be alive, that she would be safe. I was a good business lady. I could see with whom I was dealing. I could see right through a person—everything—and I knew they were all right. I don't think it was easy for them, because they were not so rich. They fed everybody with the food they had. This was my impression. The whole family was good to me, and I had to trust them. To tell you the truth, in that situation you would give your child away to a bandit, too.

If it wasn't for Basha my daughter wouldn't be alive. I am thankful that we are both alive, that my sister is also alive, because of Basha. Basha doesn't know about this, but it was because she gave me the address of a woman by the name of Mrs. Unger that I was able to save my sister. When I left Rebecca there Basha gave me this woman's address, in a little town near Warsaw. She was an engineer and Jewish, but her husband was in the Polish army in Germany and they had good papers; they passed as Gentile. Later, I was able to take my sister out of a small concentration camp and send her to them. Mrs. Unger found a good place for my sister as a servant in a rich Polish home, and that's how she survived.

There were some Jews who tried to escape, but very few. They threw us out of the ghetto and killed most of us. All over Poland there were ghettos. We had no chance to run away. I used to go to Warsaw where there was a closed ghetto, a big one. You could hear people crying, "I'm hungry! I'm hungry!"—and they dropped dead in the street. I was there sometimes for two or three days, and I always heard that cry, "I am hungry!" I'm telling you, if you didn't see it for yourself, you cannot understand what happened. I can talk, explain, and you can write about these things, but you cannot understand anything at all if you didn't go through that hell, day and night, from 1939 until 1945—so many years.

It was like being in a fire—unbelievable. At the time you don't stop to think. If you're going to be killed, you run. When I left Rebecca, at first I went back to Sandomierz where my husband was, but later I was here and there, in so many different places. Sometimes I could find a place to hide in the home of Gentiles. I took chances: I went out, knowing that if they caught me they would kill me. If I stayed in hiding they would kill me too. I was not the type to sit in a concentration camp, so I would run away, and they always caught me. If they caught you, they would usually kill you, but listen, I had nothing to lose; it was such an awful situation. They killed my husband at Buchenwald.

I don't know why I survived. So many times they got me—so many times. Whenever I could, I escaped, except from Auschwitz. From Auschwitz I couldn't run away, but I ran away from everywhere else—from Sandomierz, from Germany. I was hiding a lot. Sometimes people helped me. Sometimes you pretend you're not Jewish, and sometimes you're in hiding, and they get you. I can't tell you about it.

I was not in Auschwitz for very long—from August, I would say, until maybe November. They took us to an airplane parts factory in Germany where I worked until February. Then they took us further into Germany, because the Russians were advancing. When we were going deeper into Germany I ran away and hid in an empty house, alone. On the eighth of May, the Russians came; Germany had already capitulated. Somebody said,

"Oh, look at what's going on in the road, there are so many cars! People are running!" In a few hours the Russians came and I knew I was liberated.

I wanted to go back to Sandomierz right away, but I was scared to go so far. I couldn't speak German, although Yiddish is not so different, but I was scared to talk, afraid that people would recognize me as a Jew. A few weeks later I went back on a train.

When I returned, the Szymanskas told me that Rebecca was in a convent in Lvov. This was not so easy because Lvov was now part of Russia, but fortunately I found out that they had moved the convent back to Poland. When I went to get her she was wearing a cross, but she understood, poor girl. Rebecca said she used to get down from her bed to pray she would be with mama and father, that we would be alive. The priests and nuns were not so bad since they knowingly took in Jewish children. They were kind to me—well, most of them—and they treated my daughter very well. She studied and was very good in school, very intelligent. They loved her.

After the war a few Jews came back for a while to Sandomierz. I was not there very long—maybe a month—then I had to run away. I could not escape the times: there was no place for us there anymore. It was dangerous. I can't tell you why. There are things that I have to hold back.

You know what Herzl said, "A Jew suffers not just for the bad things but for the good things, too." It's true. We didn't do anything bad. We didn't drink, we didn't kill. You know the story: you go to the jail, you don't find Jews there—well, very few, very, very seldom. But still they complain that the Jews are no good. I am talking about the world in general. Here in Canada it is different, you don't come across this. You are not treated badly here. You have freedom. Some people may complain, but I'm telling you, I cannot complain about what I have seen on this continent. I have never had trouble as long as I've been here, not from the government, not from the neighbors, not from anyone. Poland was different.

6 ～ The Important Thing Was to Survive

John Damski was born in Germany in 1914 to Polish parents. At the end of World War I, his mother and father returned to newly independent Poland to raise their family: John and his two brothers and sister. From an early age he excelled in sports, especially track and field, and soccer; John once placed second in the Polish national championship triple jump event. When World War II broke out, twenty-five-year-old John was serving in the Battalion for the Defense of the Seashore of the Polish army. He was stationed at Gdynia, on the Baltic coast.

A few months after the Polish army fell to the German invaders, John was caught trying to cross the Polish border illegally. His awakening to the ruthless nature of the Nazi regime came when he barely escaped execution—the fate of most of his fellow inmates—at the prison for Polish political prisoners, where he was held for many months. Upon his release, he found work as the chief electrician of construction projects for the German air force. Despite the German threat of the death penalty for anyone caught helping Jews in Poland, John helped many. He found work for Jewish men on his construction projects, obtained lifesaving false identity papers for others, and at one point smuggled ten Jews out of the sealed Warsaw ghetto.

John had been helping his Jewish neighbors, the Rozen family, in small ways for months before the dramatic incident that brought him together with the Rozen's beautiful young daughter, with whom he fell in love. From that point until the end of the war, John used all of his considerable talents to ensure the safety of Christine and her mother, obtaining false identity papers, a false marriage certificate making Christine his "wife," and moving with them from city to city whenever there were warnings of imminent betrayal and arrest.

Christine Damski was born Sara Rozen in Chelm, Poland, in 1918, the daughter of an upper-class assimilated Jewish family. Christine's father owned seven breweries, a distillery, and a bank, in Zamosc, Chelm, and Lublin. She grew up in Zamosc, a town of thirty-five thousand, of which about one-fourth were Jews. Christine spent the long war years trying to protect herself, her mother, and beloved brother, moving frequently, always just one step ahead of the Nazi terror. In 1943, she met John Damski in a most unexpected manner: fleeing an imminent SS raid, she literally landed in his lap as she jumped out of a bedroom window. The following year, passing themselves off as a married couple, they were caught in the 1944 Warsaw uprising. After several days of surviving by their wits, they managed to escape together.

At the war's end, John and Christine married officially. From Zamosc, they moved to Gdansk and subsequently emigrated with Christine's mother to the United States. About the same time, Christine's father, Samuel Rozen, emigrated to Israel. John and Christine settled in the Los Angeles area, where they live today, and where John, still in good form, participates in track and field events. They told their stories in their home on May 14, 1988.

John Damski

I'll tell you about my first association with Jewish people. We lived in a small town named Solec-Kujawski when I was growing up—just five thousand people, and only one Jewish family. Their name was Dalman. They had three sons and one daughter; she was a very good friend of my sister. Their son Jacob—we were pals until we were eighteen or nineteen years old—always came to our family's big Sunday meal. We served dishes Jacob liked that he couldn't get at home because his family was kosher.

All three brothers belonged to our gymnastic organization, the Polish Falcons. We called our local organization "the nest." There was also a district level, and so on, up to the national level. One day a fellow from the district organization came to our meeting and made a fuss about Jews being in our group. The oldest of the three Dalman brothers stood up and told him that the Jews were just as patriotic as the Poles, they had fought for Poland too, and other such sentiments. It didn't take very long before the local organization just fell apart. First, all the teachers from our little town who belonged to this club resigned. They didn't say it was in protest—they were just no longer interested. My brother and I dropped out of the organization, and so did many of our friends; half of the membership resigned. Nobody said, "I'm quitting because the district officer made an anti-Semitic speech." We just didn't like what was happening; we simply did not see any difference between us and the Jews.

My next encounter with Jews was in 1935, one year before the Olympic Games in Berlin. I was in the state training camp, but I wasn't quite good enough to be chosen for the Olympic team. A fellow named Israelowicz, the state champion in the hundred-meter run, was also in our camp. He was the first Jew to really show me what anti-Semitism was all about. One day as we were walking down the street, we stopped to look at a poster of Joan Crawford; it was advertising travel to the United States.

"Look at that," Israelowicz said. "They ask us to travel, but they won't let us go."

He told me how he couldn't just go to the foreign ministry, like I or anyone else could, and get a passport. That's when my eyes were first opened to the difficulties of the Jews—that they were being treated differently. But then, as a young fellow, you think to yourself, who cares? You live in your own little world.

When I was already a grown man living in Gdynia, my third encounter with Jews took place. One evening I ran into an old school pal and his girlfriend in a nightclub. We were sitting there having a few drinks, when all of a sudden she said, "Take a look! Those are Jews over there! To hell with the Jews!" I was so ashamed—my brother and I knew those Jewish girls. My friend slapped her face, and we left the club. That someone could say a thing like that in public showed me how ignorant people could be. Sure, we saw the signs posted everywhere saying "Don't Buy from a Jew." People were still doing business with the Jews, but no one took the signs down, and we didn't protest.

PRISONER

On September 1, 1939, the Germans invaded, and being in the army, I was taken prisoner of war. On the way to the prisoner-of-war camp, I managed to escape. It was not such a big deal—escaping at night was easy. I returned to Gdynia and took a job working for the power and water company. One day some Germans came around and said that since I was born in Germany and spoke German almost as well as Polish, I should declare myself a German national. I said no, I would never do it. I was not a German; it was as simple as that.

They kicked me out. I got a paper saying I had to leave town within twenty-four hours. This happened to most of the Polish people in that area. The Germans resettled all the Poles to the area they named the General Gouvernement, under the jurisdiction of the famous Nazi Hans Frank.

It was early in December 1939. Two friends and I decided to try to get to Hungary, and eventually France. On December 9 we were close to the Hungarian border when German soldiers caught us and delivered us to the Gestapo. They made us undress completely. As we stood naked against the wall, the Gestapo made all kinds of insinuations, threatening to shoot us. Then they sent us to a jail at Sanok near the Ukraine, for "preventative," that is, political prisoners—mostly doctors, lawyers, professional people—345 men altogether. The conditions were dreadful. We had forty-five guys in a cell meant for seven or eight; there was so little room, we could only sleep on our sides. The toilet was a single bucket in the cell. We were never allowed to go out. Fleas, flies—whatever you want—they were all there.

On the night of June 13—it must have been three or four o'clock in the morning—we heard big trucks come into the prison yard. I looked through the window—just peeked—because we were not allowed to look out. The sky was still gray. I saw two SS men walking in the yard with rifles on their shoulders. One stopped and kicked what I think must have been a dead mouse, and said, "One is already dead." It gave me a shiver. Then I saw them load prisoners on the trucks. All night long the trucks kept coming back and taking more out again. It went on until seven or eight in the morning.

Right away we got the news about what was happening. Each truck had five or six benches. They put one prisoner on a bench and an SS man with a gun next to him to guard him—maybe six prisoners in one truck—they were not packed in. Before loading them into the trucks, they had cut the buttons off of the prisoners' trousers, so that they had to hold up their pants with their hands. There was no possibility of escape. The trucks stopped on the outskirts of town, and they killed them. They killed 115 men that night—one-third of the prison's inmates. We were told that the rest of us would go the next night.

When we realized that we all faced death, there wasn't much to say. Most of us were praying. No matter how brave or how atheistic we were, when we came to face death, almost everybody started to pray. But it didn't happen. At three or four o'clock in the afternoon the trucks and the SS unit that was killing us suddenly left.

A short time later, they sent the remaining prisoners to Auschwitz, but for some reason I was not among them; I stayed on in that prison. One day an SS man came to my cell.

"Something's wrong. I don't seem to have any record of you."

He started asking me questions. How did I get there? I told him a little lie, that I was arrested at the local railroad station. What was I doing in this town? I said I was looking for a job in the battery factory—it was somewhat related to my trade as an electrician. I thought this up on the spur of the moment.

Christine and John Damski, 1945

He didn't believe me. For two hours he interrogated me. I told him that my mother spoke German because she had attended school in Germany and that I felt as if I was a German.

"Oh, so now you feel like a German?"

"Well, do you know any Poles who speak German as well as I do?"

I used a German expression that means "my mother tongue," and that impressed him.

"Okay, I'll let you out," he said. "But I want you out of this town immediately."

After the interrogation I was waiting to go back to my cell, holding my arm behind my back. A female warden passing by stuck something in my hand. Not wanting to call attention to myself by raising my hand, I didn't look. Later I saw that it was five zloty—about five dollars—enough to have a good meal.

On August 9 I was released from the prison, but in very bad condition; I weighed only ninety-seven pounds. I wanted to go to Lublin to find my brother Zygmunt, but I didn't have enough money for a railway ticket. I walked down the track about a half mile from the station and boarded the train without a ticket. The train, however, traveled only a hundred miles. I got out and did the same thing with the next train, and the next, and in this way I made my way as far as Cracow. There I boarded a train in the same manner, but this time a Polish railroad attendant came to check my ticket.

"I just came out of prison," I told him. "I don't have a ticket and I don't have any money."

"Come with me," he said, and he locked me in a compartment. A few miles before Lublin he let me out.

ZAMOSC

When I finally reached my brother, we talked over our situation. Zygmunt figured it would be easier for us to survive the war in a small, quiet, out-of-the-way place, like Zamosc, about eighty kilometers away. I had never been there and knew it only from history books. Two weeks later we moved to Zamosc.

Having no money, we needed to find work. The Zamosc unemployment office told me that the Germans were planning to build an airfield nearby. I wasted no time going to their office—it was just across the street. The outfit was a civilian construction company called Bauleitung der Luftwaffe, which means "Building Management for the Air Force," and they were building not one but six military airfields. In charge of the project was a famous engineer, an energetic man named Walter Enderlein. When he heard me speaking German, he said, "I could use a fellow like you," and so I went to work for him as chief electrician.

"I have to go to Berlin for two weeks," he said to me one day. "When I come back I want you to have fifty electricians working here." Well, I couldn't get fifty electricians because, according to my standards, there were not fifty electricians to be found in that town.

Then I had the idea to look in the Zamosc Jewish forced labor camp. There were at least a couple of hundred Jewish men garrisoned in a former armory. Every morning they went out to dig irrigation ditches for the Germans. A fellow named Walter Reuter from the Bauleitung der Luft-waffe supervised that camp. I went over there and told Reuter what I want-ed. He brought all the men out of one of the barracks and yelled, "Is any-one here an electrician?" Six or seven guys came forward. Only one of them was actually an electrician—a fellow named Friedman. Another one, Feigenbaum, told me his father had a factory that made electrical fixtures; I knew he could not be an electrician. The other guys just wanted to get out. It was October 1940, still near the beginning of their internment, but you could see they were already getting a little bit worn down from their terrible living conditions. I needed a few guys to sort out the materials, so I took them all. It worked out well. In fact, Feigenbaum became my chief assistant, in charge of materials. He was no electrician, but he was very able and intelligent. I liked him.

I found some blankets and fixed up a storage place in a former school for the Jewish men to sleep in—it was more like a compartment than a room. The German construction workers for the airfield were living in the same building. The arrangement worked just fine for two or three months, until one day one of the Germans said to me, "Say, what's going on up there?"

"Those are just the guys who work for me."

"What! Jews under the same roof with me?" He moved them all out in a big hurry. Somehow they found sleeping quarters elsewhere.

My boss, Enderlein, liked me; I became his right-hand man. He did not actually belong to the Nazi party, but he was a very strong German nationalist, and he thought Hitler was doing a fine job. He told me many interesting stories that gave me real insight into the thinking of the Nazi leaders. By now it was Eastertime '41, and Germany had just invaded Greece. Enderlein asked me to have lunch with him in the hotel.

"Fine," I said. After all, he was my boss.

On the way, he said, "Can you keep your mouth shut?"

"Naturally."

"Did you hear that Germany invaded Greece?"

"Yes, I heard the news this morning."

He rubbed his hands together, "The English are pulverized! It will begin now."

He told me that the Germans were going to fight Russia. Then after they finished off England and Russia, they would take care of the "dirty Italians." At that point they were still allies! How did he even know these things? It seems that just before the war began, Enderlein was the chief engineer at the construction of an airfield in Gleivitz, close to the Polish-German border. When it was completed, Hitler himself came to the dedication and wanted to meet the engineer in charge. In admiration of Enderlein's efficiency, Hitler invited him to come to certain meetings that occurred every two or three months in Berlin. At those meetings Enderlein became privy to all the details of the Nazis' plans. He was no small fry or a mere dreamer.

"So first we'll take care of the dirty Italians, and then the war begins," he told me.

"With whom?" I asked him.

"With the Yellow Peril."

In 1941 they were already planning a war against Japan! I never read that in a book, but this is the truth; that was what they planned. The day before Germany invaded Russia he told me, "We have one foot in our neighbor's garden now." So I knew they were going to start any minute. Next day, June 22, 1941, the war started.

But something happened in relation to Jews and myself just before the war with Russia. Again, my boss told me we needed more electricians. I gave him an idea about how to find them.

"Why don't you send me to the Warsaw ghetto? I'll find some Jewish electricians there."

I also needed to buy welding equipment for the company that I knew I could get in the ghetto. Enderlein thought it was a brilliant idea. The truth is, I also had a little business to do there on the side; after all, I had to make a living.

Every one of those Jews who were working for me was from Warsaw; they all had relatives in the ghetto. When I announced I was going to the Warsaw ghetto to find electricians, they all wanted to come with me, to see their families and bring them some food.

"Okay, I'll take four or five of you, but no food."

It was dangerous; we could have been stopped. They all agreed; they just wanted to see their families. I got a special travel permit from my boss that said, "John Damski is going to Warsaw to arrange for some electricians, badly needed for airfield construction work."

We left early in the morning in an Opel-Blitz, a very fast truck. Up front with me were two German Luftwaffe guys, the driver and his assistant. We were speeding down the road pretty fast—it was just great—then we had the accident. Coming out of a curve too fast, the driver lost control, and our truck rolled over three times. The two Germans and I weren't hurt, although I was pretty lucky because a piece of glass had cut right through my shoe. Then I remembered the Jews in the back with the big heavy propane bottles. I went to see what had happened. They were screaming. One fellow got it in the back, and Feigenbaum had a big gash in his forehead.

"I'm mutilated!" he cried.

He was an extremely handsome fellow, and all he could think about now was that he might have a permanent scar.

I had a different worry: a huge seventy-kilo slab of pork that I was planning to smuggle into the Warsaw ghetto was laying in the ditch a few yards off. As soon as we could, one of my drivers and I picked it up and walked over to the nearest farmhouse, where I left it with the farmer for temporary safekeeping.

When I got back to the truck I could see a line of troops coming down the road. At the head of the column was a colonel in his black car. Seeing our overturned truck, he stopped to ask what was going on. My two German drivers were still shaking; I think I was the only one who stayed cool.

"We had an accident," I said.

"Do you have any injured people?" the colonel asked.

"I have several."

"Okay, take them to the hospital."

Impossible—they were Jews. The colonel assumed we were all Germans. He ordered his men to turn our truck upright, but they couldn't budge it. So he gave me his car and driver, and I loaded all five Jews into it. What else could I do with them? My two Luftwaffe drivers stayed behind with our truck, while the Jews and I went on to Warsaw. They were not too badly injured, and in any case, I couldn't very well take them to the Warsaw hospital. The only place for us was the ghetto, and that's where we went.

Jewish seller of Jewish star armbands, Warsaw ghetto, c. 1943

When we arrived we found the place surrounded by a high wall with an entrance gate and an SS guard standing watch. It was all right with him that I brought Jews into the ghetto, but when he realized I was bringing them in a German car he became suspicious and started to come after me. However, I just disappeared into the crowd.

Entering the Warsaw ghetto was a shock. It was as if somebody suddenly dropped you into an entirely different world. The buildings and the streets were the same as the rest of Warsaw, but the atmosphere overwhelmed you. There was something about it that you could not describe. I went about fifty yards and saw a guy lying on the sidewalk with his hand outstretched. He must have been sixty years old. He said, "Give me a piece of bread." Just that. I will never forget it in all my life.

Staying in the ghetto those five days was a devastating experience. As a Gentile I really had no business being there and could not move around easily. To make myself less conspicuous, I put on an armband with the star of David. Wearing it gave me a very strange feeling. You feel that you are not human. You feel like a marked man. It's hard to believe—just from an armband—but once you put it on, it's like having a number in a prison. The armband made me feel so bad, finally I said to hell with it and took it off.

We made contact with the people we needed. I also got in touch with my boss in Zamosc and told him about the accident; he said he would send another truck. I bought the welding equipment and some other items only obtainable in the ghetto. The Germans could get us the equipment too, but it took a long time, and we needed it right then. The Jews were manufacturing everything imaginable in the ghetto, even Swiss watches. I still have a gold watch from those days. The movement was from Switzerland, but the watch was made in the ghetto.

Finally the new truck arrived from Zamosc to pick us up. First thing, I went back to the farmer for my pork. "What pork?" he said. Without a word, I turned the truck around and left, returning pretty soon with my two German drivers and their pistols. Right away the pork appeared, and the pork fat too. During the war, fat was very important. You might not have much to eat, but if you had a little fat and some potatoes, it was a meal; it didn't matter whether or not it was kosher.

Back in the ghetto, we pulled the truck up to a gate, sold the pork and fat, and loaded up our new equipment. It all had to be done very fast, so that no one would be caught. For some reason it was taking longer than it should have.

"Is everybody ready?" I asked at last. Something seemed odd to me; it was too quiet. I looked over at the Jewish guys I had brought with me. One had disappeared into the ghetto, but the other four were going back. Then I happened to glance under the canvas covering the back of the truck and I saw about ten other Jews pressed flat on the floor. They thought I wasn't going to see them.

I had to make a split-second decision. I don't know why I risked it; you never know why you do things like that. I said, "Okay, fellows, keep quiet," and off we went. I didn't say anything to the German drivers. When we got to the ghetto entrance gate the SS guard looked in the cab and saw two German soldiers—the drivers—and me, a civilian. He probably thought we were all right. He never looked in the back.

About twenty miles out of Warsaw we made a stop. I told the Jewish guys, "Now get out, you're on your own. You're well out of the ghetto." I asked each one to give me what he could—one or two hundred zlotys— I don't remember exactly how much, but it was a very small sum. Altogether I collected three thousand zlotys and gave it to the drivers to keep them quiet. It was not much, but for the drivers, who were paid 150 German marks a month, it was like getting ten times their monthly wages on the black market; they were happy. The money shut them up, and after that no one ever mentioned it. Those ten guys disappeared and I never saw them again. They may still be alive. I hope so.

CHRISTINE

In Zamosc my brother and I rented the front room of an apartment in a two-family house. In the back were three rooms with a separate entrance. A family named Rozen lived there. I had met their daughter Helena before we became neighbors; she was a young girl, I was a young fellow. Although she had once introduced me to her mother and father, there was nothing special between us—just friendship. Then in October 1941, the other daughter came from Lvov to be with her parents. The walls were very thin; I could hear her speaking to her mother. I liked the way they spoke to each other. From the first moment I heard her voice, I fell in love.

But Christine had come from Lvov illegally, and a few days later, October 4, the Gestapo came to the house looking for her. Whenever the Gestapo came everybody was scared; you never knew what they would do. They could take you with them, and that would be that. Since my apartment was in the front, they banged on my door first, barged in, and asked me where the Rozens lived.

"Not here. They're in the next apartment," I told them. They went around to the back. I was anxious to find out what was happening, so I went outside and sat on the bench under the Rozens' window. Suddenly, Christine jumped out of the window, into my lap! That's how we first met.

Hide! That was the first thing that came to my mind. She had the same idea. We went across the backyard, through some fields, to the Jewish cemetery—it was not far—and waited there until about ten o'clock at night. She stayed that night with her family's friends, the Garfinkles. A few days later she moved to another place. For the next several weeks I was the only person who knew her whereabouts, acting as the contact between her and her family, bringing her food and money. Then she left for Lublin, to try to help her brother who was arrested and in jail there.

When the Germans told the Jews that they had to wear the armband with the star of David, I knew that they were not going to fool around. I had no doubts in my mind about it, no illusions. I saw how the Germans were shooting people when I was in prison. I knew what they were capable of; they were already killing Poles; they would kill Jews the same way, or worse.

Knowing the danger they were in, I arranged to meet Christine and her mother, Helen Rozen, in Warsaw to help them get Aryan identification papers. I had some connections in the Warsaw underground and was able to get them genuine birth certificates of people who had died, whose deaths had not been recorded by the priests. Her mother, who was very

Jewish-looking, became Zophia Olszewska, while Sara—her real name—who didn't look at all Jewish, was now Christine Paderewska. Zophia became my "aunt," and Christine, my "wife." We even had a false marriage certificate. While they were in Warsaw waiting for their papers, Christine and her mother stayed with a woman I knew who probably never suspected they were Jews. This woman was making some very nasty remarks to me about the Jews being killed in the ghetto. She said the Germans were stamping them out like bedbugs. Perhaps she said that intentionally, to warn me; I don't know.

Most of the Jews in Zamosc lived in their own district. One day the Germans rounded up a big group from the Jewish quarter and marched them to the railroad station a mile away. In that short stretch they shot about fifty people: because they couldn't walk, or were too slow, or maybe just because they didn't like them. At the railroad station they made them walk up a ramp, where they were loaded into little boxcars. They shot another fifty people right there, for no reason at all. The few who were left had to throw the bodies into the boxcar. Then the Germans made them climb on top of the corpses, and they locked them up. It was the most horrible thing that I have ever seen.

Quite a few people saw this, and it really shook them up. Who could comprehend it? People in that town had not taken much notice of what the Germans were doing to the Jews up until then, but now they all knew exactly what was happening. Today, the Jews and the Gypsies, but next will be us. People who knew the Germans believed that. I believed that. So did my brother.

After they took away those first Jews from Zamosc, those who were left became panicky. It seemed as if they had all been told the same thing: "If you need help, go see Damski." Someone was always coming to me needing papers, like Ringard, for instance, a very nice fellow who worked for me. I went to Warsaw and helped him. Even Israelowicz, the athlete, came to Zamosc. Blond hair, blue eyes—he looked like ten Germans put together—but he was Jewish.

Sara Rozen (Christine Damski), 1935

"What are you doing here?" I asked him. Here was a guy with whom I had participated in sports, but what could I do? I had so many problems already: Christine, her mother—I had a hundred problems. He didn't ask me to help him, but I told him what I would do if I were him: move to Tomaszow, a smaller town about twenty miles from Zamosc. Like my brother and I moving to Zamosc, I thought that in a smaller town he might be able to survive, but I don't know what he did. I never saw him after that.

CZESTOCHOWA AND OLSZTYN

After Christine and her mother got their Aryan papers in Warsaw we all went back together to Czestochowa, where Christine had found a place to live. There we decided to split up; I thought we had a better chance for survival that way. I rented a room in a farmer's house for my "widowed aunt"—Christine's mother—in Olsztyn. It was a little village of about a thousand people, just twelve kilometers from Czestochowa. Soon after, I quit my job in Zamosc and moved to Czestochowa to be with Christine. We lived there for about a half a year, commuting every weekend to Olsztyn to visit her mother. Everyone believed Christine and I were married.

It was about that time that I came under suspicion myself. The janitor of our building knew that we were visiting Christine's mother every weekend, coming back at a certain time every Monday morning. One Monday he was waiting for me in front of the apartment house.

"Mr. Damski, the Gestapo from Zamosc have been here looking for you. They said your wife is from a Jewish family in Zamosc."

Apparently somebody from Zamosc recognized Christine on the street, followed her home, and reported it to the Gestapo. I went inside, quickly gathered everything up in a bed sheet, and left with my bundle. I took the next train to Olsztyn to live with Christine and her mother.

For a brief time I had a second "aunt" in Olsztyn, the mother of a Jewish man whose friend I helped to obtain false papers. When this woman left Olsztyn for Kielce, she was betrayed and arrested. In separate incidents her son was also arrested, released, and later shot. As a result of the connections between the two "aunts," rumors began to circulate in Olsztyn that my aunt, "Mrs. Olszewska," might be Jewish. Christine and I decided we needed to send her to a safer place.

At the Czestochowa employment office we discovered that they were recruiting Polish volunteers to work in Germany. Christine's mother had good papers saying she was a Polish widow, so we signed her up to work in a restaurant in Bad Reichenhall, a spa town in Bavaria. We felt she would be safe in Germany; no one there would suspect that she was Jewish. The Poles could recognize Polish Jews—they were their own people—but the Germans couldn't. We were much more afraid of Poles who might blackmail or betray her than we were of Germans. To the Germans she would simply be a Polish peasant woman. In Germany, people were not so interested in these things anymore. By then the Jews were nonexistent for them; they had all been deported.

In Olsztyn I found work as a photographer, taking pictures of communions and weddings, trying to make a buck however I could. It was the autumn of 1943. I was photographing a wedding one day when a fellow who I did not particularly like came up to me and said he wanted to speak to me in private. We went outside.

"Mr. Damski, some people here are saying that your wife is Jewish."

"What are you talking about?"

"I'm not asking you if she is or isn't, but I think it would be better for you if you left."

Such a nice fellow. In the same village there were four or five Jewish families hiding on Polish papers. At least half of the town knew about them. Nevertheless, I didn't want to take any chances. At five o'clock the next morning I put Christine on the train to Warsaw. I stayed behind to pack up our belongings.

In Warsaw I found a job managing a fruit and vegetable store that sold exclusively to Germans. Now that we were starting over in a new place, I arranged for a very fine false marriage certificate, so that there could be no questions about that. Nobody knew Christine was Jewish, but nevertheless, we had to live quietly, on the side; we had to be careful. We were used to the hard conditions; that was not the bad part. The important thing was to survive, not to be caught.

The terror in Warsaw went on all the time; it was not just directed against the Jews in the ghetto, although that was on a different scale. I was once on a truck, coming back from a buying trip for the store, when suddenly we saw the SS drive up in two or three trucks. It was a place where people had little garden plots to raise vegetables. The men from the trucks just started shooting at them. They shot maybe ten people, jumped back on their trucks, and took off again. Random killing like that was going on all over Poland.

THE WARSAW UPRISING

Christine and I were getting by, living in a room across the street from the Opera House. On August 1, 1944, I came home about five o'clock in the afternoon. I was home only a few minutes when suddenly we heard shooting coming from all over the city. We knew what it was: the Warsaw uprising. Everyone knew the underground was preparing for a revolt. The Russians were already on the other side of the Vistula; we could see their tanks in Praga from the third floor of our building. So we were a little bit prepared for such an eventuality. We had amassed some food—a few pounds of bacon, two or three loaves of bread.

We attempted to make our way to the Old Town in the center, where the partisans had their stronghold, but you were not allowed out in the street unless you were in the fighting forces. We made our way from our basement through the basements of the next four houses—Warsaw had an old sewer system with large tunnels connecting one building's basement to the next; you could go a whole block through these tunnels. Then we needed to go above ground, to run across a street that had no tunnel.

I gave Christine instructions: "When I say run, then run! Then, flat on your belly!" I knew I could make it, even though there were machine guns firing from every building, but I was afraid for Christine. We were still in the basement; she didn't want to come up to the first floor. I had to drag her out. It was the only time during the war that she panicked.

"Down here you're going to die," I said. "The house will collapse and we'll be buried. If we go up we still have a chance."

Somehow I got her out of that basement, and just at that moment a bomb fell on the building. It lodged on the second floor. Everything was collapsing. She fell. I thought she got hit by something, but it was the impact. "Well," I said, "that's a sign we should get out of here."

We were two buildings away from the Polish Ministry of Agriculture, when the Germans started burning out the houses. Our apartment building, across from the opera, was already on fire. We were trying to put out the flames with buckets of water, but I couldn't keep it up for long; the fire was too much for me. When I gave up, a woman took over from me. We moved to the next building, then that house burned out. We moved again, and that house burned too. Now we were out on the street. We saw what must have been the remains of a garden plot; somebody had dug a

Partisans dash across street, first days of Warsaw uprising, August 1944

hole, just large enough for the two of us to slide into. Cinders were flying everywhere. You couldn't see the sun for all the ashes; it was like a huge orange ball. All of Warsaw was burning. I had to urinate on my handkerchief and cover Christine's head with it, to keep her hair from burning. I found an empty cement bag to put over our heads, to conceal us from view. We stayed in that hole for three days.

The second evening it was so very quiet, I said, "I'm going out to see what is happening. Maybe the war is over." In front of the second house where we had been I saw people we knew lying there, dead. The heat had burned up the noses and ears, but I could still recognize them. From a big heap a man called out a woman's name, "Hanka! Hanka!" I don't know if he was crazy or what. Every dog in Warsaw was howling.

I went back to our hole. The morning after the third night, we heard a shout, "Out! Everyone out! If you don't get out I'll throw a grenade!" I said to Christine, "This is it. We have to get out." They had found us with their dogs.

The German military in that part of Warsaw was a battalion of the worst criminals from the SS, sent there to rehabilitate themselves—they called it the Rehabilitation Battalion. In the whole world you couldn't find a more rotten bunch than those guys. As I came out of the hole, I could hear that the fellow who roused us out had a Rhinelander accent. The people from the Rhineland speak German very well, but a bit softer than the Berliner.

"Are you from the Rhineland?" I asked.

"Yah."

I told him I was from the Rhineland too; I was born there.

"So what are you doing over here?"

I told him I was a businessman, caught in Warsaw by the uprising, and Christine was my Polish wife. I couldn't say she was German because she didn't speak German.

We were saved, for the moment. They took us to the basement under the Opera House. It was a very large space; there were probably two or three hundred women in there, and not more than six or seven men. There was no light, no electricity—just a few candles. After a few days, some of these convict SS came in saying, "All the men, out!" I could hear what was happening to each one as he went out. "Pppfook!" They shot them on the spot. They weren't particular about whether or not they were partisans; they shot them all.

Christine was wearing her fur coat—in August! Quickly she covered me with the coat and sat on top of me, keeping me hidden. A very young SS— only about eighteen or twenty years old—was strolling back and forth with his rifle, singing: "Mother, give me a horse, a horse is my paradise." That was his song. He had seen Christine put her coat over me. He stopped singing to lean over and say to her, "There's always time to go to heaven." Then he turned around and began his song again. He didn't say a thing. That was a moment we will never forget.

The next day, people came around asking for helpers for a makeshift hospital they were setting up in the basement of the Foreign Ministry building. They took Christine, a few other women, and me. We stayed there a couple of days, until a fellow came along whom I'll remember always: an SS man, tall, cross-eyed, carrying a basket loaded with fine crystal glassware, obviously stolen; the Germans were looting all the houses.

He looked at me and said, "You Polish swine, why are you looking at me like that?"

I replied in German, "I'm sorry, but I'm not Polish."

"Oh, forgive me. What are you doing over here?"

I told him my businessman story, that I got caught by the uprising. Then he said, "Look, everyday at four o'clock we take our packages for Germany to Jablonna." They couldn't send anything to Germany directly from Warsaw because of the fighting, so they drove their stolen goods about twenty-five or thirty miles out of town, filled a big truck with the loot, and sent it from there to Germany.

"You and your wife can come with us tomorrow," he said. Well, it was a chance to get out. The next day at four o'clock they showed up, drunk. "Come on!" they yelled. They gave me a bottle, and I had to have a drink too. Then they warned us, "When the truck turns the corner at this particular intersection, duck as low as you can. They're going to shoot." They explained that the partisans' guns were aimed at a certain height; if we got down, they couldn't hit us. They made this trip every day and had it figured out. The partisans could hear us as our truck came down the street, and they were ready. As we went by they shot twice, but just as they said, the bullets went over our heads, and we got out safely.

They made a stop about fifteen miles from Warsaw, in a place called Bielany. Everyone in the village was scared; they didn't know what was going on in Warsaw. They had set up beds in the church basement and were all staying there. We took shelter with them for the night. The next day we decided to leave the Germans and strike out on our own.

We were walking through the woods when we came upon a large villa;

it was a vacation resort for the city employees of Warsaw. Everybody there wanted to know our story—how we got out of Warsaw. Some of them thought we were traitors, not because we didn't stay to fight, but because I was not in favor of the uprising. I said that it was unwise, in fact suicidal, for the Poles to attempt the uprising; we didn't stand a chance against the Germans; we should let the Russian army finish them off.

We stayed on at that villa for a week or two. Every night we had to stand watch in the surrounding forest; I couldn't figure out why. Then one day, in the daytime, someone called to me, "Mr. Damski! Come quick! Germans are coming! Try to talk to them." They were a group of German officers—medical doctors—who were looking for a place to put a hospital. They were all from Bavaria, from the regiment that had retreated from Stalingrad. Hitler had blocked the promotions in that division because they had given up the fight. They said something to me about "Polish bandits," meaning the partisans. I said I didn't consider them to be outlaws, just fighters from the Polish Home Army. We talked for a while, and then they left.

After they had gone, I found out why the people in the villa had wanted me to stall the Germans with this conversation: they were operating a secret hospital for Polish partisans hiding in the nearby forest. While I was talking to the Germans in the front, they were taking the wounded partisans out the back door. A few days later one of the doctors came back, saying that they were organizing the collection and delivery of local farm produce, and they needed a translator. So every day I went to their military hospital to translate for the people working for the agricultural department. And every day they gave me a big can of soup, that I brought back to the villa for everyone to eat.

One day, Christine was walking down the road when a car stopped, and a guy jumped out. "Mrs. Damski, I'm looking for your husband." He was an inspector for all the fruit and vegetable businesses in the Warsaw district; I knew him from my last job there. He explained that Warsaw had a population of over two million people, cut off now from the farmers' production. And what do you do with all the vegetables in the fields? Let them rot? He wanted me to organize a fruit and vegetable wholesale operation.

So Christine and I moved to the little town of Ozarow, and there I organized a wholesale business which grew very quickly; we employed 119 people, and at peak time we were selling as much as four thousand tons of vegetables. I could get all the vehicles I needed from the Germans; we had six large trucks with trailers. Every month we loaded between twelve and fifteen railroad cars with vegetables that were shipped to Hamburg, to Brussels—everywhere. There had never been such a wholesale business in all of Poland before; it was a terrific success.

In January 1945 the Russians entered Ozarow, and that was the happiest moment; we had survived.

I did the right thing—no, I don't mean the right thing—it was what everyone should have done. Certainly there were Poles who didn't care about what happened to the Jews, but there were others who did. That one hundred dred thousand Jews survived in Poland must have meant about one million people helping them. In our case, at least a dozen people knew my wife was Jewish. I have an inner sense of satisfaction for what I did, and that is my reward. And, I have a wonderful wife.

Christine Damski, 1943

Christine Damski

I always knew I was Jewish; our family observed Passover and the other holidays. In Zamosc everyone accepted us as equals. Growing up, my girlfriends were both Polish and Jewish. At my Polish high school about ten of the girls in my class were Jewish, but I was the only one in the entire class to get an "Excellent" in Polish language; no Polish girl received that grade. Really, I didn't feel different while I was in high school. The shock came in September 1938, when I went to the university in Warsaw.

My first choice was to study engineering at the Polytechnic, but I was refused admission because of numerus clausus [a quota system to limit the number of Jews admitted]. My second university application, to study journalism, was accepted. I was a good student. My class did everything: we attended court to report on trials, went to the opera and concerts to write reviews, wrote political articles; we even learned typesetting, so that in case of an emergency we would know how to print a paper. With eleven required subjects, it was a tough program.

One day they announced that all the Jewish students had to sit on the left side of the lecture hall, to show that Jews were leftists—Communists. It was very hard; I was very patriotic, and this was a Polish university. To protest, we stood in the back, on the right side. It was at the same time that my uncle Nathan, my father's youngest brother, left Warsaw University because he was beaten up for being Jewish. Like me, he was from a prominent family and very patriotic. He didn't feel he was Jewish.

At the end of my first year I came home for vacation, knowing that I couldn't return to Warsaw in the fall to study; I didn't even want to be in Poland anymore. I applied to the Sorbonne and was accepted. I got a passport and visa for France for the middle of September, but on the first of September, the Germans came into Poland. We knew that the first people they would look for would be journalists and other writers who were against Hitler and Nazism. As a student I was required to write political articles, so I was in some danger. On October 9, 1939, my father gave me three thousand gold rubles—quite a lot of money—and sent my brother Julian and me across the border to Russian territory. We settled in Lvov, a beautiful city—people used to call it "the Little Vienna." We found it was full of Polish refugees, people who didn't want to be under the Germans.

Julian was three years younger but just one grade behind me; he was such a genius, he skipped two grades. I loved him very much. When we left for Lvov, I promised my parents I would be responsible for him. I still had my passport and visa for France and thought we would go there together, but Julian couldn't get a passport, so I decided not to go. My father and mother didn't see any need to leave Zamosc. This was at the beginning of the war; they didn't realize the danger yet. They had gone through the First World War and knew that away from the battlegrounds, people survived. No one thought that the Nazis were going to eliminate the whole Jewish population.

I still blame myself that I took Julian to Lvov. He was not quite nineteen when we arrived there. Just after his birthday the Russians drafted him into the military and assigned him to Vladivostok. I was beside myself! Vladivostok is on the other side of Siberia, near Japan. Julian meant everything to me; I was determined that he not go. I arranged to meet the Soviet in charge of the draft board and gave him a very beautiful oriental rug. He deferred Julian's draft. I had only the best intentions, but it was a big mistake. Julian would have been safe in Vladivostok; he would have lived. I have very bad dreams.

While I was in Lvov the Germans threw my parents out of their house and confiscated my father's business. But he was lucky: his business was given to a very honest man, a Pole whom the Germans had resettled from Poznan when that area was annexed to Germany. He had a German name, but he didn't feel he was German.

"Mr. Rozen," he said to my father, "they turned me out of my business, too. Just pay me a monthly wage and consider this to still be your business."

The Germans considered this man to be a German national, so my father had some protection; he employed my father all through the war. They lost their house, but my parents stayed financially well off until the end.

Julian and I stayed in Lvov until the Germans returned in 1941. We were coming home from a concert the night of June 21, when all of a sudden we heard bombs explode; we knew that the terrible war had started again. For more than two weeks the Germans bombarded Lvov in a ferocious battle. Lvov was a Ukrainian city, and many Ukrainians hated the Polish people. While the Russians were in charge, the Ukrainians pretended to be friendly, but they hated the Russians as much as the Poles. When the war started again, they massacred Poles, and Jews too, because quite a few Jews worked for the Russians. The Ukrainians turned to the Germans as friends.

Julian and I were in a terrible situation in Lvov. There was still a recognized border between the Soviet and German territory. My father sent word that he was sending someone to bring us back; in September the brother of my best girlfriend from school arrived with a car. My father paid him a lot of money to do this—he had known him since he was a very young boy and trusted him. He took Julian first, then two weeks later returned for me.

We still had big problems. The Germans considered every Jew returning from Lvov to be a Communist. When my cousin's father brought my cousin back from Russian territory, the Germans executed both of them for supposedly being Communists. Julian and I had to hide.

We went to our relatives' estate at Siedliska, a little village near Lublin where they had a big house and farmland. All the peasants around there once worked for them. When the Germans came, my relatives had to move out of their house to one of the outer buildings, something like a stable. But the peasants were very friendly; one of them gave up his little hut to Julian and me and three of our friends who were in a similar situation. Of course, we paid him well.

The five of us lived there for a month. None of us had false papers yet. One day a Gestapo car pulled up to the house. I wasn't alarmed; I thought that probably my father had sent for Julian. Our father still had his brewery, and we were used to a lot of SS and military men coming to buy beer.

There was only one entrance to our hut. The Gestapo never knocked; they pushed the door and barged in. We were sitting at the table—Julian and I, and our three friends.

"Which one is Julian Rozen?" they asked.

Slowly, my brother stood up. They put handcuffs on him and took him away.

My heart stopped. I couldn't think. There was no telephone; I couldn't communicate with my parents. Early the next morning I walked seven kilometers to the railroad station. Only one car at the end of the train was allowed for the Poles, and you had to give a bribe for a ticket. I got a ticket for Zamosc and went straight to my parents' home.

It was a very tense situation. I found out that the man my father had hired to bring Julian and me safely back across the border—my girlfriend's brother—had betrayed us to the Gestapo. He told them that my father had brought us back illegally, and that Julian was in hiding. They arrested my father and tortured him so terribly, he broke down

Julian Rozen, 1939

and told them where Julian was. I know just how badly they treated my father because a few days later I saw him myself.

My sister Helena and I were talking in the kitchen. I was wearing a fur coat, without an armband; at that time Jews no longer had fur coats—the Germans had taken them all away. My mother had gone out, to find money for bribes to release my father and brother. Suddenly, the door was pushed in, and there was the Gestapo—two big, tall guys—and behind them, my father, all beaten up: a big gash in his temple, no teeth, his nose smashed in.

My father looked straight at me. "What is this Polish girl doing here?" he said. "She doesn't belong here. Make her leave!"

They didn't ask me anything. "You! Out!" I flew out. He saved my life.

The next day my sister told me that they had thought she was me. They even went through all the picture albums to find out what we looked like. My father just kept telling them she was not the one they were looking for, and finally they believed him.

A few days later they let my father out of jail, for a big bribe, but not my brother. Julian was sent to the Polish prison in Zamosc. Not realizing he was Jewish, the prison authorities put him in a cell with Poles. Then they transferred him to Zamek, the biggest prison in Lublin.

I stopped speaking to my father. I couldn't believe he would tell the Gestapo the whereabouts of his only son. It was hard to forgive him.

JOHN DAMSKI

Zamek was situated in the middle of the small Lublin ghetto. Lublin never had a closed ghetto; the Germans simply told the Jewish people to get out of their homes and move to another part of town, so in the big Lublin ghetto there were Polish and Jewish houses mixed together. They did the same thing in Zamosc, and that's how my parents ended up living in the same house with John Damski.

John was friendly with my parents; they had lived in the same house for two years, almost in the same apartment. He always knew everything that was going on in our place and had been helping my parents with many small things.

When the Germans confiscated all the furs belonging to Jews, John took my mother's coat to his German friend in Cracow for safekeeping. Because they had money from their business, my parents could always afford to buy coal on the black market, but Jews were not allowed to keep coal for heating their homes. There were two coal bins at the back of the house, one on the owner's side, the other on my parents' and John's side. When the Gestapo came around asking whose coal was in our bin, John always said, "This is mine." When Julian was sent to the Zamek prison, John brought him my parents' packages. And when Julian contracted typhus in the prison, it was John who brought him medicine. He did a lot.

I was going from place to place in Zamosc, one night here, one night there, visiting my parents and sister in the evenings. One day I ran out of places and went back to my parents' apartment for a few days. October 4, 1941, I spent the whole day in their bedroom. It was about eight o'clock at night—dark—when we heard a car. We knew it was the Gestapo because no Poles had cars at that time. I was scared. When they knocked on our kitchen door, I jumped out of the window. Johnny caught me.

He grabbed my hand. "Let's get away," he said. I didn't have time to be surprised; I just wanted to get out of there. We had never met, but I knew who he was; I had heard his voice when I was with my parents. Johnny told me not to go back. He said I didn't look Jewish, that I should never wear the armband, or go into the ghetto, or tell anyone I was Jewish. He promised to help me get Polish papers.

A few days later I left with Johnny for Warsaw. But first we went to Lublin to bring Julian a package. In Lublin, I spent the night with my mother's cousin. Around two o'clock in the morning there was a lot of commotion in the small ghetto where the Zamek prison was. Believe it or not, that was the night they surrounded the place to liquidate it. But my cousin was on the Aryan side. The next morning I entered the ghetto to deliver my package to the prison. As I was leaving, a Ukrainian military policeman stopped me and tried to keep me from crossing to the Aryan side. I found a German officer and explained that I had only been delivering a package to my brother in the prison. He let me cross the street.

CZESTOCHOWA

I stayed in Warsaw only a few days, just until Johnny could get my Polish papers. Then Johnny went back to his job in Zamosc, and I went to Czestochowa; it was a big industrial city without a closed ghetto, and as far away as possible from Zamosc. In Czestochowa I didn't know a single person.

Rozen family, 1935

For the first few days I stayed in a hotel while I looked for a place to rent. Because the Germans had taken over all the best apartment buildings, many people were renting out their rooms. I knew that the most dangerous thing for Jews in hiding was simply to sit in a room all day. If you didn't go out, and never had visitors, right away you were under suspicion. Before long someone would report you to the Gestapo. I immediately started looking for a job and soon was working as a manicurist in a beauty salon. So I had a job and a nice room with a young family—an engineer and his wife, and their seven-year-old girl.

It was about this time that we learned Julian had contracted typhus. He survived the illness, but while he was sick they saw that he was Jewish and shipped him to Majdanek concentration camp. I was going back and forth to Lublin, trying everything I could think of to get my brother out.

The German practice in Poland was to take the best dentist, the best doctor, best tailor, shoemaker, and so on, in every town, and let them live in the gentile districts, so the Germans could have their services available to them. My cousin's husband was such a dentist in Lublin; they still lived in their beautiful house, where he had his dental office. All the SS big shots came to him—he knew them all. We knew that once in a while, for a lot of money, the SS would arrange to release someone from prison. My cousin's husband started working on it. One month I made at least five trips to learn if my cousin had found a contact who could get Julian out of Majdanek. Each time he said the same thing, "Come next week. Next week So-and-So from the SS is coming to have his teeth fixed."

Then I got a telegram: "Bring four thousand American dollars and a new suit of clothes." That meant civilian clothes, to replace Julian's prison uniform. I got the suit and money and set off for Lublin. I arrived at my cousin's door. The lady from across the street had seen me coming there before; she probably thought I was a patient. "Ohhh, lady," she said. "They are all gone. They took the dentist and all his family—everybody who lived there." My cousin, her husband, her father, an uncle, her children—they liquidated them. And now I lost all contact with Julian, completely.

John Damski and
Samuel Rozen,
Christine's father,
1946

In the spring I got a letter from my mother in Zamosc, saying that they were beginning to liquidate the Jews in Zamosc; she wanted to come out.

Johnny had gone to Warsaw to help my mother get Polish papers. When he returned to Zamosc he discovered that the cab driver who had brought him and my mother to the railroad station was blackmailing his brother Zygmunt. Unless Zygmunt paid him, the cab driver would turn Johnny over to the Germans, for helping a Jew. Johnny told him to go to hell and refused to pay. But he couldn't go back to Zamosc now. He gave up his job and moved to Czestochowa. We told everyone we were married.

My mother was close to us, in Olsztyn, but my father stayed on in Zamosc with my sister. Johnny offered to help her get Polish papers, too, but she said no. She and my father thought they were safe; she was young—only sixteen years old—and was working for my father's brewery business, which the Germans considered essential. My father went to work all day long, coming home only at night; there was no reason for him to run away. Besides, it was dangerous to live on Polish papers, especially for a man. If the police asked him to pull down his pants, they would know immediately he was a Jew. And if you didn't have the best looks? Polish people recognized Jews.

Everything was going well for us in Czestochowa until we had a warning from the apartment janitor that somebody from Zamosc had recognized me. We immediately packed up for Olsztyn, to be with my mother.

The farmer's family she was living with rented us their one room. The five family members slept in the kitchen, by the stove; they were that poor. My mother had settled in and become quite friendly with the farmer's wife; she was even going to church every day. The wife was expecting a baby. They had one cow—their main livelihood—and the cow was pregnant too. The wife said if the cow gave birth first, they would be able to afford a nice party when her child was born, and my mother would be the godmother. This prospect scared my mother—she was afraid of the attention it would bring to her.

Every day the wife went to the forest to gather firewood to sell in Cze-stochowa. One day she came back, carrying the wood on her back, but now there was a baby in her shawl as well. She had delivered the child by her-self in the woods. The cow didn't have its calf yet, so my mother was saved.

Even in Olsztyn the rumors started again; we knew we had to find a safer place for my mother. Oddly enough the only safe place seemed to be in Germany. The Germans had employ-ment offices in nearly every town in Po-land, to recruit volunteers for work on German farms, in factories, and business-es. Nearly the entire German population had been drafted into the military, and they badly needed a workforce. It was so hard for a poor person to make a living in Poland, a lot of Polish people were vol-unteering. In Germany they would at least have a place to live, food, and a lit-tle money.

Christine's mother and sister, Helen and Helena Rozen, 1937

I took my mother to register her at the Czestochowa recruitment office. She was wearing a babushka, looking very much like a peasant woman. But I didn't stop to think: I was dressed elegantly, in silk. This guy in the office looked at me, looked at my mother, then at me again. He walked to the front of the office and looked up and down the street. He was suspicious. Then he came back and said, "Okay. Come tomorrow for the physical examination." We didn't know what to do with ourselves for the rest of the day. We went to the biggest church in Czestochowa, the holiest church in Poland, where they held

*Christine and John
Damski, Los Angeles,
1988*

masses every hour, all day long. We moved from one part of the church to another until the evening curfew. The next day we went back and finished the registration; my mother signed up to go to Bavaria, to work in a family restaurant in the German Alps.

WARSAW

Spring '43, shortly after my mother left for Germany, it happened again; somebody in Olsztyn told Johnny that he thought I wasn't really his wife, that I was Jewish. We left right away for Warsaw. At first we lived in the beautiful villa of Johnny's friend Danuta Majewska. Her house was full of people working for the underground—pilots, refugees from western Poland; everybody was involved. There was an arsenal as well. The house had belonged to Danuta's late father-in-law, a doctor. Before the war it had been a private institution for mentally ill patients. Located in a quiet street, with an orchard and garden, surrounded by high walls, it was a very safe place for the underground. We lived there with all the others, as many as twelve people in one room.

While we were at Danuta Majewska's I learned that the Polish government-in-exile in London was sending money every month to be distributed to Jewish people in hiding. They needed couriers to help deliver the money, so I volunteered. That's how I discovered that my father was in hiding in Warsaw.

One day I was told to bring some money to six people from Zamosc; the contact was a man named Veigler. When I went to see him his first words were, "Your father is here!" He told me the story. As the Germans were rounding up the last Jews from Zamosc, my father and several others were able to bribe the railroad station attendants and escaped by boarding the train for Warsaw. One of them—our family friend Mr. Garfinkle, who was also the president of the Zamosc Judenrat—had a relative in Warsaw who was married to a Polish lady.

This lady had a friend, an old widowed lady, who was living in a tall apartment house—six or seven stories high—that was damaged by a bomb in '39. One section was almost completely destroyed, but a few rooms were left hanging, somewhat intact. The old lady ran a small hotel in the building, something like a pension, next to the destroyed section. Due to the danger, she had been ordered to close it off. She placed a large armoire in front of the door of the only room leading to the destroyed part, and behind that door she was hiding my father, another lady from Zamosc, and fifteen other Jews. She asked for absolutely nothing from them in return—not one cent.

I hadn't talked to my father since he was released from jail in Zamosc; it was so hard to forgive him for betraying Julian. My mother never did. But I had been through so many things myself by then, of course I went to see him. We became close again. It was a place where I could go and spend a few hours each day. I brought him food and tobacco. He made cigarettes from the tobacco, which I sold.

Johnny and I found a room of our own on the top floor of an apartment house near the Polish Opera building. Everyone on that floor shared one bath, but we were by ourselves at last, not sleeping on the floor with ten other people. I was so happy. I hung beautiful curtains in the window. Johnny was working. I was visiting my father and getting letters from my mother. I was even baking cookies for my mother, making up packages to send to her. She was living in an attic without heat in the Alps. About all they gave her to eat was black bread, ersatz coffee, and one bowl of soup a day, and this was a restaurant!

August 1, the uprising started. When they started burning out the houses, instinctively I grabbed the bacon, some stale bread, and my fur coat. The city was burning, it was summertime—an inferno all around us—and I was wearing a fur coat. I didn't even feel the heat. You see, inside the shoulder pads I had sewn in diamonds and golden rubles; it was the money I had lived on through the whole war.

LIBERATION

When the Russians finally liberated us, Johnny and I thought we would return to Zamosc, back to this town where I had grown up, gone to school, where before the war I was really somebody. No one wanted to see me now; no one greeted me on the street, and no one invited me to their home. Before the war I had never felt any anti-Semitism in Zamosc, but when I returned, people turned their backs. I didn't want to stay.

Thank God, my mother and father survived. My sister died in Treblinka. She had to dig her own grave. After the war, my mother was still hoping that my brother had survived. When he didn't come back, she divorced my father; she said she couldn't live with him. I have a letter from my father after the divorce, full of tears. He wrote that my mother was an angel, and he was the most unhappy man. I keep it with me all the time.

APPENDIX: PLACES, EVENTS, AND TERMS

Bad Reichenhall: This spa town in southeastern Germany, close to the Austrian border, is very near Berchtesgaden, where Hitler entertained guests at his mountain retreat, the Berghof.

Battle of Arnhem: On September 17, 1944, General Montgomery's army launched the Battle of Arnhem, a bold attempt to capture a strategic bridgehead over the lower Rhine. Poor planning and unexpectedly fierce resistance caused the Allies to withdraw after ten days of bitter fighting and heavy casualties. In spite of the losses, the Dutch viewed the battle as a sign of strong Allied resistance on their own territory and the beginning of the end of the detested German occupation.

Czestochowa: This city has long been considered the spiritual capital of Poland. Situated on the Jasna Gora (Bright Mountain), the Pauline monastery's Basilica of the Virgin Mary is the sight of several annual festivals attracting Catholic pilgrims from all over the world. The basilica houses the legendary icon called the Black Madonna. Brought from Jerusalem in 1384, the icon is considered by the faithful to be the work of St. Luke the Evangelist, painted on cypress wood from a table used by the Virgin Mary.

The Jewish community in Czestochowa dates back to 1765. By the start of World War II, close to thirty thousand Jews lived there, participating in every economic activity of the wealthy industrialized city. When the Germans took political control shortly after the September 1, 1939, invasion of Poland, the persecution of Jews began immediately, following the same pattern practiced throughout Poland: denial of civil rights, confiscation of property, harassment, confinement to ghettos, and deportation.

Chronology of Events during the Nazi Occupation of Czestochowa

August 1940	One thousand Jews sent to forced labor camps at Ciecha-now.
August 23, 1941	Twenty thousand Jews from other Polish towns and villages forced into the sealed-off Czestochowa ghetto.
September 22–October 8, 1942	Thirty-nine thousand Jews deported from Czestochowa ghetto to Treblinka death camp. Residents of orphanages and old-age homes killed before deportation of the able-bodied.
September 1942–January 1945	Three forced labor camps in the region around Czestochowa supplied ten thousand Jews from Poland, Germany, Austria, and Slovakia to work in three German munitions factories and a steel mill. Few survived the ordeal.
December 1942	A branch of the Jewish resistance group ZOB (Jewish Fighting Organization) formed, with three hundred members. After their resistance to a German raid in January 1943, severe reprisals resulted in many Jewish deaths and deportations.
June 1943	Another ZOB group resisted liquidation of the Czestochowa ghetto.

Friesland: A region in northeastern Holland located between the Scheldt and Weser Rivers. Many present-day natives are descendants of the Frisians, a Germanic tribe conquered by the Franks in the eighth century. The Frisians were notable for maintaining their native language and for their fierce independence.

German-Soviet War: Hitler's alliance with Stalin's regime, as marked by the Molotov-Ribbentrop Treaty, was never one of real trust. Hitler always considered communism to be a major enemy of his world scheme, and his early writings reveal a strong desire to acquire the vast natural resources of Russia for the German state.

As early as December 18, 1940, Hitler's Directive Number 21 called for the German army "to erect a barrier against Asiatic Russia on the general line Volga-Archangel."

The actual attack—code-named Barbarossa—didn't begin until June 22, 1941. The aim was to destroy the Red Army completely and penetrate far enough into

Soviet territory to prevent Soviet air reprisals against Germany. Intended to take only six months, the battles—stretched out along an 1,800-mile front, from the Arctic Ocean to the Caucasus—lasted until Germany's ultimate defeat in 1945.

Hatikvah: The anthem of the Zionist movement and now the national anthem of Israel, composed by Naftaly Hertz Imber in 1878. The lyrics express the Jews' wish for redemption and their desire to return to Zion, or Palestine.

Herzl, Theodor: Born in Hungary but living most of his life in Austria, Herzl (1860–1904) was a leader of the Zionist movement. He founded the Zionist World Congress in 1897.

Hitler Jugend: In 1936 Hitler outlawed all youth groups except for the national organization, Hitler Jugend, or Hitler Youth. As an important aspect of the National Socialist (Nazi) program, the aim of Hitler Jugend was to gain complete control over the social and political education of German children.

Hunger Winter: For over four years the German Reich systematically emptied Holland of its agricultural produce, sending it across the border to Germany. By the winter of 1944–45, a particularly bitter cold season, finding sufficient food and heating fuel had become the primary concern for virtually the entire Dutch population. In Holland it is still called the "Hunger Winter."

Jewish Quarter of Amsterdam: Centered around Amsterdam's Jodenbreestraat, this quarter was renowned from the late nineteenth century until World War II for its lively, vibrant atmosphere. The streets were lined with Jewish shops and street vendors selling all manner of goods, creating a special ambiance that attracted artists and writers. It was also one of the poorest districts of Amsterdam, filled with alleys and slums, and housed Eastern European Jewish immigrants in appalling conditions.

Joodsche Raad: The German occupation authorities in Holland decreed the formation of a Joodsche Raad, or Jewish Council, composed of former Jewish community leaders, to govern the Jewish population of the Amsterdam ghetto. Following the model used in other occupied countries, the members of the Dutch Jewish Council were charged with maintaining order in their demoralized, disease-ridden, and economically desperate community. Most important for the

Germans, the council acted as their intermediary to carry out their increasingly oppressive dictates, such as providing forced labor battalions for German war factories, and eventually even delivering Jews directly to the trains bound for the death camps.

Kristallnacht: On the evening of November 9, 1938, an organized pogrom was unleashed against Jews all over Germany. Synagogues were burned, businesses destroyed, and Jews were pulled from their homes to be harassed, beaten, and murdered. The infamous event was named Kristallnacht in reference to the enormous quantity of shattered glass from Jewish shop windows that littered German cities and towns the next day. In the aftermath, Nazi actions to eliminate Jews from German economic life intensified greatly. Detailed plans were put into action to confiscate Jewish businesses and property, restrict civil rights for Jews, and finally deport all Jews to concentration camps.

Letter to Dutch Jews: The German occupation authorities in Holland were particularly efficient at rounding up the Dutch Jewish population for eventual transport to death camps in Poland. Their first step was to make sure that all Jewish people living in Holland were officially registered. Then on certain dates in each city, registered Jews were sent a letter telling them when and where to report for transport either to the Amsterdam ghetto or directly to Westerbork, the transit camp in Holland from which trains left weekly for the death camps in Poland. Those who went to the Amsterdam ghetto were later deported to Poland via Westerbork.

Lvov (Lemberg): Founded in the thirteenth century in eastern Galicia, the city of Lvov, known to Jews as Lemberg, was ruled by Austria, from 1772 to 1918; Poland, from independence in 1918 until annexation to Soviet Russia in late September 1939; Germany, after the German offensive of June 1941; and the Soviet Union again, following the defeat of Germany in 1945. Presently it is within the borders of the independent state of Ukraine.

Prior to World War II, Lvov had the third-largest Jewish community in Poland. The city was known as both a cultural and industrial center, with a particularly lively Jewish culture. Following the German invasion of Poland on September 1, 1939, and the annexation of Lvov into Soviet territory three weeks later, approximately one hundred thousand Jews from Nazi-occupied Poland found refuge in

Lvov. Because most of the Jews refused the offer of Soviet citizenship, Soviet authorities exiled tens of thousands of them to Siberia the following year. Eventually they were permitted to enter central Asia—Tashkent and Sammarkand—where the vast majority survived the Holocaust.

When the Germans took control of Lvov in June 1941, during the German-Soviet War, extremely harsh anti-Jewish measures were immediately put into action. During the summer a series of massacres of the Lvov Jews by both the Germans and the Ukrainians became known as the "Petluria Days." Thousands of Jews were killed in the pogrom of July 25–27, 1941. Simon Petlurian was the general of the White Russian Army that slaughtered tens of thousands of Ukrainian Jews during the civil war of 1918–20, between the Communists and White Russians. He was the last premier of an independent Ukraine before the Communist takeover.

The Germans forced the city's Jews into the newly established ghetto by December 1941. There the Nazis enacted their usual pattern of confiscation of Jewish property, personal humiliations and deprivations of every sort, forced labor, and deportation to concentration camps.

Mensch: A Yiddish word literally translated as "human being." It is used when referring to a person who is considered to be fundamentally solid, decent, and good.

Molotov-Ribbentrop Treaty: On August 23, 1939, Hitler and Stalin signed a non-aggression pact, called the Molotov-Ribbentrop Treaty. Secret protocols of the treaty defined the territorial spheres of influence Germany and Russia would have after a successful invasion of Poland. Hitler had been creating justifications and laying plans for such an invasion since April.

According to the agreement, Russia would have control over Latvia, Estonia, and Finland, while Germany would gain control over Lithuania and Danzig. Poland would be partitioned into three major areas. The Warthland area, bordering Germany, would be annexed outright to the German Reich and all non-German inhabitants expelled to the east. Over 77,000 square miles of eastern Polish lands, containing a population of over 13,000,000, would become Russian territory. The central area would become a German protectorate, named the General Gouvernement, governed by a German civil authority. The Soviet-German agreement was emended on September 29, 1939, by the Soviet-German Friendship

Treaty, which ceded Lithuania to the Russian sphere. On September 1, 1939, Hitler's forces invaded Poland from the west. According to plan, Soviet troops invaded Polish territory from the east on September 17. Poland surrendered on September 27. The next day Poland was partitioned according to the treaty's scheme, ending a brief, twenty-year period as an independent nation.

Munich Agreement of 1938: In the summer of 1938, Hitler voiced active support of the highly publicized demands of the German population of the Sudetenland, in the Republic of Czechoslovakia, for annexation of the region into Germany. Fearing the outbreak of war, European leaders met in a conference at Munich on September 29. Present were Edouard Daladier, from France; Neville Chamberlain, from England; Mussolini, representing Italy; Hitler; and Ribbentrop. Representatives of Czechoslovakia and the Soviet Union were not invited.

Wanting to avoid the possibility of a new European war, Chamberlain and Daladier submitted to Hitler's demands very quickly; the conference was over the next day. The treaty ceded three areas of Czechoslovakia to other powers: the Sudetenland was annexed into Germany, the Teschen district was given to Poland, and parts of Slovakia went to Hungary.

Chamberlain boasted after the conference that they had achieved "peace in our time," but the agreement quickly became a symbol of the western powers' appeasement of Hitler, which led to the outbreak of World War II one year later.

Numerus Clausus: A Latin term meaning a "restricted number," numerus clausus refers to the practice of setting a quota for the number of persons of some category—usually Jews—who will be admitted to an educational institution, most often a university. This type of discrimination was normal in Czarist Russia. After World War I, the use of numerus clausus was formalized in Hungary, where the number of Jews who could be admitted to the universities was officially designated as no more than 5 percent of the total enrollment. It became a common practice at universities in other European countries as well; in Poland, the quota for Jewish admissions was 10 percent.

Beginning in the 1920s a similar practice allowed unofficial but widely observed quotas on Jewish enrollment at universities in the United States, particularly at the more prestigious schools in the northeastern states. It was to these schools that the children of recent Jewish immigrants were more likely to apply.

In recent years several major American universities in the western states have been investigated for following a similar policy to restrict the number of Asian-American student admissions.

Pogrom: Derived from the Russian word meaning "to wreak havoc," a pogrom is an organized attack, often a massacre, against a minority group, particularly Jews. For centuries the Jews in Russian lands were periodically victims of such persecutions, often with the encouragement of local officials.

Sephardic Jews: Sephardic Jews are descendants of the large Jewish community living in Spain and Portugal in the Middle Ages. In 1492, Spanish Jews who would not convert to Christianity were forcibly expelled. They scattered to all countries of the Mediterranean basin, including North Africa, Italy, Greece, Turkey, and Palestine. Over one hundred thousand Spanish Jews went to Portugal, where four years later they faced the choice of conversion or death. Many escaped to the Netherlands (then part of Spain) and the New World. Sephardic Jews never lost their identity and today are found living all over the world.

Sobibor Concentration Camp: The Nazi regime set up three different kinds of concentration camps. The first were labor camps, where Jews and nationals from occupied countries were conscripted to work, under appalling conditions, as slave laborers for the German Reich.

The second type was the transit camp, which served as a concentration point in an occupied country from which to transport the inmates to either labor or death camps. Westerbork, in Holland, was a transit camp.

The last to be established were the death camps. These camps, designed specifically for killing on a mass scale, were built starting in 1942. Most were located in Poland. Sobibor, a camp in the Lublin district of Poland, opened in May 1942. Most of the Dutch Jewish population that suffered deportation to the camps was sent there or to Auschwitz. Before it closed, an estimated 250,000 Dutch, French, and Polish Jews were murdered at Sobibor.

Sudetenland: The Sudetenland is a historical region comprising areas of the Czechoslovakian provinces of Bohemia and Moravia, in the vicinity of the Sudeten Mountains. Although the majority of inhabitants in the area were German-speaking, in 1919, at the conclusion of World War I, the Treaty of Saint-Germain incorporated the area into the Czechoslovak Republic. In subsequent years, control over the territory became a point of bitter contention between Germany and Czechoslovakia.

Matters worsened in the 1930s when, as a result of the worldwide economic depression, the heavily industrialized area suffered massive unemployment. The laid-off workers were susceptible to the anti-Semitic, anti-Czechoslovakia, pro-German rhetoric of Konrad Henlein and his cohorts, who founded the Sudeten German (Nazi) Party. Coupled with discriminatory actions of local Czechoslovakian officials, publicity of the ensuing unrest caused the leaders of the western democracies to fear the possibility of war. The result was the infamous Munich Agreement of September 30, 1938, which sanctioned the annexation of the region into Germany.

Todt Organization: The Todt Organization was a German construction company run by the engineer Dr. Fritz Todt until his death in 1942, after which it was under the control of Albert Speer. The company was quasimilitary in nature and oversaw the construction of roads and military installations in Nazi-occupied countries.

Warsaw Uprising, August 1–October 2, 1944: By summer 1944, as the Red Army was advancing from the east, the German occupying forces were perceived to be on the defensive in Poland. The Soviets were encouraging the Polish Home Army, directed by the Polish government-in-exile in London, to wrest Warsaw from German control; the Germans at that point had a comparatively small military presence in the Polish capital.

But the Polish partisans were troubled that as the Soviets liberated eastern Poland from German power, they left in their wake a pro-Communist civil authority, exemplified by the Lublin Committee in Lublin. Hoping to establish a non-Communist postwar government in their homeland, the Polish leaders in London and General Bór-Komorowski, the leader of the Polish Home Army, decided to attack the Germans in Warsaw in advance of the Red Army, with the understanding that Soviet reinforcements would be available if needed. Indeed, the Red Army entered the Warsaw suburb of Praga, across the Vistula River, late in July 1944.

On August 1, 1944, the Polish Home Army, a force of between 35,000 and 50,000 partisans, attacked the Germans in Warsaw. Joined in the fight by the city's Polish population, they took control of most of the city by August 4. But the Germans sent reinforcements: SS police units, a brigade of Russian ex-prisoners, and a brigade of ex-convicts, all of whom Hitler had previously ordered removed from the front because of their excessive brutality. The Polish forces became fragmented and isolated. The cut-off fighters were pursued without mercy into the city's refuges—burned out buildings and sewers—where virtually all perished.

During the sixty-three days of fighting, the Red Army—encamped within sight across the Vistula—never attempted assistance. The Soviets refused permission to the Americans and British to use their airfields to drop ammunition and relief supplies. In September, when a German victory seemed certain, the Russians allowed a small amount of ammunition to be dropped in, but it was useless: it was made for Soviet armaments and did not fit the Poles' weapons.

When hostilities ceased, 85 percent of the city had been razed and the Polish Home Army annihilated. The Germans deported the remaining population. When the Germans were eventually defeated there were no forces left to oppose Soviet political domination in Poland.

The Warsaw uprising should not be confused with the earlier Warsaw ghetto uprising of April 19–May 16, 1943. In that instance, the Jewish fighters, in the first anti-Nazi uprising anywhere, received virtually no help from the Polish underground.

Westerbork: Camp Westerbork was the main transit camp used by the Germans during their occupation of Holland to send people—mostly Jews—to the death camps in Poland. The second, smaller, transit camp in Holland was Vught. Between July 1942 and September 1943, approximately 110,000 Jewish people passed through the two camps.

Westerbork was located near Assen, in northeastern Holland. It was actually set up by the Dutch government before the Nazi invasion, as a refugee camp for Jews fleeing persecution in Germany. After the Nazi takeover, the Germans employed the German Jewish refugees to run their camp in an orderly, efficient manner. Every Monday evening a list of the week's 1,020 deportees was announced to the inmates in their sealed barracks. The next morning the trains carrying them to Auschwitz, Sobibor, Theresienstadt, or Bergen-Belsen death camps in Poland left Westerbork promptly at 11:00 A.M.

Camp Westerbork was used immediately after the war to intern Dutch collaborators and then, from about 1950 until 1970, as a relocation camp for dislocated people returning from the former Dutch colonies. In the early 1970s the camp was completely demolished and turned into a World War II memorial.

Westerweel, Joop: In late February 1944, Joop Westerweel traveled to the foot of the Pyrenees to say farewell to the group about to cross into Spain, which included Joseph Heinrich and thirteen other young people Joop and his underground group had helped to escape from Holland. His memorable speech was later vividly recalled by many who were present. He wished them well and that they should build Palestine into a place where there would be no war, only food and work for everyone. As the young pioneers left for Spain, Joop turned back to Holland. On March 11, he was arrested by border police while helping two young Jewish girls cross illegally from Holland to France. Five months later he was executed in prison.

Youth Aliyah: Youth Aliyah, or Youth Immigration, was an offshoot of the Zionist movement, with the aim of helping Jewish children and young adults emigrate to Palestine. Initially organized in Germany by Recha Freyer to help German Jewish youths who lost their employment as a result of anti-Semitism, the group provided agricultural training to prepare its largely urban-dwelling members for life on kibbutzim.

The first group to emigrate left Germany in 1934. By 1948, Youth Aliyah was responsible for the resettlement of 30,353 young adults and children from many European countries, including Romania, Italy, Sweden, Denmark, Yugoslavia, Bulgaria, Hungary, Turkey, and Cyprus. Of these, 5,012 arrived between 1934 and the outbreak of the war in 1939. During the war years, 9,342 left Europe for Palestine, and the other 15,999 came between 1945 and 1948. (These figures come from *Encyclopaedia Judaica* [Jerusalem: Macmillan, 1972].)

Zamosc: Founded in the late sixteenth century, Zamosc is the principal city of a province of the same name in eastern Poland. Before World War II, the majority of the city's population was Jewish. During the German occupation, native residents—Jewish, Polish, and Ukrainian—were subject to particularly harsh treatment.

The Germans declared the area to be the "First Resettlement Area" of the General Gouvernement in November 1942, which resulted in the "ethnic cleansing" of hundreds of the region's villages to make room for German nationals. Tens of thousands of Poles were deported to labor or extermination camps or killed outright, while others were singled out to be "Germanized" and resettled in the Reich.

After visiting Zamosc and finding it a beautiful town built on the model of Padua, Heinrich Himmler considered turning it into a German city named Himmlerstadt. To accomplish this aim he sent out a special commission to examine the population and decide who was German and thus could remain; everyone else was expelled. John Damski's brother Zygmunt reported that he was checked for eye and hair color. Even the length of his fingers was measured.

Zegota: This Warsaw group, founded in October 1942, grew out of the Polish underground resistance. Organized specifically to funnel money, provide false identity papers, buy food on the black market for Jews in hiding, and to give all other forms of aid necessary for survival, Zegota was the only formal organization directly to help thousands of Jews in Nazi-occupied Poland.

Zionism: Zionism originated in the late nineteenth century as a movement expressing secular Jewish nationalism. Prior to that time, Zionism had been an entirely religious concept, found chiefly in Jewish liturgy and in pseudomessianic movements.

Theodor Herzl (1860–1904) founded the modern political Zionist movement at the First Zionist Congress, held in Basel, Switzerland, in 1897. The initial aims of the Zionist movement were to settle Jewish people in the traditional land of Palestine, revive Hebrew as a language of daily discourse, and reconstitute the ancient nation of Israel as a modern Jewish state.

The context for the development of the modern Zionist movement was similar to that of other European ethnic groups with aspirations for national liberation, such as the Irish, Polish, and Czech peoples. The rationale was this: because so many were forbidden or chose not to assimilate to the cultures of the countries where they lived, Jews had retained a unique identity throughout their long history. They were a people without a state. Jewish persecution throughout history spoke to the need to establish a place of safety that would have international recognition and the protection of international law.

Since its inception, modern Zionism has been met with opposition by strictly religious Jews who believe that only God is sanctioned to restore Jews to Palestine. Secular Jews, moreover, do not consider Jewish people to form a distinct ethnic group. They feel Jews are a community simply by virtue of their religion.

Contemporary Zionist activities focus on the support and development of the state of Israel.

Zuider Zee: This large body of water in northeastern Holland was originally a lake, but heavy flooding joined it to the North Sea. A dike created the southern part, called the Ijsselmeer, where drained land is used for agriculture.

Anger, Per. *With Raoul Wallenberg in Budapest: Memories of the War Years in Hungary.* Translated by D. M. Paul and M. Paul. New York: Holocaust Library, 1981.

Arnold, Elliot. *A Night of Watching.* New York: Scribner, 1967.

Bacque, James. *Just Raoul: The Private War against the Nazis of Raoul Laporterie, Who Saved Over 1,600 Lives in France.* Rocklin, Calif.: Prima Publishing, 1992.

Barfod, Jorgen H. *The Holocaust Failed in Denmark.* Copenhagen: Frihedsmuseets Venners Forlag, 1972–81.

Bartoszewski, Wladyslaw, and Zofia Lewin. *The Righteous among the Nations.* London: Earls Court, 1969.

———. *The Samaritans: Heroes of the Holocaust.* New York: Twayne, 1970.

Bauer, Yehuda. *Flight and Rescue: Brichah—The Organized Escape of the Jewish Survivors of Eastern Europe, 1944–1948.* New York: Random House, 1970.

———. *A History of the Holocaust.* New York: Franklin Watts, 1982.

———. *They Chose Life: Jewish Resistance in the Holocaust.* New York: American Jewish Committee, 1973.

Baumel, Judith Tydor. *Unfulfilled Promise: Rescue and Resettlement of Jewish Refugee Children in the United States, 1934–1945.* Juneau, Alaska: Denali Press, 1990.

Bauminger, A. L. *The Righteous.* Jerusalem: Yad Vashem, 1983.

Benchley, Nathaniel. *Bright Candles: A Novel of the Danish Resistance.* New York: Harper and Row, 1974.

Berenbaum, Michael. *The World Must Know: The History of the Holocaust as Told in the United States Holocaust Memorial Museum.* Boston: Little, Brown, 1993.

Berenstein, Tatiana, and Adam Rutkowski. *Assistance to the Jews in Poland, 1939–1945.* Warsaw: Polonia Foreign Languages Publishing House, 1963.

Bertelsen, Aage. *October '43.* New York: Putnam, 1954.

Bierman, John. *Righteous Gentile: The Story of Raoul Wallenberg, Missing Hero of the Holocaust.* New York: Viking, 1981.

Bishop, Claire Huchet. *Twenty and Ten.* New York: Viking, 1952.

Biss, Andreas. *A Million Jews to Save: Check to the Final Solution.* New York: A. S. Barnes, 1975.

Blond, Shlomo. *The Righteous Gentiles.* Tel Aviv: S. Blond, 1983.

Boehm, Eric H. *We Survived: Fourteen Histories of the Hidden and Hunted of Nazi Germany.* New Haven: Yale University Press, 1949; Santa Barbara, Calif.: ABC-Clio Information Services, 1985.

Brecher, Elinor J. *Schindler's Legacy: True Stories of the List Survivors.* New York: Dutton, 1994.

Breznitz, Shlomo. *Memory Fields: The Legacy of a Wartime Childhood in Czechoslovakia.* New York: Knopf, 1993.

Dawidowicz, Lucy S. *The War against the Jews, 1933–1945.* New York: Holt, Rinehart and Winston, 1975.

Drucker, Malka, and Michael Halpern. *Jacob's Rescue: A Holocaust Story.* New York: Bantam, 1993.

Edelheit, Abraham J. *The Yishuv in the Shadow of the Holocaust: Zionist Politics and Rescue Aliya, 1933–1939.* Boulder, Colo.: Westview, 1996.

Fabre, Emil C., ed. *God's Underground.* Translated by William and Patricia Nottingham. St. Louis: Bethany, 1970.

Feingold, Henry L. *The Politics of Rescue: The Roosevelt Administration and the Holocaust, 1938–1945.* New Brunswick, N.J.: Rutgers University Press, 1970.

Fensch, Thomas, ed. *Oskar Schindler and His List: The Man, the Book, the Film, the Holocaust and Its Survivors.* Forest Dale, Vt.: Paul Eriksson, 1995.

Fittko, Lisa. *Escape through the Pyrenees.* Translated by David Koblick. Evanston, Ill.: Northwestern University Press, 1991.

Flender, Harold. *Rescue in Denmark.* New York: Simon and Schuster, 1963; Holocaust Library, 1963.

Fogelman, Eva. *Conscience and Courage: Rescuers of Jews during the Holocaust.* New York: Anchor Books, 1994.

Ford, Herbert. *Flee the Captor.* Nashville, Tenn.: Southern Publishing Association, 1966.

Friedenson, Joseph, and David Kranzler. *Heroine of Rescue: The Incredible Story of Recha Sternbuch, Who Saved Thousands from the Holocaust.* Brooklyn, N.Y.: Mesorah Publications, 1984.

Friedlander, Saul. *When Memory Comes.* Translated by Helen R. Lane. New York: Farrar, Straus, Giroux, 1979.

Friedman, Philip. *Their Brothers' Keepers: The Christian Heroes and Heroines Who Helped the Oppressed Escape the Nazi Terror.* New York: Crown, 1957; Holocaust Library, 1978.

Frye, Varian. *Assignment Rescue: An Autobiography.* New York: Scholastic, 1945.

Gies, Miep, with Alison Leslie Gold. *Anne Frank Remembered: The Story of the Woman Who Helped to Hide the Frank Family.* New York: Simon and Schuster, 1987.

Goldberger, Leo, ed. *The Rescue of the Danish Jews: Moral Courage Under Stress.* New York: New York University Press, 1987.

Green, Gerald. *The Legion of Noble Christians: The Sweeney Survey.* New York: Trident, 1965.

Greenfeld, Howard. *The Hidden Children.* New York: Ticknor and Fields, 1993.

Gross, Leonard. *The Last Jews in Berlin.* New York: Simon and Schuster, 1982.

Gutman, Israel, Editor-in-Chief. *Encyclopedia of the Holocaust.* New York: Macmillan, 1990.

Gutman, Yisrael, and Schmuel Krakowski. *Unequal Victims: Poles and Jews during World War Two.* New York: Holocaust Library, 1986.

Gutman, Yisrael, and Efraim Zuroff, eds. *Rescue Attempts during the Holocaust: Proceedings of the Second Yad Vashem International Historical Conference, Jerusalem, April 8–11, 1974.* New York: Ktav, 1978.

Haesler, A. *The Lifeboat Is Full: Switzerland and the Refugees, 1933–1945.* Translated by Charles Lam Marksmann. New York: Funk and Wagnalls, 1969.

Haestrup, Jorgen. *Passage to Palestine: Young Jews in Denmark, 1932–1945.* Odense: Odense University Press, 1983.

Hallie, Philip Paul. *Lest Innocent Blood Be Shed: The Story of the Village of Le Chambon and How Goodness Happened There.* New York: Harper and Row, 1979.

Hellman, Peter. *Avenue of the Righteous: Portraits in Uncommon Courage of Christians and the Jews They Saved from Hitler.* New York: Atheneum, 1980; New York: Bantam, 1981.

Henry, Frances. *Victims and Neighbors: A Small Town in Nazi Germany Remembered.* South Hadley, Mass.: Bergin and Harvey, 1984.

Herzer, Ivo, Klaus Voigt, and James Bugwyn, eds. *The Italian Refuge: Rescue of Jews during the Holocaust.* Washington, D.C.: Catholic University of America Press, 1989.

Hilberg, Raul. *The Destruction of the European Jews.* Chicago: Quadrangle Books, 1961; New York: Holmes and Meier, 1985.

———. *Perpetrators, Victims, Bystanders: The Jewish Catastrophe, 1933–1945.* New York: Aaron Asher Books, 1992.

Horbach, Michael. *Out of the Night.* Translated by Nina Watkins. London: Valentine Mitchell, 1967.

Huneke, Douglas K. *The Moses of Rovno: The Stirring Story of Fritz Graebe, a German Christian Who Risked His Life to Lead Hundreds of Jews to Safety during the Holocaust.* New York: Dodd Mead, 1985.

Iranek-Osmecki, Kazimierz. *He Who Saves One Life: A Documented Story of the Poles Who Struggled to Save the Jews during World War II.* New York: Crown, 1971.

Isaacman, Clara. *Clara's Story.* As told to Joann Adess Grossman. Philadelphia: Jewish Publication Society of America, 1984.

Keneally, Thomas. *Schindler's List.* New York: Simon and Schuster, 1982.

Kranzler, David. *Japanese, Nazis and Jews: The Jewish Refugee Community of Shanghai, 1938–1945.* New York: Yeshiva University Press, 1976.

———. *Thy Brother's Blood: The Orthodox Jewish Response During the Holocaust.* Brooklyn, N.Y.: Mesorah Publications, 1987.

Kranzler, David, and Eliezer Gevirtz. *To Save a World.* 2 vols. New York: CIS, 1991.

Kranzler, David, and Gertrude Hirschler. *Solomon Schonfeld: His Page in History.* New York: Judaica Press, 1982.

Kren, George M., and Leon H. Rappoport. *The Holocaust and the Crisis of Human Behavior.* New York: Holmes and Meier, 1980.

Lampe, David. *The Savage Canary: The Story of Resistance in Denmark.* London: Casell, 1957.

Lazare, Lucien. *Rescue as Resistance: How Jewish Organizations Fought the Holocaust in France.* Translated by Jeffrey M. Green. New York: Columbia University Press, 1996.

Leboucher, Fernande. *The Incredible Mission of Father Benoit.* Translated by J. F. Bernard. London: W. Kimber, 1970.

Lester, Elenore. *Wallenberg, the Man in the Iron Web.* Englewood Cliffs, N.J.: Prentice-Hall, 1982.

Leuner, Heinz David. *When Compassion Was a Crime: Germany's Silent Heroes, 1933–45.* London: Oswald Wolff, 1966.

Levine, Hillel. *In Search of Sugihara: The Elusive Japanese Diplomat Who Risked His Life to Rescue Ten Thousand Jews from the Holocaust.* New York: Free Press, 1996.

Lewy, Gunther. *The Catholic Church and Nazi Germany.* New York: McGraw-Hill, 1964.

Lifton, Betty Jean. *The King of Children: A Biography of Janusz Korczak.* New York: Farrar Straus Giroux, 1988.

Lowrie, Donald Alexander. *The Hunted Children.* New York: Norton, 1963.

Lowry, Lois. *Number the Stars.* Boston: Houghton Mifflin, 1989.

Macaulay, Jacqueline R., and Leonard Berkowitz, eds. *Altruism and Helping Behavior: Social Psychological Studies of Some Antecedents and Consequences.* New York: Academic Press, 1970.

Marshall, Robert. *In the Sewers of Lvov: A Heroic Story of Survival from the Holocaust.* New York: Scribner, Maxwell Macmillan International, 1991.

Marton, Kati. *Wallenberg: Missing Hero.* New York: Random House, 1982.

Melchior, Marcus. *A Rabbi Remembers.* Translated by Werner Melchior. New York: Lyle Stuart, 1968.

Meltzer, Milton. *Rescue: The Story of How Gentiles Saved Jews in the Holocaust.* New York: Harper and Row, 1988.

Mendelsohn, John. *Relief and Rescue of Jews from Nazi Oppression, 1943–1945.* New York: Garland, 1982.

Milton, Sybil. *Rescue to Switzerland: The Musy and Saly Mayer Affairs.* New York: Garland, 1982.

Muus, Flemming Brunn. *The Spark and the Flame.* Translated and edited by Varinka Muus and J. F. Burke. London: Museum Press, 1956.

Oliner, Pearl M., ed. *Embracing the Other: Philosophical, Psychological, and Historical Perspectives on Altruism.* New York: New York University Press, 1992.

Oliner, Samuel. *Restless Memories: Recollections of the Holocaust Years.* Berkeley, Calif.: Judah L. Magnes Memorial Museum, 1986.

Oliner, Samuel P., and Pearl Oliner. *The Altruistic Personality: Rescuers of Jews in Nazi Europe.* New York: Free Press, 1988.

'Omer, Devorah. *The Teheran Operation: The Rescue of Jewish Children from the Nazis: Based on the Biographical Sketches of David and Rachel Laor.* Translated by Riva Rubin. Washington, D.C.: B'nai B'rith Books, 1991.

Opdyke, Irene Gut, with Jeffrey M. Elliot. *Into the Flames: The Life Story of a Righteous Gentile.* Edited by Mary A. Burgess. San Bernardino, Calif.: Borgo Press, 1992.

Orenstein, Henry. *I Shall Live: Surviving against All Odds, 1939–1945.* New York: Beaufort Books, 1987.

Orlev, Uri. *The Man from the Other Side.* Translated by Hillel Halkin. Boston: Houghton Mifflin, 1991.

Paldiel, Mordecai. *The Path of the Righteous: Gentile Rescuers of Jews during the Holocaust.* Hoboken, N.J.: Ktav, 1993.

———. *Sheltering the Jews: Stories of Holocaust Rescuers.* Minneapolis: Fortress, 1996.

Perl, William R. *Operation Action: Rescue from the Holocaust.* New York: Ungar, 1983. Rev. ed. of *The Four-front War* (1979).

Phayer, Michael. *Protestant and Catholic Women in Nazi Germany.* Detroit: Wayne State University Press, 1990.

Ramati, Alexander, with Padre Rufino Niccacci. *The Assisi Underground: The Priests Who Rescued Jews.* New York: Stein and Day, 1978.

Rautkallio, Hannu. *Finland and the Holocaust: The Rescue of Finland's Jews.* New York: Holocaust Library, 1987.

Reilly, Robin. *The Sixth Floor.* London: Leslie Frewin, 1969.

Reiss, Johanna. *The Upstairs Room.* New York: Bantam, 1973.

Rittner, Carol, and Sondra Myers, eds. *The Courage to Care: Rescuers of Jews during the Holocaust.* New York: New York University Press, 1986.

Rochman, Lieb. *The Pit and the Trap: A Chronicle of Survival.* New York: Holocaust Library, 1983.

Roi, Emilie. *A Different Story: About a Danish Girl in World War Two.* Jerusalem: Yad Vashem, 1990.

Rose, Leesha. *The Tulips Are Red.* South Brunswick, N.J.: A. S. Barnes, 1978.

Rosenfeld, Harvey. *Raoul Wallenberg, Angel of Rescue: Heroism and Torment in the Gulag.* Buffalo, N.Y.: Prometheus Books, 1982.

Rotenberg, Alexander. *Emissaries: A Memoir of the Riviera, Haute-Savoie, Switzerland, and World War II.* Secaucus, N.J.: Citadel Press, 1987.

Roth-Hano, Renée. *Touch Wood: A Girlhood in Occupied France.* New York: Four Winds Press, 1988.

Rubinek, Saul. *So Many Miracles.* New York: Viking Penguin, 1988.

Ryan, Michael D., ed. *Human Responses to the Holocaust: Perpetrators and Victims, Bystanders and Resisters. Papers of the 1979 Bernhard E. Olson Scholars' Conference on the Church Struggle and the Holocaust.* New York: E. Mellen Press, 1981.

Silver, Eric. *The Book of the Just: The Silent Heroes Who Saved Jews from Hitler.* London: Weidenfeld and Nicolson, 1992.

Staden, Wendelgard von. *Darkness over the Valley.* Translated by Mollie Comerford Peters. New Haven: Ticknor and Fields, 1981.

Stein, André. *Quiet Heroes: True Stories of the Rescue of Jews by Christians in Nazi-Occupied Holland.* Toronto: Lester and Orpen Dennys, 1988.

Sugihara, Yukiko. *Visas for Life.* Translated by Hiroki Sugihara. San Francisco, Calif.: Edu-Comm Plus, 1995.

Tec, Nechama. *Dry Tears: The Story of a Lost Childhood.* New York: Oxford University Press, 1984.

———. *When Light Pierced the Darkness: Christian Rescue of Jews in Nazi-Occupied Poland.* New York: Oxford University Press, 1986.

Ten Boom, Corrie, with John and Elizabeth Sherrill. *The Hiding Place.* New York: Bantam, 1974.

Tokayer, Marvin, and Mary Swartz. *The Fugu Plan: The Untold Story of the Japanese and the Jews during WWII.* New York: Paddington Press, 1979.

Tomaszewski, Irene, and Tecia Werbowski. *Zegota: The Rescue of Jews in Wartime Poland.* Montreal: Rice-Patterson, 1994.

Troen, Selwyn Ilan, and Benjamin Pinkus, eds. *Organizing Rescue: National Jewish Solidarity in the Modern Period.* London, and Portland, Ore.: F. Cass, 1992.

Vlcko, Peter. *In the Shadow of Tyranny: A History in Novel Form.* New York: Vantage, 1973.

Waagenar, Sam. *The Pope's Jews.* LaSalle, Ill.: Open Court Publishing Company, 1974.

Weinstein, Frida Scheps. *A Hidden Childhood, 1942–1945.* New York: Hill and Wang, 1985.

Werbell, Frederick E., and Thurston Clarke. *Lost Hero: The Mystery of Raoul Wallenberg.* New York: McGraw-Hill, 1982.

Wolfe, Jacqueline. *"Take Care of Josette": A Memoir in Defense of Occupied France.* New York: Franklin Watts, 1981.

Wood, E. Thomas, and Stanislaw M. Jankowski. *Karski: How One Man Tried to Stop the Holocaust.* New York: Wiley, 1994.

Wuorio, Eva-Lis. *To Fight in Silence.* New York: Holt, Rinehart, and Winston, 1973.

Yahil, Leni. *The Holocaust: The Fate of European Jewry, 1932–1945.* Translated by Ina Friedman and Haya Galai. Oxford: Oxford University Press, 1991.

———. *The Rescue of Danish Jewry: Test of a Democracy.* Translated by Morris Gradel. Philadelphia: Jewish Publication Society of America, 1969.

Zassenhaus, Hiltgunt. *Walls: Resisting the Third Reich—One Woman's Story.* Boston: Beacon, 1974.

Ziemian, Joseph. *The Cigarette Sellers of Three Crosses Square.* Translated by Janina David. Minneapolis: Lerner Publications, 1975.

Zuccotti, Susan. *The Italians and the Holocaust: Persecution, Rescue, and Survival.* New York: Basic Books, 1987.

ILLUSTRATION CREDITS

page

INDEX

der in, 73; life in prewar, 124–26; Olympics in, 255–56; Polish Jews deported from, 177–78; refugees from, 20–21, 169; restrictions in, 124–26; Soviet Union's relations with, 192, 261, 292–96; teenage refugees from, 109–10, 112. *See also* Emden (Germany)

Gestapo: betrayal to, 280–82; Czech village searched by, 169, 170, 187, 188; fear of, 174; as highest Dutch authority, 46, 118; searches by, 166–67; tactics for handling, 27–28; terror tactics of, 124–25, 235, 271; underground spy in, 25; workers for, 128. *See also* arrests/interrogations; raids; SS (Schutzstaffel)

Gittler, Sieg, *44*

god-trees, use of term, 219

Goering, Hermann, 12, 32–33, 34

Greece, invasion of, 261

Greenbaum brothers, 153

greenhouse, as hiding place, 24–25

Gross-Rosen concentration camp, 178, *179*

The Hague: Gestapo headquarters in, 28; old-age home in, 64, 99–100; people from, 63, 70

Hamerslag, Tsuika Araten, *123*

Hatikvah (Zionist movement anthem), 153, 293

Heinrich, Asher: escape of, 154; hiding of, 145, 147–48, 150; photo of, *146;* sent to Holland, 141

Heinrich, Joseph: on arriving in Israel, 156; background of, 109–10; on Children's Werkplaats, 143, 144; escape of, *151,* 153–55, 300; hiding of, 145, 147–53; home of, *143;* on Kristallnacht, 140–41; on Mirjam Waterman, 144, 148–49; photos of, *141, 146, 150, 156;* sent to Holland, 141; on Westerweel group, 145–47

Heinrich, Lorle, 141, 145, *146*

Henlein, Konrad, 298

Herzl, Theodor, 252, 293, 301

Hesteren, Erika van: arrest and imprisonment of, 12, 55, 59; assistance for, 12, 32; on hiding, 56–62; illness of, 35–36, 60; photo of, *62*

hiding: communications in, 50; creating places for, 25, 68–71; moving from place to place in, 47–48; occupations during, 47–48, 284–85, 289; payment for, 89–90, 97–98; psychological effects of, 81, 147–48; relations among hiders, 74, 76; relations with hosts and, 22–23, 29, 48; resistance to, 28–29, 49, 132; "rules" in, 60–61; skepticism about, 114–15; visits to places of, 19–20, 29, 50, 231, 237; of weapons, 15

Hilberg, Raul, 3

Himmler, Heinrich, 35, 301

Hirschberg (Poland), Jewish population of, 189

Hitler, Adolf: attitudes toward, 139–40, 261; Czechoslovakian Republic takeover by, 158; directive Number

21 of, 292; Jewish businesses under, 124–25; Munich Agreement and, 296; Poland invaded by, 192–93, 296

Hitler Jugend (youth organization), 293

Holland: chronology of events in, 7–9; geographic disadvantage of, 4; German authority in, 46, 118; Hunger Winter in, 61, 81–90; Jewish orphans in, 122–23; Jewish situation in, 3, 4–5, 7, 109; liberation of, 38–40, 39, 53–55, 90–91; map of, 7; misperceptions in, 7; refugee children's reception in, 129, 141–42; registration in, 145–46, 294; restrictions in, 4–5, 7–9, 43–44, 56, 63, 79; visas from, 128–29. See also Amsterdam; Huizen (Holland); Hunger Winter; Jewish Council (Holland); underground resistance (Dutch)

Holocaust: Czech Jews in, 159; Dutch Jews in, 7, 53, 98, 99, 100, 107; German Jews in, 140; Polish Jews in, 179, 189, 200, 228; reading and talking about, 106–7; unawareness of, 279

hothouse (greenhouse), as hiding place, 24–25

Huizen (Holland): community support in, 88; hospital in, 104, 106; Hunger Winter in, 81–90; liberation of, 90–91; post office in, 70–71; raids in, 102. See also drugstore (Huizen, Holland)

Hungary, restrictions in, 296

Hunger Winter: descriptions of, 36–40, 81–90, 95, 95–96; overview of, 61, 293

identification papers: for Dutch population, 9; history to back up, 29, 150; obtaining false, 16–17, 59, 60, 93, 115, 139, 186, 266–67, 270–71, 283; problems with false, 118–19; stamped with "J," 18, 46. See also passports; registration

Ikkersheim, Peter (Lou), hiding of, 70–71, 72, 77–78, 79, 81

Imber, Naftaly Hertz, 293

International Red Cross, 222–23

Israel: Bergen-Belsen prisoner exchange and, 121; children sent to, 108–10, 118, 123, 156, 156; emigration to, 64, 107, 254, 300. See also Zionist movement

Israelowicz (athlete), 255–56, 267, 269

Janowicka (work camp), 209

Japan, Nazi attitudes toward, 261

Jewish Agency, 156

Jewish Council (Holland): description of, 293–94; establishment of, 5, 8, 115; influences on, 132; Jews registered by, 5; sent to transit camp, 9, 19; special papers provided by, 100

Jewish Council (Poland), 194, 195, 232

Jewish Fighting Organization (ZOB, Poland), 292

Joodsche Raad. See Jewish Council (Holland)

208–9, 278, 279–81; imprisonment in, 213–18, *214*, 236–37; Jewish situation in, 240–41; Ukrainians in, 210; work camp in, 209

Lvov ghetto: assistance for people in, 198, 230–31; construction of, 195; deportations from, 196; history of, 294–95; liquidation of, 232–33

Lvov Polish Socialist Party, 198

Majdanek concentration camp, 285

Majewska, Danuta, 288–89

Makuch, Barbara (Basha) Szymanska: arrest and imprisonment of, 199, 210–17, *214*, 235–39; background of, 197–98, 200–201; character of, 191, 233–34, 238; emigration of, 200; on liberation, 222–27; Lilien assisted by, 204–6, 241–43; on Lvov, 207–9; Marysia (Rebecca) and, 202–3, 247, 249; Meisel assisted by, 217–18; photos of, *201, 225;* Polowicz assisted by, 204; on Ravensbruck, 218–22; Sophie assisted by, 206–7; Stefan assisted by, 203; teaching of, 197–98; underground activities of, 209–10, 233–35

Makuch, Stanley, 200

Marx, Karl, 14

Maryna (Halina's friend), 231–33

Marysia. *See* Litowitz, Rebecca (Marysia)

medical care: for childbirth, 104, 106; difficulties of, 12, 35–36, 60; doc-

tors' provision of, 86, 172, 174, 185, 188, 205; home remedies for, 171–72; for laborers, 151–52, 166; for prisoners, 119–20, 282–83; underground classes in, 17, 37, 61; Warsaw uprising and, 276

Meisel, Felka, 229, 230, 233

Meisel, Henryk: assistance for, 199; imprisonment of, 217–18, 240; occupation of, 198, 228–30; photo of, *216*

Melkman, Tamar, 20

memoirs, approach to, 1–2

Mendels, Ans: hiding of, 68, 74, 78, 101; money of, 90; on number of people, 86; sister of, 99, 107

Mendels, Bob (father), 100

Mendels, Bobbie (son), 101, *102*

Mendels, Henny. *See* Juliard, Henny

Mendels, John, 101, *105*

Mendels, Max, 99

Mendels, Yettie Malachi: background of, 64; on hiding, 98–103; occupations of, 103–6; photos of, *98, 100, 102, 105;* postwar activities of, 106–7; on raids, 100, 102–3

mensch, definition of, 295

Meyer (banker), 73–75, 86, 90

Molotov-Ribbentrop Treaty: components of, 198, 295–96; context of, 192, 292–93; knowledge of, 239

monuments, from desecrated tombstones, *248*

Moravia: history of, 297–98; Hitler's takeover of, 158; map of, *159*

Werkplaats Kinder Gemeenschap (Children's Community Workshop), 111–12, 143, 144

Westerbork transit camp (Holland): avoidance of, 85–86; description of, 299–300; establishment of, 9, 297; imprisonment in, 121; Jews shipped to, 21, 99, 100, 114, 130, 140, 294

Westerweel, Joop: arrangements in Spain escape, 153–54; arrest and imprisonment of, 118–19, 119–20; children rescued by, 108, 115–17, 118; death of, 116, 300; group of, 115, 136; Heinrich on, 145–47, 153–54; motivation of, 138–39; photo of, *116;* teaching by, 109, 112; Yaari on, 137–38

Westerweel, Willie, 137–38, 146–47

White Russian Army, Ukrainian Jews slaughtered by, 295

Wolf, Bob, 64

Wolf, Yettie. *See* Mendels, Yettie Malachi

women: attack on Nazi officer by, 223; deportation of Polish Jewish, *204*

Woubrugge (Holland): business in, 63; farms in, 83–84

Yaari, Ruth, 136; hiding of, 133–34, 136; Kristallnacht and, 128; liberation of, 140; meeting Westerweel and, 137; sent to Holland, 129

Yaari, Sophie: background of, 109, 110; on Kristallnacht, 126–29; on life in prewar Germany, 124–26; on Mir-

jam Waterman, 132, 138–40; photos of, *124, 127;* on Pinkhof, 129, 130, 139; postwar activities of, 139–40; on underground, 131–36; on Westerweel, 137–38

yellow stars: for Czech Jews, 165; for Dutch Jews, 9, 18, 43–44, 48, 56; gentile wearing, 264; for German Jews, 149; in Holland, 18, 43–44, 48, 56; for Polish Jews, 195, *263,* 266

Young Palestine Pioneers: emigration to Israel, 156; escape to France, 150, 153–55; hiding of, 115–18, 132–33; origins of, 108; photos of, *130, 156;* training of, 112–13, *118, 119*

Youth Aliyah movement: activities of, 108–10, 112, *119,* 145; experience of, 129, 131–32; leaders of, 149; leisure time and, *147;* overview of, 300; second group of, 113–15

Zamek jail (Lublin), 282–83

Zamosc (Poland): description of, 300–301; housing in, 265–66, 282; Jewish population of, 254, 267, 277–78, 282, 286; liquidation of Jews in, 286, 289; return to, 281, 290; work situation in, 259–60

Zeeland, Youth Aliyah group in, 145

Zegota (resistance group): activities of, 209–10, 230–31, 301; Basha's imprisonment and, 218, 236; members of, 198, 199, 209, 233–34

Zihle train station, 183, *184*

Ellen Land-Weber is a photographer/artist and a professor of art at Humboldt State University, Arcata, California. She has exhibited her work in solo or joint exhibitions every year since 1968. Her photographs are in the permanent collections of museums in twelve states and in France, Japan, Canada, and Australia. She is the author of and photographer for *The Passionate Collector* (1980).

Typeset in 10.5/14 Minion

Designed by Erin Kirk New

Composed by Barbara Evans

at the University of Illinois Press

Manufactured by Friesens Corporation

University of Illinois Press

1325 South Oak Street

Champaign, IL 61820-6903

www.press.uillinois.edu